EISENHOWER
as Military Commander

1 (*overleaf*) *Eisenhower in March 1943*

EISENHOWER

as Military Commander

E. K. G. Sixsmith

A DA CAPO PAPERBACK

Library of Congress Cataloging in Publication Data

Sixsmith, E.K.G. (Eric Keir Gilborne)
    Eisenhower as military commander.

    (A Da Capo paperback)
    Reprint. Originally published: New York: Stein and Day,
1973
    Bibliography: p.
    Includes index.
    1. Eisenhower, Dwight D. (Dwight David), 1890-1969 —
Military leadership. 2. World War, 1939-1945 — Campaigns
— Western. 3. Generals — United States — Biography.
4. United States. Army — Biography. I. Title.
[E836.S53   1989]   355'.0092 [B]   89-11821
ISBN 0-306-80369-0

This Da Capo Press paperback edition of *Eisenhower as
Military Commander* is an unabridged republication of
the edition published in New York in 1972. It is reprinted
by arrangement with the estate of the author.

Published by Da Capo Press, Inc.
A Subsidiary of Plenum Publishing Corporation
233 Spring Street, New York, New York 10013

Manufactured in the United States of America

To
My Father

Contents

List of Illustrations

Maps

Acknowledgments

I have to acknowledge with gratitude the help I have received from many sources both in the United States and in this country. The principal source has been the Eisenhower Papers, edited by Professors Alfred Chandler and Stephen Ambrose. Although I read through all the papers I should like to pay tribute to the editors for the remarkable way in which the work has been cross-referenced, annotated and indexed. Professor Ambrose has been most helpful to me in elucidating further information. General of the Army Omar Bradley, Generals Alfred Gruenther, Lauris Norstad and Andrew Goodpaster, and His Excellency Colonel John Eisenhower have all taken great trouble to answer my questions and to provide me with valuable information and background.

Of the British officers who served under or worked with Eisenhower I have been able to talk to or correspond with Field Marshal Lord Montgomery, the late General Sir John Whiteley, Lieutenant-Generals Sir Brian Horrocks, and Sir Ian Jacob, Major-General Sir Kenneth Strong and Brigadier Lionel Cross. Closest to him of all was Brigadier Sir James Gault; he has been assiduous in answering my questions, in providing information and in doing everything possible to facilitate my work and to give a picture of the man as he was. In my study of the part played by the Canadian forces in North-West Europe I have had great help from a most interesting correspondence with Lieutenant-General Guy Simonds.

No British officer who tries to write a book on a military subject ever fails to go to Mr D. W. King, Chief Librarian of the Ministry of Defence (Army and Central) Library. He has been a fund of useful information and has spared no pains to get me the books and documents which would be helpful to me. Miss Meg Shuff of the South-West District Library has also been most helpful to me. My thanks also go to Mr Ray Joynt who has helped me with the maps and to Miss Greta Williams who typed the manuscript for me.

I must give special thanks to my elder brother, Mr Guy Sixsmith, who read each chapter, and to Brigadier L. F. Heard, who read all except the first two. I have benefited from uncompromising but constructive criticism of both. My brother has not let any loose phrase or punctuation go unquestioned and has tried to keep me within the bounds of lucidity and good English. Brigadier Heard has called on his experience of many of the events described and his wide reading to help me. I am also grateful to Mr Eversley Belfield, Senior Lecturer at Southampton University for his criticism of three of the chapters, and to my son Angus, who has helped with some of the phraseology.

Acknowledgment is made to the authors and publishers of the books quoted in the text. Full details are given in the notes and Bibliography. Acknowledgment for the illustrations is made to the Imperial War Museum (*frontispiece*, 2, 9–14, 16–29, 32, 35); Associated Press Photo (15, 31, 34); the Dwight D. Eisenhower Library (3–8); Topix (33) and Brigadier Sir James Gault (30).

Finally, I should like to pay tribute to Mr Samuel Carr, Miss Suzy Powling, and the Staff of B. T. Batsford for their unfailing care and courtesy.

NOTES

1. The rank of officers is not given except where it is significant and is not apparent in the text. The highest rank reached by all the officers mentioned will be found in the index.
2. 'Chiefs of Staff' is used throughout to mean the British Chiefs of Staff Committee and 'Joint Chiefs of Staff' its American equivalent. 'Combined Chiefs of Staff' is the Committee of both acting in concert.
3. The use of code-names has been kept to the minimum and a Glossary provided on page 222. Only a very few of the most familiar abbreviations have been used.

E. K. G. SIXSMITH

THE ENGLISH CHANNEL AND
THE MEDITERRANEAN

North
Sea

DENMARK

EIRE

GREAT
BRITAIN

GERMANY

Dover
Ostend
HOLLAND
Boulogne
Dunkirk
BELGIUM

ENGLISH CHANNEL
Cherbourg

Brest

LUX.

Bay of
Biscay

FRANCE

SWITZ.

AUST.

Bordeaux

ITALY

Rimini

Pisa
Leghorn

Marseilles

PORTUGAL

CORSICA

La
Maddalena

Naples

SPAIN

SARDINIA

BALEARIC ISLANDS

Decimomannu

Tyrrhenian
Sea

Cagliari

Gibraltar

MEDITERRANEAN   SEA

Bizerta

Trapani
Skerki
Bank
Palermo
SICILY
Cata
Syrac

TANGIER

SP. MOROCCO

Oran

Algiers

Bône

Tunis

PANTELLERIA

Comisa

The

Narro

Casablanca

MAL

LAMPEDUSA

MOROCCO

Sfax

KERKENAH
IS.

ALGERIA

TUNISIA

Tripoli

0   500
Miles

TPIPOLITANIA

~ARTHUR BANKS~

LITHUANIA

Baltic Sea

EAST PRUSSIA

POLAND

U.S.S.R.

CZECHOSLOVAKIA

HUNGARY

RUMANIA

YUGOSLAVIA

Black Sea

BULGARIA

Bosporus

ADRIATIC SEA

ALBANIA

Valona

GREECE

Dardanelles

TURKEY

Taranto

Ionian Sea

Aegean Sea

Reggio Calabria

Athens
Piraeus

Aleppo

Messina

Navarino

SYRIA

C.Matapan

Maleme

RHODES

DODECANESE Is.

CYPRUS

CRETE

Haifa

MEDITERRANEAN

SEA

Derna

Gazala

Sidi Barrani

Mersa Matruh

Alexandria

Port
Said

PALESTINE

TRANS-
JORDAN

Buerat

Benghazi

Bomba

Tobruk

Suez
Canal

Gulf of
Sirté

Bardia

Sollum

El Alamein

Cairo

Suez

LIBYA

El Agheila

CYRENAICA

EGYPT

ARABIA

Early Years and Pre-War Career

An account of the abilities and accomplishments of a great soldier can usually show how he earned his apprenticeship under fire and how in lesser tasks in battle he showed those qualities which marked him out for the ultimate responsibilities of high command. Not so with Eisenhower: he was, so to speak, thrown in at the deep end before he had even learnt to paddle. His first active command was not only a considerable military venture, but it involved him in political problems of great complexity. Moreover, if the short lived experience of Wavell in South East Asia be discounted, he became the first supreme allied commander responsible not only for the army but also for the naval and air forces committed to the campaign. He may therefore be said to have set the pattern for a new type of military commander, never perhaps in so urgent and decisive a role as that given to Foch in 1918, yet far transcending it in scope and responsibility.

Dwight David Eisenhower was born at Denison in Texas on 14 October 1890. He was the third of seven sons, the fifth of whom died in infancy. The family had no military background: Dwight's father, David, was a Kansas man who had been given a farm by his own father as a wedding present. David had disliked farming and had sold the farm to buy a partnership in a general store in Hope, Kansas. In a year of drought and grasshopper pests the farmers on whom the store depended had run into difficulties but the store had continued to give credit. David's partner could not stand the resultant stress and had absconded with what cash there was. As a result the store had become bankrupt and the Eisenhowers moved to Texas where David became a railway worker. Two years after Dwight was born the family returned to Kansas and set up home in Abilene. David was successively an engineer in a creamery, a manager of a gas plant, and a director of a savings group.

Dwight's home was frugal and pious, but his boyhood was very happy. He says that he never heard his parents exchange a cross word and that they shared an ideal partnership in bringing up their six sons. 'Father was the breadwinner, Supreme Court, and Lord High Executioner. Mother was tutor and manager of the household.'[1] Family tradition had it that in her youth his mother had won a church prize for memorizing 1365 verses from the Bible. The early family disaster naturally had its effect on the parent's outlook. David was determined to owe no man anything and if there was not cash to pay the family did without. The boys were made to feel that they were contributing to the survival and happiness of the home. Their mother ensured that they helped in the house and that she never had cause to bemoan the lack of a daughter. In the rural life that they led there was plenty of outdoor work too: gardening, the haymaking, feeding the chickens and milking the cow.

The boys led a free robust life, but were certainly aware of parental discipline as well as love. They knew that if one of them overstepped the limits of reasonable order—certainly if it was deliberate—chastisement would inevitably follow. Both parents were determined that their sons should learn to look after themselves in a hard world. Self-dependence and self-discipline were demanded. Dwight remembers that whenever one of the sons was faced with a difficult decision or wanted something apparently out of reach, his mother's advice was almost always 'sink or swim' or 'survive or perish'. The parents insisted that their sons should seize the opportunity for a full education which was available to all in America, but the boys were left free to choose their college course and to find their own vocation.

At school Dwight worked hard, especially at history, and played hard. Probably for no better reason than as a way of getting a college education he decided to try for West Point—he would have gone to Annapolis but by the time he had made up his mind he was just too old. He entered West Point in 1911 and graduated four years later. He can hardly be said to have shown particular distinction there but was always in the top third of his class. His own account of his time[2] makes much of the number of 'Demerits'—the equivalent of a black mark—he received, but he admits that he enjoyed life at West Point and was by no means below the average as a cadet. From the first his easy and above all optimistic nature earned him many friends. Among those in his own class was Omar Bradley and in the same company, but two years his junior, was Mark Clark. Each confesses to admiring Eisenhower but neither pretends that

[1] Eisenhower, *At Ease*, p. 31
[2] *Ibid.*, Ch. 1

2 *The Eisenhower family with the 12-year-old Dwight on the far left*

he foresaw in him the great Allied commander of the future. Cadets did not think in that way and few of them aspired beyond field rank. So far as his own thoughts went Eisenhower was of the same mind. Towards the end of his life he confessed that the rank and appointments to which he attained were 'far beyond his loftiest ambition.' Yet there was in that carefree cadet at West Point something that moved him to great purpose. He knew how to achieve his aim. This was partly due to the ease with which he got on with his fellows, not necessarily as the dominant and obvious captain of his class, but as a man of sympathy and understanding who could carry others willingly with him. But there was more in it than that. He had a belief in himself that refused to allow him to succumb to difficulties, that told him how, whether the matter was trivial or important, he must work out his own solution. Whether consciously or not he was thus carrying out his mother's most cherished precept.

Eisenhower's reaction to the oath of allegiance that he was required to take on his first day at West Point illustrates the serious vein that ran through his character. On the evening of a day on which the cadets had been hustled and harassed, and put in their lowly place to a degree almost beyond comprehension, they were brought together to repeat the official oath. The wording is:

I pledge allegiance to the flag of the United States of America and to the Republic for which it stands – one nation, indivisible, with liberty and justice for all.

Eisenhower tells us: 'Whatever had gone before, this was a supreme moment. The day had been one of confusion and a heroic brand of rapid adjustment. But when we raised our right hands and repeated the official oath, there was no confusion. A feeling came over me that the expression "The United States of America" would now and henceforth mean something different than it ever had before. From here it would be the nation I was serving, not myself. Suddenly the flag itself meant something. I haven't heard other officers speak of their memories of that moment but mine have never left me. Across half a century, I can look back and see a rawboned, gawky Kansas boy from the farm country, earnestly repeating the words that would make him a cadet.'[3]

Eisenhower did not resent the meticulous rules, regulations and conventions that seemed designed only to persecute and torment the cadet in his early days. He saw that they were in fact designed to get him into the

[3] *Ibid.*, pp. 4–5

habit of immediate obedience to legitimate orders. But there was nothing too easily submissive in his character. His sense of humour prevented his taking either the petty restrictions or himself too seriously. He was not slow to take advantage of puny authority when reasonable opportunity offered. He tells how he and a fellow cadet were ordered by a cadet corporal to appear 'in full dress coats'. They decided to take the order literally and appeared before the corporal in full dress coats 'and not a stitch of other clothing.' Eisenhower suffered for his temerity but he enjoyed it.

Eisenhower did not show any particular brilliance in his academic work. His own explanation was that he was too idle a student. He did however achieve one minor triumph which illustrated his refusal to accept defeat and his rugged mode of thought. Through inattention to his tutor's explanation of a complicated problem of integrated calculus, Eisenhower found himself in difficulties when called upon to expound the solution to his section on the next day. He wrestled with the problem until he eventually worked his way to the answer. His tutor was not prepared to accept Eisenhower's version and accused him of memorising the answer and inventing the reasoning. It so happened that the head of mathematics appeared during the discussion and decided that Eisenhower's solution was more logical and direct than the 'school solution' and would henceforth be adopted as such.

One of Eisenhower's reasons for going to West Point was his love of games and sports. He went there with great ambitions both for football and for baseball. In his first year he was disappointed to find that although he was strong and agile he was too light to be considered for football. By the next year he had put on 22 pounds and began to show up well. He played regularly for the West Point team and had a reputation for extreme toughness. But in the week before the Navy match he suffered a knee injury which kept him out of field games for ever and nearly caused his rejection for commissioning on medical grounds. He did not however lose his interest in games and he was much in demand as a coach and as a cheer leader. In his early service he earned many an honest dollar as a coach to local colleges. His earnings and his winnings at poker, of which he seemed inordinately fond, helped him to pay off the debts which he incurred in his early service and increased by his early marriage.

Less than two years after Eisenhower was commissioned the United States was at war. Mobilisation and expansion brought the opportunity for advancement and added responsibility. Eisenhower was soon the

Colonel's right hand man in training the newly formed 57th Regiment in Texas. An ability as an instructor seems to have been the obstacle which prevented him from achieving his ambition of going to the war. Several times he was promised he would go in command of the next draft, but always his commanding officer found that he could not be spared. The disappointment was sugared with quick promotion and Eisenhower became a temporary Lieutenant-Colonel on 14 October 1918, his twenty-eighth birthday. Earlier that year Eisenhower had been put in charge of the training of the newly organized Tank Corps under the general direction of an infantry officer, Colonel Welborn, whose office was in Washington. Eisenhower, largely left to his own devices at Camp Colt, was required 'to take in volunteers, equip, organize and instruct them and have them ready for overseas shipment when called upon'. There was no flow of information from France on the technical skill or type of training that was required. At first there were no tanks: later three small Renaults arrived without either the machine guns or the one pounder cannons which they were designed to take as alternative weapons.

After the war Eisenhower felt that he had 'missed the boat'. He knew that he would have to go down in rank: he did in fact lose his Lieutenant-Colonelcy a few months later and did not regain it until 1936. This, added to the uncertainty about the future of the Tank Corps, caused him to contemplate leaving the army. He had the offer of a highly paid job from an Indiana business man who had served under him. Yet he realised that short of active service he had had the best of all possible experience— the conversion of a slice of American civilian life into first-class fighting officers and men, a task accomplished by using his own ability rather than textbook or official guidance. He therefore decided to stay on.

His first post-war task was to add to the variety of his experience. He went as one of two Tank Corps officers in an all service motor convoy from coast to coast—from Washington to San Francisco. With modern vehicles and roads this is nothing, but in those days it was a formidable task. On the first three days a total of 29 hours driving took them only 165 miles. Later, on some days only a few miles were covered. Heavy lorries sometimes broke through the surface of the road and had to be towed out by tractors. Nevertheless, in a journey which took from 7 July to 6 September, only three vehicles were lost, one of which had rolled down a mountain.

When Eisenhower returned to Camp Meade after this journey some of the officers who had been in action with tanks had returned from Europe. One of these, Colonel George Patton, struck up a friendship with Eisenhower. Both were keen students of military technique and both believed passionately in the efficacy of the tank. They did not accept the official doctrine that the tank was an infantry support weapon that moved at infantry pace. They wanted a faster weapon that could make use of surprise to disorganise enemy resistance. In Eisenhower's own words: 'By making good use of the terrain in advance, they could break into the enemy's defensive position, cause confusion, and by taking the enemy front line in reverse, make possible not only an advance by infantry, but envelopments of, or actual break-throughs in, whole defensive positions.'[4] They were interested not only in the tactics but also in the design of the tank and with a man named Christy they took one tank completely to pieces and reassembled it in working order.

Both Eisenhower and Patton began to write about their theories. Patton for the *Cavalry Journal* and Eisenhower for the *Infantry Journal*. Eisenhower was brought before the Chief of Infantry and told that his ideas were not only wrong but dangerous. He was informed that what he wrote must be compatible with official doctrine. The next year the two officers were parted because the Tank Corps, which had been an independent arm, was merged into the infantry. Patton, feeling that a more independent outlook would be found in the cavalry, decided to go back to his old arm. There is no doubt that this period of study and experiment with Patton had a great influence on the development of Eisenhower's military thought. It also reserved in his heart a soft corner for Patton so that when the time came he could make use of that magnificent leadership, despite the erratic streak in him and even though, as Eisenhower said, it sometimes needed 'all the friendship we could muster'. An interesting sidelight on their characters in these early days is their attitude to the game of poker. The addiction of Eisenhower, the steady calculating planner, has already been mentioned; Patton, the dashing leader with an eye for a chance and all the attributes of a gambler, had no use for the game.

One of the by-products of friendship with Patton was an introduction to Brigadier-General Fox Conner, who had been Pershing's operations staff officer in France. Conner asked for Eisenhower as his staff officer with his brigade in Panama. In their service together Eisenhower learnt much, not only of the direct duties of a staff officer but also about the

[4] *At Ease*, p. 170

meaning and value of military history. Eisenhower had taken away from West Point a hearty contempt for the routine instruction in military history. He had been made to learn by heart the name of every brigade commander in the opposing armies at Gettysburg and his action at every stage of the battle. No attempt had ever been made to show what was in the mind of the various commanders or what was the meaning of the battle. Conner, who had an excellent library, gradually introduced Eisenhower to the art of reading, and to thinking and talking about what he had read. Naturally much time was devoted to the Civil War but they roamed further afield not only to Julius Caesar and Tacitus but even to Plato and to Shakespeare. The three years Eisenhower spent with Conner in an isolated post in Panama were undoubtedly the most formative of his military life.

As a result of Conner's recommendation Eisenhower went to the Command and Staff School at Fort Leavenworth in August 1925 for a one-year course. Conner's instruction had been so complete and so relevant to the duties of a staff officer that Eisenhower took the work in his stride and revelled in the war-games and the problems with which he was faced. He decided to regulate his private study sensibly and not to exhaust himself by late poring over books. He decided on two and a half hours work each evening five days a week. This work was carried out with an officer slightly senior to him, Leonard T. Gerow, with whom he was subsequently to work in the Plans Division. Eisenhower graduated top of his class.

After Fort Leavenworth Eisenhower was appointed to Pershing's staff to assist in the task of writing a guide book to the action of the American forces in the war. Pershing does not seem to have had much influence on Eisenhower's thought or outlook. Eisenhower found him colourless, and it seems that most of what Eisenhower wrote for him was altered in a rather petty way. There was one exception: Eisenhower persuaded Pershing that a cohesive military study of the St Mihiel and the Argonne operations would be more valuable than the lifeless day-to-day account which Pershing had written. Pershing was satisfied with the new draft. He thought however that before accepting it he would show it to Colonel George Marshall, a man generally expected to rise to the highest position in the army. Marshall decided against Eisenhower's approach and Pershing reverted to the diary form. This was Eisenhower's first direct contact with Marshall.

During his time with Pershing, Eisenhower had had an interregnum to graduate at the War College where his old mentor, Conner, was Commandant, and afterwards he served on the staff of the Assistant Secretary of War. His duties were particularly suitable for a recent graduate at the War College: a study of ways to mobilize American industry in a future war. Working directly under General Moseley, who had served on Pershing's staff during the war, Eisenhower visited firms and factories to see what plans there were should it be necessary to turn again to the warlike production of which they had recent experience. Not unnaturally it was difficult to interest firms at all. In the late 'twenties thoughts were centred on the depression and few believed that there was ever going to be another war, certainly not one in which the United States would be involved. There were exceptions. Eisenhower got valuable help and advice from Bernard Baruch, who had been chief of the War Industries Board in 1918. Baruch believed that as soon as war could be seen to be imminent, an agency should be set up for the control of prices, wages and raw materials. There was naturally much opposition to Baruch's views but a congressional commission was working on the problem of how to take the profit out of war and this gave an opportunity to the War Department to do something. Eisenhower, working with an engineer, Colonel Williams, drafted a plan for industrial mobilization and for the reform of the technical services. The arrival of a dynamic figure, General Douglas MacArthur, as the Chief of Staff, and his reception of these advanced ideas, added strength to the reformers. Eisenhower considered that the plan put forward was far from a masterpiece but it did make an impression. In particular the status of the technical service and of supply and production was raised in the eyes of the General Staff, and officers of ability from the army and the navy were sent to the recently established Industrial College to study this essential side of the national war potential.

His duties in the War Department introduced Eisenhower to a wider concept of war. It also brought him in touch with MacArthur on whose staff he was to serve from February 1933 to December 1939. First he became Military Assistant in the rank of major, where he had the task of drafting MacArthur's statements and letters, and was generally responsible for the organization of the personal office. From MacArthur Eisenhower learnt how it was not always possible to draw a clear line between the political and the military. MacArthur was a hard taskmaster but in most ways a rewarding one. He gave a task and asked no questions—all he required was that it should be done.

Towards the end of MacArthur's term as Chief of Staff much of his time was taken up with preparations for a defence programme for the Philippines. A bill, approved by the President in 1934, had provided for independence in 1946. In the intervening years the Philippines were to have Commonwealth status and it was the desire of the United States government to do everything possible to prepare the people for independence. As so often with a country emerging to independence the obstacle to effective defence was the cost of the necessary forces. Eisenhower's task was to provide a force which would be ready to take the full burden of defence when United States protection was removed and yet fall within the cost which the Philippines would be prepared to bear. Little did Eisenhower know that of the intervening years about half were to be taken up with war or Japanese occupation.

Eisenhower was to be taken even closer to the Philippine problem because of the spell which the name MacArthur had in those islands. General Arthur MacArthur, father of Douglas, laid the foundations of a free and independent Philippines based on liberal concepts. He introduced free education and established a sound legal system which included the essential writ of habeas corpus. Manuel Quezon, then head of the Commonwealth government, asked that Douglas MacArthur should become Military Adviser. MacArthur enthusiastically accepted and when he went out took Eisenhower as his Military Assistant.

Despite his long service with MacArthur, Eisenhower does not appear to have been unduly impressed by him or even to have held him in very high personal regard. Possibly this was due to an incident early in their time in Manila. MacArthur had, despite warnings from his staff of the expense involved, set on foot certain elaborate preparations for a ceremonial parade to show the army to the people. When the preparations were seen to be objectionable MacArthur appears to have disclaimed responsibility and failed to give his staff the support which Eisenhower believed they deserved. Nevertheless, the experience which Eisenhower gained in the Philippines was invaluable and one small incident can serve to show the scope of his duties. In Washington Eisenhower's work had shown him that a navy and air force would be impossibly expensive for the Philippines and that they must rely on the United States for external defence. But soon after he arrived in Manila, Eisenhower saw that it was essential to have some small air force, both as a foundation stone for the future and to get about the military stations which were necessarily widely scattered over the islands. Eisenhower involved himself so deeply in the project that he decided to learn to fly himself and at the age of 46 he obtained a pilot's certificate. This practical approach reveals an important facet of the character of the man, just as his understanding of the importance of the air factor shows his ability to grasp essentials. It was also a forerunner of the future, because this same understanding was to be one of the outstanding features of his ability as a military commander.

In his quarter century of service before the outbreak of the Second World War, Eisenhower had benefited from his varied military experience. For the first ten years he had always been at duty with troops. There he developed his capacity as an instructor and showed his ability to get the best out of his men. It was the association with Patton and the working out with him of new ideas and then the guidance of Conner that taught him to look and think more widely. He was thus able to get the most out of his year at Fort Leavenworth and to give of his best there. After that he had gone to broader spheres where he came in contact with men like Pershing and MacArthur and where he had the political experience of shaping the forces of the Philippines. In those years he had grown from the carefree but determined young officer into a mature and thoughtful but still extrovert and gregarious staff officer. Wherever he served he hated anything that savoured of War Department rigidity or inflexibility. He was always ready to protest and, more important, to use his imagination and enthusiasm to make his own unit or group work happily and efficiently. Protest he might, but Eisenhower had an abiding faith in the Republic and its central direction. He knew that frustrating rules and regulations were always the result of stupidity or thoughtlessness on the part of individuals. His loyalty, his sense of service, and his reverence for the flag never slipped from that moment of deep conviction when he had taken the oath at West Point.

One of Eisenhower's gifts was his understanding of the nature of the American Army and the characteristics of the American soldier. He foresaw that in war the army would consist largely of citizen soldiers and that they must be responsible thinking men who understood the purpose of conflict. He knew from the history of George Washington's army and the American Civil War that 'Americans either will not or cannot fight at maximum efficiency unless they understand the why and wherefore of their orders'. Eisenhower based his views on morale on this understanding. In his final report to President Quezon when he left the Philippines he put some of these thoughts on paper:

Morale is born of loyalty, patriotism, discipline, and efficiency, all of which breed confidence in self and in comrades. Most of all morale is promoted by unity – unity in service to the country and in determination to attain the objective of national security. Morale is at one and the same time the strongest, and the most delicate of growths. It withstands shocks, even disasters of the battlefield, but can be destroyed utterly by favoritism, neglect, or injustice. . . .

The army should not be coddled or babied, for that does not produce morale, it merely condones and encourages inefficiency. But the army should be taught to respect itself and to render a quality of service that will *command* respect throughout the nation. Thus the population will come to look upon the uniform as the badge of loyalty, of duty, and of efficiency, and this feeling will be reflected, inescapably, in still higher performance in the army.[5]

When news came that Britain and France were at war with Germany Eisenhower immediately went to MacArthur and asked that he might go home. He had been promoted Lieutenant-Colonel in July 1936 and felt that he must do everything possible to ensure that he was in at the beginning of a war which he believed was now inevitable for the United States. Neither the counsel of MacArthur nor the generous financial provisions of a new contract offered by Quezon availed and in the new year of 1940 Eisenhower was back in the United States.

Eisenhower's first task at home was again to make use of the instructional and organizational talent that he had shown in the first war. He was required to arrange the concentration of the Regular Army and the National Guard of the whole west coast for a large-scale exercise in California. However, he soon got his heart's desire, duty with troops, and was given command of a battalion of the 15th Infantry Regiment. He also got a letter from Patton, who said he expected to get command of one of the new armoured divisions and was going to ask for Eisenhower as a regimental commander. Another who was after his services was Gerow, his companion in study at Leavenworth. Gerow was chief of the War Plans Division in the War Department. Eisenhower was able to make his point that he wanted to remain with troops, but he left the decision with Gerow, who withdrew the request. But by December 1940 direct command was over and Eisenhower became Chief of Staff of the division in which he was serving. Three months later rapid expansion of the army took him first to be Chief of Staff IX Corps as Colonel and then Chief of Staff to General Krueger commanding the Third Army. The Third Army covered an enormous area of largely unsettled country from New Mexico

[5] *Ibid.*, pp. 383-4

to Florida and the problems of training and administration were enormous. The officers and men of the new formations had little understanding of the realities of war and few had had experience in the first war, so there was little to leaven the lump. Eisenhower saw that the principal aim of the training must be to harden the troops and to teach them to look after themselves. But no opportunity was lost to ensure that the lessons of each stage were brought home to the officers and that useless officers were eliminated. Eisenhower wrote of this time:

> During manoeuvres, my tent turned into something of a cracker-barrel corner where everyone in our army seemed to come for a serious discussion, a laugh, or a gripe. These visitors prolonged my hours and considerably reduced sleeping time. But I never discouraged those that came to complain for I was often astonished to see how much better they worked after they had unloaded their woes; and, of course, the harder they worked the smoother things went for us at army headquarters.[6]

At Third Army Eisenhower was promoted Brigadier-General. He remained there until the Japanese attack on Pearl Harbour. Within five days of that attack he was summoned to Washington.

[6] *At Ease*, p. 243

2

Eisenhower at the Operations Division

On 14 December 1941, one week after the Japanese attack on Pearl Harbour, Eisenhower was selected by Marshall to join the War Plans Division where, in the rank of Brigadier-General, he would be deputy to his old friend Gerow. Eisenhower strongly resisted this move into the War Department. He felt he had been trapped in the United States during World War I and he was determined that the same thing was not going to occur again. He asked a contemporary, Brigadier-General Haislip, then chief of the Personnel Division, to intervene with Marshall on his behalf. Marshall however was adamant and Eisenhower was ordered forthwith to Washington.

Marshall chose Eisenhower because he understood the problems of the Far East and had the added advantage of knowing MacArthur well. Eisenhower was given the task of studying Far Eastern strategy in the light of the fact that the greater part of the United States Pacific Fleet had been destroyed or disabled. At that time United States strategy was torn between the purely defensive and the offensive. On the one hand was the need to protect the still undamaged fleet installations at Pearl Harbour, the aircraft factories on the west coast of the United States and the locks of the Panama Canal, and on the other the offensive possibilities of counterstroke if the Japanese overreached themselves. In this dilemma the position of the Philippines, where MacArthur had taken over command on 26 July 1941, was critical. Luzon was a strategic area for naval and air bases from which offensive operations could be conducted against Japan and her sea communications. But the strong air forces necessary for this purpose—and to keep the United States fleet in being—had not been provided before the Japanese initiative. MacArthur believed that the battle for the Western Pacific would be decisive and that 'if the Western Pacific is to be saved it will have to be saved here and now'.[1]

[1] Matloff & Snell, 'Strategic Planning 1941-2', (1953), p. 84

The result of Eisenhower's first study was the recommendation that the Pacific lines of communication between the United States and Australia must be kept open and that the United States must go ahead and set up a military base in Australia. On 17 December Marshall approved the concept and appointed Eisenhower as 'Action Officer'. A few days later Eisenhower, together with his chief Gerow, attended the Arcadia Conference, the first war-time meeting of Churchill and Roosevelt and the British and United States Chiefs of Staff. The impact of the high-level discussions on Eisenhower may be imagined. The leaders of the two great nations were discussing the long-term plans for the Alliance at a time when desperate action was necessary to stave off further disasters of the moment. The British, who had been living with disasters for more than a year, came to the conference better prepared to steer the discussion their way: the entry of the United States into the war made virtually certain the consummation of their national faith in ultimate victory—a faith which had never wavered. In this light Roosevelt saw eye to eye with Churchill and there was a much closer accord than that between Roosevelt and his Joint Chiefs of Staff or even than that between Churchill and his own military advisers. Similarly in the military staffs the division of thought was more often by service than by nationality. The soldiers saw the problem one way and the sailors saw it rather differently. In this matter of services it must be remembered that there was no independent United States Air Force but only their Army Air Force and the carrier-borne naval airmen. Thus Eisenhower was brought up to look at a problem as much from an air as from an army point of view—a factor which was to show throughout his development and performance as a commander.

The essential agreement which came out of the Arcadia Conference was the confirmation of the pre-war assumption that in a war against the Axis and Japan the United States would combine with her allies to defeat Germany first. Eisenhower himself did not doubt the wisdom of this decision nor did he believe that it could be questioned by any student of strategy.[2] Nevertheless it was a brave decision. In the eyes of the American people Japan was the enemy at the gate and the nation whose assault had brought them into the war. However right the decision, it made it little easier to decide what to do at once and how to bring to bear the forces that would lead to the quick defeat of Germany. No time must be wasted because the decision could only seem right for the United States if she

[2] Eisenhower, *Crusade in Europe*, p. 31

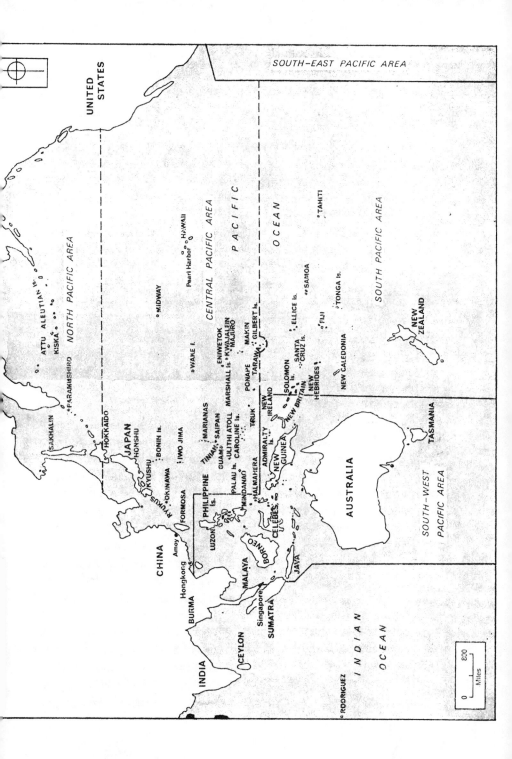

could move quickly to the defeat of Germany. Two factors weighed heavily in the question of timing: it was not known how long Russia could continue to withstand the attacks of the German Army nor how far Japan could consolidate or extend her gains in the Pacific.

One of the important points raised at the Arcadia Conference was the machinery for consultation and command in the Far East. On the day of discussion, Christmas Day 1941, the battle for the mainland of Malaya had been virtually lost; Hong Kong had fallen; the Philippines were isolated and attacked, and the Japanese had established bases in North Borneo and several Pacific islands. Marshall took the opportunity to put forward his views on unified command. He believed that there must be in each theatre of operations one commander to receive instructions from and to report to the various national governments and staffs concerned and to direct the sea, land and air forces to a common purpose. Marshall's views were not altogether acceptable to the British Chiefs of Staff, who favoured their traditional practice of commanders equal in authority for each of their three services. Nevertheless, after the meeting Marshall instructed Eisenhower to draft a paper which might serve as a vehicle to establish unity of command in the critical situation in Southeast Asia—or what was to the Americans the South Western Theatre. Eisenhower was thus set on the first steps of what was to be his chief contribution to the military art, the construction of a sound and workable unified command system. Having set out the immediate tasks of the armed forces in the theatre, Eisenhower's paper authorised the commander to co-ordinate the tactical and strategic operations of all the forces to this end and organize task forces to execute special operations. In the climate of the discussions at which he had been present, Eisenhower found it necessary to hedge the chosen commander with many restrictions so that he could not impede direct communications between national commanders and their own military authorities and government.[3] With these safeguards Marshall got his way and the Australian-British-Dutch-American Command (ABDA) was set up under Wavell and was directed to report to a newly constituted Allied committee, the Combined Chiefs of Staff (CCS). The CCS consisted of the American Joint Chiefs of Staff and either the British Chiefs of Staff or such officers as they would appoint to represent them. For this purpose, Field Marshal Dill, the former Chief of the Imperial General Staff, became their permanent chief representative in Washington.

[3] The paper in full is Papers I, No. 24

As chief War Department operations officer for the Pacific Eisenhower was concerned with the provision of army forces essential for minimum security in the Pacific. Admiral King put forward extensive proposals for island garrisons in the South Pacific and believed that the security of the navy and possibility of offensive action depended on land-based, and thus army, air forces. Marshall wanted to do anything reasonable that would make offensive action by the fleet possible but he feared demands for occupational troops and air forces that would undermine efforts to provide and train an effective United States Army. Eisenhower's views are clear from notes made at the time:

> The struggle to secure the adoption by all concerned of a common concept of strategical objectives is wearing me down. Everybody is too much concerned with things of his own.
> We've got to go to Europe and fight – and we've got to quit wasting resources all over the world – and still worse – wasting time. If we're to keep Russia in, save the Middle East, India and Burma; we've got to begin slugging with air at West Europe; to be followed by a land attack as soon as possible.[4]

On 16 February Eisenhower became Chief of the War Plans Division and one of his first studies set out the problem of the South West Pacific in the light of world strategic objectives. This paper[5] began by substantiating the soundness of the decision to concentrate on Germany first because of the greater accessibility of Germany, the position of Russia—not at war with Japan—and the fact that it took three or four times as many ships to transport and maintain a given American force in the Pacific as in the Atlantic. Nevertheless the decision on priorities did not remove the necessity to face the immediate problem of the Pacific and 'to be as careful to avoid unwarranted weakness as to abstain from unnecessary commitments'. He saw the enormous advantages that would accrue to the enemy powers through conquest of India, domination of the Indian Ocean and the possible junction of Germany and Japan. He saw the defence of Australia and adjacent islands as being important but less critical. Thus Eisenhower sought to differentiate between the things that were necessary and those that were 'merely desirable because of their effect in facilitating such defeat'. He considered that the loss of Malaya and much of the Netherlands Indies had removed one of the original reasons for action in the South-West Pacific—it was no longer possible to deny the

4 Papers I, No. 73
5 Papers I, No. 160

natural resources of the area to the Japanese. In setting out the tasks to be faced in the Pacific he concluded:

> The United States' interest in maintaining contact with Australia and in preventing further Japanese expansion to the Southeastward is apparent ... but ... they are not immediately vital to the successful outcome of the war. The problem is one of determining what we can spare for the effort in that region, without seriously impairing performance of our mandatory tasks.

The necessary tasks as Eisenhower saw them were:

(a) Maintenance of the United Kingdom, which involved relative security of the North Atlantic sea lanes.
(b) Retention of Russia in the war as active enemy of Germany.
(c) Retention of a position in the India-Middle East area which would prevent physical junction of the two principal enemies, and would probably keep China in the war.

In developing his ideas of what might be necessary to keep Russia in the war he urged action both through lend-lease and by the early initiation of action to draw off sizeable German army and air forces from the Russian front. He concluded:

> We should at once develop, in conjunction with the British, a definite plan for operations against North West Europe. It should be drawn up at once, in detail, and it should be sufficiently extensive in scale as to engage from the middle of May onward, an increasing portion of the German Air Force, and by late summer an increasing amount of his ground forces.

Thus Eisenhower begins to show himself as the principal advocate of the assault on Europe in 1942.

During early March Eisenhower was taken up with a reorganization of the War Plans Division. The wide authority of Marshall as Chief of Staff of the Army and his use of the Division as his executive staff gave it a central position in the prosecution of the war. Apart from direct planning and operations duties the Division was now concerned with co-ordination with the navy and with the British; with resources and requirements, and with such new developments as psychological and economic warfare. Eisenhower saw Marshall as the central commander and considered that his Division should be known as 'Command Headquarters'. There was some logic in this idea as the Division existed outside the four normal branches of the War Department, G1, G2, G3 and G4. However Marshall decided otherwise and did no more than change the name to the 'Operations Division'.

5 *With MacArthur in the Philippines, 1935*

In all this period we see the moulding of the Eisenhower of the future: the man who saw things with very much the same mind as Marshall; the advocate of the quick assault on Germany; the airman cum soldier, and the planner who looked to the broad structure for the future rather than the commander with his eye on the battle of the moment. The contemporary remarks of Eisenhower himself and of his close friend, George Patton, confirm this view. Patton, just promoted to command 1st Armoured Corps, wrote to say with what certainty he regarded the future with Eisenhower in the War Plans Division: 'Your self-assurance and to me, at least, demonstrated ability, give me a great feeling of confidence for the future . . . we will eventually beat the hell out of those bastards—you name them I'll shoot them.' Eisenhower replied: 'I don't have the slightest trouble naming the helions I'd like to have you shoot; my problem is to figure out some way of getting you to the place you can do it.' He added that he had reconciled himself to being in Washington against his personal inclination and had put away in mothballs his ideas on troop training and troop leadership.[6]

The exchanges between Roosevelt and Churchill after the loss of the Netherlands East Indies and the dissolution of ABDA led Roosevelt to propose that for war direction the world should be divided into three areas or, as Marshall later called them, theatres: the Pacific, a United States responsibility; the Middle East and Far East, a British responsibility; and the European and Atlantic area, a joint responsibility. Eisenhower thereupon set out clearly a staff paper which, approved by Marshall, was sent by Roosevelt to Churchill and informally accepted. This paper set out what became the established practice throughout the remainder of the war. It gave the Combined Chiefs of Staff general direction over all theatres and direct control over the joint theatre, while the United States and British Chiefs of Staff were respectively responsible in the other theatres for strategy and operations and for co-ordination with their allies. This is just one example of the questions, usually requiring decision at the highest level, which came before the Operational Division at this time. Some, although less important, yet held within them the possibility of serious friction between the Allies if not properly handled at the staff level. There might have been controversy and bitterness if the United States had initiated a proposal to make MacArthur Supreme Commander in an area in which the primary purpose was the defence of Australia—yet

[6] Papers I, No. 157

Roosevelt was determined that he should be. In the course of military operations it was logical to arrange for MacArthur to slip secretly away from the Philippines to Australia so that almost as a matter of course the Australian Government would ask for him as Supreme Commander. Similarly in Burma there was the possibility of endless complications. The Americans had poured equipment into the country and the presence of such characters as Chiang Kai Shek and Stilwell made for difficulties. A false step could have caused considerable embarrassment to Alexander, who was at that time trying to extricate his forces and to ensure at any rate the security of the northeastern borders of India. On the material side as well as on the command side there were immense problems. The United States was being asked to pour weapons and equipment into the Middle East, into India and into Australia for use by British Commonwealth forces. Admiral King was calling for all sorts of static defence units and land-based aircraft for naval support. There was also the deeper question of division of control of air forces between army and navy. Each of these calls on the military resources of the United States was in some way justified, but taken together they would have the effect of putting off the moment when the United States would have the trained and equipped army for the major task which Roosevelt, Marshall and Eisenhower all saw before them. In the many notes and memoranda drafted by Eisenhower[7] it will be seen how clear was his mind and how politic his influence. Posterity with all the advantage of hindsight will not often have cause to criticise his judgment.

The United States were bent on efforts for a cross-Channel invasion in 1942 but information received from the British Chiefs of Staff in mid-March showed that they had very different views about the timing. The British believed that even in 1943 a landing would be possible only under conditions of severe deterioration of German military power. The Combined Chiefs of Staff therefore set the Combined Planning Staff to reconcile the two views. Meanwhile Eisenhower was working to bring the War Department to a co-ordinated view on the major tasks of the war. On 25 March he put before Marshall a paper requiring first of all the decision on the theatre in which the major offensive effort of the western Allies would first be made. That was a decision which would govern the United States training and production programme and the other tasks which might be undertaken. Again Eisenhower emphasised that because

[7] Papers I, especially Nos. 143, 152, 154, 181, 187-8

the United States must devote considerable resources to keep open the lines of communication to Britain, and because Britain must keep great forces for the security of her own islands, a cross-Channel operation would take advantage of naval and air forces which could not be used elsewhere. Such an operation in fact offered the only feasible method for employing offensively a major portion of the British combat power. It was on this operation that the Allies should fix their sights. Shipping, air forces and landing craft should be accumulated and husbanded to make the operation feasible as soon as possible and all temptation towards dispersion should be resisted. At the end of the paper was an ominous warning that if such a policy could not wholeheartedly be accepted the United States must turn her back on Europe and go full out, as quickly as possible, against Japan.[8]

Marshall accepted Eisenhower's paper and took it straight to the President. He decided, with Stimson, the Secretary of War, and Hopkins, his own confidant, that the question should be taken up not in the Combined Chiefs of Staff but direct with Churchill. Eisenhower and his staff were thereupon directed to put up proposals for presentation, and after Marshall had worked on these proposals they became known as the 'Marshall Memorandum'. The President directed that it should be taken to London by Marshall and Hopkins for presentation to the Prime Minister and his military staff.

While all this hard work was going on there occurred an incident which throws light on the characters of Marshall and of Eisenhower and the relationship between them. Marshall spared a moment in his office to give Eisenhower his philosophy about promotion and the duty of officers. Marshall believed that in the First War staff officers had been favoured at the expense of outstanding fighting leaders. He intended that this time promotion should go to commanders in the field and not to the staff who cluttered up the War Department and the higher headquarters. He directed his thoughts on to Eisenhower's own case and said that although he knew Eisenhower had been recommended for divisional and corps command he was going to stay where he was and fill his position, unjust as that might seem. Eisenhower's past frustration and his protests at being called to the War Department welled up within him and he burst out: 'General, I'm interested in what you say, but I want you to know that I don't give a damn about your promotion plans as far as I am concerned. I came into this office from the field and I am trying to do my duty. I expect

[8] Papers I, No. 207, Matloff & Snell, *op. cit.*, p. 181

to do so as long as you want me here. If that locks me to a desk for the rest of the war, so be it!' Both were somewhat surprised at this outburst but neither could quite resist a slight smile at the situation. A few days later Eisenhower heard that he had been promoted Major General. Marshall in making the recommendation to the President said that Eisenhower was his operations officer rather than a staff officer. As such he was in effect a subordinate commander responsible for the disposition of all army forces, including the Air Corps—a function which had to be performed without constant reference to Marshall.[9]

Eisenhower did not accompany Marshall to London, but from the Operations Division went Colonel A. C. Wedemeyer, later to become Stilwell's successor in Burma and China. Out of the discussions in London came the three concepts which were to govern planning for the next year: Bolero,[10] the concentration of United States forces and material in the United Kingdom ready for the cross-Channel operation whenever it might come; Round-Up, a major British–United States attack across the Channel in 1943, and Sledgehammer, a limited attack in 1942 to seize a bridgehead in France. On Bolero there was no disagreement, but the other two were regarded very differently by the two nations. The Americans wanted to make Round-Up a firm commitment for 1 April 1943 and were willing to take risks in the Middle East and the Indian Ocean and to accept losses in the Pacific. Above all they were determined that operations on the Continent should not become the residuary legatee for which nothing was left. They set much store by Sledgehammer which they thought might have to be launched in September or October 1942, either because it was necessary to save Russia from defeat, or because critical weakening of the German position in Western Europe presented the opportunity. The British were anxious lest premature concentration for operations on the Continent should weaken their position, particularly in the air, in the Middle East and Indian Ocean. They were most sceptical about the possibility of Sledgehammer: Brooke, the British C.I.G.S., thought Marshal's ideas on this operation 'just fantastic'.[11] Moreover Churchill had other ideas about fruitful operations and had not given up hope of interesting the Americans in his ideas for North Africa nor of a

---

[9] *At Ease*, pp. 248–9
[10] In United States papers Bolero is sometimes used loosely to cover Round-Up but in British documents and in this book it is used only in its proper sense.
[11] Bryant, *Alanbrooke Diaries*, I, pp. 354

British operation in Norway. Nevertheless Churchill realised the vital necessity of marching with the United States lest they should decide to direct their main efforts against Japan. For all their mental reservations the British accepted the American proposals for offensive action in 1943 and possibly in 1942. The differences were all the more important because of the balance of forces available. The shipping and landing craft requirements had not been worked out but it was clear that by mid-September 1942 only three and a half United States divisions and 700 combat aircraft would be available. It was thought that enough landing craft to maintain five divisions, half British half American, would be available by the autumn. It was apparent therefore that the operations on which the Americans set so much store would have to be carried out largely by British forces. Eisenhower saw this clearly and was constantly trying to get the War Department to grapple with the shipping problem and to stir up interest in the production of landing craft. If the shipping problem could be solved some 30 United States divisions and 3,250 combat aircraft could be made available in the United Kingdom by 1 April 1943. Eisenhower believed that these with 18 British divisions and 2,550 combat aircraft would be sufficient to establish air superiority and make a landing on a six-division front between Le Havre and Boulogne. Even at this early stage Eisenhower emphasised the necessity for the early seizure of the port of Antwerp.

It must not be imagined that Eisenhower was able to devote himself exclusively to these matters although they were nearest his heart. While Marshall was in London, events in the Pacific were showing the bitter price the Americans were having to pay for their inability so far to hold the Japanese. At the beginning of April the United States forces in Bataan were at their last gasp. Eisenhower realised only too clearly the harsh realities of an emaciated army fighting without hope and facing an inexorable fate. But he had to grapple with the conflicting pulls of Roosevelt's instruction to MacArthur that resistance should be 'as effective as circumstances will permit and as prolonged as humanly possible' and MacArthur's utter opposition to capitulation in any form. MacArthur was determined that if the force was to be destroyed 'it should be upon the actual field of battle taking full toll from the enemy'. The facts and orders were cogently summarised by Eisenhower for the acting Chief of Staff and the President[12] but in such a situation the answer could not rest with

[12] Papers I, Nos. 229 & 230

Washington and on the night of 8 April the commander of the Luzon force surrendered.

Eisenhower did not allow the tragedy in the Bataan Peninsula to obscure his strategic vision and in a review of the situation for the Secretary of War he said: 'The significant strategical development of the last few days was not the loss of Bataan, but the bold and extensive incursion of Japanese air and naval power into the Bay of Bengal and the Indian Ocean.' He was fully alive to the problem that was at that moment exercising the British Chiefs of Staff and was responsible for some of their mental reservations about the Marshall Memorandum. Although both the United States Army and Navy authorities regarded the Japanese attack on Ceylon as a raid and believed that the real Japanese threat was in the Pacific, Eisenhower, in his review of priorities, was dispassionate enough to put the security of the Middle East and the Indian Ocean above that of the South Pacific.

Marshall returned from London aware of the fact that he had brought agreement only in principle and that everyone had reservations on one aspect or another. Nevertheless a start had been made and after talking to Marshall, Eisenhower wrote: 'I hope that—at long last . . . we are all definitely committed to one concept of fighting! If we can agree on major purposes and objectives, our efforts will begin to fall in line and we won't just be thrashing about in the dark.'[13] There was however still plenty of competition with Bolero and Eisenhower was soon once more immersed in questions of air forces for Stilwell in China and reinforcements for Australia. The complications in the South West Pacific are illustrated by an occasion when the demand for reinforcements for Australia reached the Operations Division from Roosevelt. Curtin, Prime Minister of Australia, had cabled to Churchill asking for two British divisions until such time as two Australian divisions could be released from the Middle East. Since this arose from a request by MacArthur to Curtin for reinforcements Churchill, fearing that MacArthur's demands might be a prelude to the recall of a valuable Australian division then fighting in Libya, cabled to Roosevelt. MacArthur, on being told that his requests for reinforcements must come to the War Department, thought that the delicacy of his position in dealing with the Prime Minister of Australia was not fully appreciated. These and other matters caused Eisenhower to note: 'Bolero is supposed to have the approval of Press and Prime Minister. But the struggle to get everyone behind it, and to keep the highest authority

13 Papers I, No. 254

from wrecking it by making additional commitments of air-ship-troops elsewhere is never ending. The actual fact is that not 1 man in 20 in the Govt (including the W. and N. Depts) realizes what a grizzly, dirty, tough business we are in! They think we can buy victory.'[14]

During May Eisenhower was working on the command of the United States forces for Bolero. He emphasised the necessity for unity of command, a principle already agreed between Marshall and King. The British must be made to realise that the officer nominated would be the effective commander of all the United States forces in the theatre, land, sea and air. Eisenhower foresaw that the President might direct that Marshall himself should eventually go to Europe to take over command and that the commander now appointed must therefore be a man acceptable to Marshall as Deputy or Chief of Staff. There is no indication that Eisenhower had himself in mind. Indeed he suggested in a second paper that if Major General Chaney, then Commanding General United States Army Forces British Isles, were not to continue in the command in its new role then McNarney (an air force officer who had just been nominated for promotion to lieutenant general and for appointment as Deputy Chief of Staff of the Army) should be appointed.[15] Before Marshall made up his mind about the command question he sent Eisenhower as his personal representative to London to discuss the progress of planning for Bolero with Chaney and the British Chiefs of Staff. Eisenhower was accompanied by Arnold, Chief of the Air Staff, Lieutenant General Somervell, head of logistics and responsible for landing craft, and Major General Mark Clark, Chief of Staff of Army Ground Forces. The party arrived at Prestwick on 25 May and after looking at a demonstration of landing craft went on to London. Before meeting the Chiefs of Staff Eisenhower attended a large-scale exercise in the south-east to test the new British divisional organization. This 'Exercise Tiger' was run by Montgomery, commanding South-Eastern Army, and was the last exercise he organized before he went on to command Eighth Army in the Desert. Eisenhower noted his impressions: 'General Montgomery is a decisive type who appears to be extremely energetic and professionally able, I would guess his age as 58 years.'[16] Montgomery was in fact 55 and the only thing he notes in his memoirs about Eisenhower's visit is that he signed his visitors' book.

In discussion with the British Chiefs of Staff Eisenhower seems to have

[14] Papers I, No. 278
[15] Papers I, Nos. 292 and 319
[16] Papers I, No. 318

concentrated on the command question. He did not like what he considered the British committee system and said so. His memorandum on his visit contains a number of diagrams of alternative command arrangements but in all of them there is a supreme commander responsible to the Combined Chiefs of Staff and under him a Commanding General United States Army (ground and air forces) and a British Army Commander. Eisenhower had several discussions with Mountbatten, then Chief of Combined Operations, and it is apparent that the two men saw eye to eye about the problem of the assault and tactics for a combined operation and in general on the types of landing craft required. This accord is all the more interesting in the light of the fact that immediately after the conferences Mountbatten went to Washington to explain that Sledgehammer in 1942 was out of the question. Later Eisenhower had discussions with Paget, Commander-in-Chief Home Forces, then responsible for planning cross-Channel operations. Paget thought the Americans should capture Le Havre and the British Boulogne and Calais, each using in the assault three divisions and following up with three more. Paget thought this the maximum that could be maintained before bringing the ports into use. The British foresaw providing 21 divisions (including Canadian and one Polish) of which eight would be armoured. Eisenhower accepted Chaney's estimate that 18 or 19 American divisions might be in England on a 'D' Day in 1943 and that 27 divisions might be in France by D plus 80.

Eisenhower returned to Washington on 3 June, noting: 'Our own people are able but do not quite understand what we want done. It is necessary to get a punch behind the job or we'll never be ready by Spring 1943 to attack. We must get going.'[17] Five days later Marshall mentioned for the first time the possibility that Eisenhower might go to England in command. Eisenhower noted: 'Its a big job—if U.S.-U.K. stay squarely behind Bolero and go after it tooth and nail, it will be the biggest American job of the war. Of course command now does not necessarily mean command in the operation—but the job before the battle begins will still be the biggest outside that of C/S himself.'[18] On 11 June the decision was made and at the same time Clark was appointed to command II Corps, the spearhead in Britain. Marshall ordered Eisenhower himself to draft the signal to Chaney telling him of his supersession. This signal was a model of tact and understanding, pointing out that the change was in no way a

[17] Papers I, No. 320
[18] Papers I, No. 328

reflection on the way Chaney had carried out his duties, but had come about because of the change in scope of the appointment. On 24 June Eisenhower arrived in London and assumed command, confident that he was set on the task of immediate preparation for the great cross-Channel operation. What he did not know was that on 11 June, the very day of the confirmation of his appointment, the British Cabinet had decided not to attempt a landing unless it could be launched in sufficient strength to be sure of remaining. This was certainly the end of Sledgehammer, and it strengthened Churchill in his desire to undertake some peripheral operation which would engage the enemy at once and would prepare the way for the more formidable assault across the Channel.

3

Planning for North Africa

A few days before Eisenhower left Washington Churchill, accompanied by the C.I.G.S., had arrived to discuss strategy for the remainder of 1942 and 1943. Eisenhower had attended an informal meeting between Marshall, Dill, Brooke and Ismay and had found the views there expressed coinciding with his own; that Round-Up remained first priority; that Sledgehammer would be justified only by compelling reasons, and that an operation in North Africa in 1942 would be an unacceptable diversion.[1] Both Eisenhower and Clark had been presented to Churchill. Churchill wrote of this meeting:

> I was immediately impressed by these remarkable but hitherto unknown men. They had both come from the President whom they had just seen for the first time. We talked almost entirely about the major cross-Channel invasion in 1943, 'Round-Up' as it was then called, on which their thoughts had evidently been concentrated. We had a most agreeable discussion, lasting for over an hour. In order to convince them of my personal interest in the project I gave them a copy of the paper I had written for the Chiefs of Staff on June 15, two days before I started, in which I set out my first thoughts of the method and scale of such an operation. At any rate they seemed much pleased with the spirit of the document. At that time I thought of the spring or summer of 1943 as the date for the attempt. I felt sure that these officers were intended to play a great part in it, and that was the reason why they had been sent to make my acquaintance. Thus began a friendship which across all the ups and downs of War I have preserved with deep satisfaction to this day.[2]

Notwithstanding this meeting Eisenhower arrived in England with no knowledge of the discussions which Churchill had had with Roosevelt at Hyde Park (New York). Churchill had indeed gone to the United States to make it clear that he believed that Sledgehammer was out of the question and that in order to engage the enemy, operations should be undertaken in North Africa and possibly in Norway too. The North African operation was then named Gymnast but was eventually called Torch, which name

[1] Papers I, No. 344
[2] Churchill, *op. cit.*, IV, p. 345

will here be used. Churchill played his hand well. On the subject of Sledgehammer he asked Roosevelt whether the War Department had a plan, 'If
so, what is it? What forces would be employed? At what points would they
strike? What landing craft and shipping are available?' He went on to say
that if a plan could be offered that gave a good chance of obtaining a
permanent footing on the Continent he would support it. If there was no
such reasonable chance he considered that such an operation would be no
help to the Russians and would gravely prejudice the main operations for
1943. But if there were to be no Sledgehammer he said: 'Can we afford to
stand idle in the Atlantic Theatre during the whole of 1942? Ought we not
to be preparing within the general structure of Bolero some other operation
by which we may gain positions of advantage and also directly or indirectly
take some of the weight off Russia?'[3] These were arguments which ap-
pealed strongly to Roosevelt and it was against this background that they
both contemplated Torch.

Eisenhower, thus unaware of the weight that was to be brought against
his own views and those of the War Department, spent his first days in
Britain in discussing the immediate tactical problems of an assault on
Europe. Although he realised Sledgehammer must be a principally British
operation, he was intensely interested in the choice of objectives and the
frontage on which the attack should be made. He was worried lest a frontage too wide to allow proper concentration of ground and air forces should
be agreed. He worked closely with Major General Spaatz, the senior Army
Air Force officer in his party. Both of them attached great importance to
air support of ground forces and to the establishment of air superiority
before a landing took place. Eisenhower seemed to think that the Royal Air
Force were discounting the value of preparatory operations and were concerned only with a fighter umbrella during the assault and later advance.[4]
He was also interested in a discussion which Mountbatten was having
with Paget, by inference the commander of any major British operation.
Mountbatten believed that an assault should be carried out by a specially
designated and trained corps. Paget believed that the seaborne assault was
the same as any other military attack and that two or three corps should
move abreast. In each corps the leading divisions would be specially
trained in amphibious operations but each corps would command not only
the assault but also the follow-through as well. Eisenhower, although not

---

[3] Matloff & Snell, *op. cit.*, pp. 239-240
[4] Papers I, No. 367

concerned to interfere in what was a British argument, strongly agreed
with Mountbatten, who was in fact recommending what was being done
by Clark and his corps. Another matter that exercised Eisenhower's mind
was the German 88 millimetre gun, then much in the military eye as the
battle-winning factor in the Desert. He had already impressed on Somervell (responsible in the War Department for weapons procurement) the
necessity for a gun that could equal the 88 in performance, and now he was
giving his mind to ways and means of defeating the anti-tank gun.

Eisenhower and Captain Harry Butcher, an old friend who was his
Naval Aide, lived in a suite in the Dorchester Hotel, looking out over Hyde
Park. They also rented a country cottage at Coombe Hill. In London, work
and meetings filled their days and much of the night. Their great relaxa-
tion was to get away when they could for a quiet evening, possibly with a
few other members of the staff or with Clark, and enjoy an informal meal.
This seems usually to have consisted of dehydrated chicken noodle soup.
As planning developed it is surprising how often these rare evenings, or the
opportunity for an early night, were interrupted by a telephone call from
the Prime Minister with a suggestion for a nocturnal visit.

Eisenhower confessed that for him smoking was an addiction rather
than a habit. At this time he smoked about 80 cigarettes a day[5] and he was
shocked to find that at many of the dinners where important business was
discussed smoking was not allowed until after the toasts to His Majesty
and to the President had been proposed. He felt so strongly about it that
at first he determined not to accept any of these semi-official invitations
to dinner. On one occasion Mountbatten overcame the difficulty by
proposing the loyal toasts immediately after the soup had been served.
Nevertheless the rule in most London clubs that smoking was not allowed
in the dining room kept Eisenhower from ever accepting dinner invitations
at those establishments. For his social arrangements Eisenhower relied
heavily on Butcher, and wrote of him:

> Butch is fine. There is a constant stream of visitors, official and semi-official,
> to this city from the United States. . . . Butch is developing a great skill in
> meeting them, going over their business with them and then, when it appears
> desirable, cutting down the time I must devote to each person. On top of
> this, he is a swell person to have about from the standpoint of my disposition.
> It is a rather lonely life I lead; every move I make is under someone's observa-
> tion and, as a result, a sense of strain develops that is entirely aside from the
> job itself. At home, a man has his family to go to. Here there is no-one except

[5] He gave up smoking in 1949

a fine friend like Butch, who can be trusted with anything and who is performing a service far more than even he realises.[6]

While Eisenhower was settling down to work in Britain, Roosevelt and Marshall were at grips with the problem with which Churchill had faced them. Marshall, strongly supported by King, considered that the British refusal to undertake Sledgehammer demanded a complete change in American policy. Both doubted whether the British had ever been in wholehearted accord with United States proposals for operations on the Continent. They now submitted a memorandum to the President setting out the objections to Torch. They believed it would be both indecisive and a heavy drain on United States resources. Moreover, it would jeopardise the chances of Russian survival until 1943 and would undermine commitments to Russia. They recommended, unless the President could persuade the Prime Minister into forceful and unswerving adherence to operations on the Continent, that the United States should turn all available forces to the Pacific for a decisive stroke against Japan and should go on to the defensive against Germany. The President answered his Joint Chiefs of Staff with some very pertinent questions and pointed out that the defeat of Japan could not contribute to the defeat of Germany, whereas 'defeat of Germany means the defeat of Japan, probably without firing a shot or losing a life.'[7] He was willing to allow his representatives in London to make one more effort to persuade the British to undertake Sledgehammer in 1942. If that failed, then the Joint Chiefs 'must decide upon another place for United States troops to fight in 1942' but he formally opposed the Pacific alternative.[8] In order to hasten the decision the President asked Hopkins, accompanied by Marshall and King, to go to London and he expressed the hope that total agreement should be reached within one week.

On 8 July Eisenhower heard that the Prime Minister and Chiefs of Staff had decided that Sledgehammer could not take place in 1942. Marshall asked Eisenhower to have ready for him 'a searching examination' of the possibilities of Sledgehammer and details of how it might be carried out. He said that the Joint Chiefs considered that Torch was out of the question because of Pacific naval requirements alone. It is clear from the paper prepared by Eisenhower for Marshall[9] that he looked at Sledgehammer as necessary for keeping Russia in the war. The Germans had already crossed

[6] Papers I, No. 390
[7] Quoted in Matloff & Snell, *op. cit.*, p. 272
[8] *Ibid.*, pp. 277–8
[9] Papers I, No. 379

the Don and, although he admitted he knew little of the power or morale of the Russian forces, Eisenhower considered the situation was sufficiently critical to justify any action by the Allies that would be of definite assistance, even though the immediate material effect would be small. He emphasised that his aim was to keep eight million Russians in the war and that unless this were achieved the chances of a successful Round-Up in 1943 were small. Although the advantages of a successful landing were cogently brought out, the paper was weak in other respects. There was no discussion of the forces that the enemy might be able to bring to bear on the one assault division—the maximum for which assault craft could be provided. Eisenhower expressed his personal opinion that the chance of getting this division ashore were two to one against, and the odds against establishing a firm beachhead with six divisions and air support were five to one. The paper was not so much 'a searching examination' of the possibilities of an effective cross-Channel operation as an essay on the advantages of keeping Russia in the war.

Hopkins, Marshall and King met the Chiefs of Staff on Monday 20 July and the following two days. Churchill presided at the first and last meetings. Eisenhower did not attend any of the meetings, but after the Tuesday morning session he was instructed by Marshall to draw up detailed proposals for Sledgehammer in time for presentation on the following morning. Eisenhower, assisted by Clark and his staff, worked at high speed and three drafts were made which were successively discussed with Marshall, King and Spaatz. The tenor of the paper was as before: The operation would undoubtedly be hazardous, but it was emphasised that the odds to be met in 1942, in relation to enemy strength, might well be better than in Spring 1943. The tactical objective proposed was Cherbourg.[10]

Neither Churchill nor the British Chiefs of Staff believed this operation was possible. The fact that the Americans were advocating an attack that would largely have to be executed by British troops did not add weight to their advocacy. Brooke wrote of Eisenhower's memorandum that it 'drew attention to the advantages, but failed to recognise the main disadvantage that there was no hope of our still being in Cherbourg by next spring'. Of the American attitude he wrote: 'They failed to realise that such action could only lead to the loss of some six divisions without achieving any results.'[11] Eisenhower, too, committed to paper his thoughts

[10] Papers I, No. 386
[11] Bryant, *op. cit.*, I, pp. 424–5

about the meetings and the part he had played in briefing Marshall. He said that the days and nights had been 'tense and wearing', that the British had shown themselves resolutely against an attack which they believed could not possibly help the Russians and that they considered 'the chances of a tactical defeat very great'. The burden of proving that an attack on Cherbourg was a possible operation had been put on Clark and himself and their final recommendation to Marshall had been 'that if he thought the Russians were in bad shape and that an attack on the French coast would have a material effect in assisting the Russians, we should attempt the job at the earliest possible date—regardless.' In putting forward what he described as 'a tough recommendation', Eisenhower did not claim that the operation would be a tactical success but he did believe that 'with whole-hearted co-operation all round' the operation had 'a fighting chance'. He concluded: 'We have sat up nights on the problem involved and have tried to open our eyes clearly to see all the difficulties and not to be blinded by a mere passion for doing something.'[12]

Eisenhower was deeply disappointed at the result of the meeting. All that Marshall could do now was to report to the President that the British were not prepared to mount Sledgehammer and to ask for instructions. Eisenhower believed that the decision could only result in dissipation of the American effort and thought that the day on which it was taken 'could well go down as "the black day in history" particularly if Russia is defeated in the big Bosche drive now so alarmingly under way.'[13] On the other hand, Roosevelt said he was not surprised by the British decision and repeated his direction to his Joint Chiefs of Staff to prepare plans to bring United States forces into action in 1942. He again ruled out the Pacific and suggested for their consideration such widely ranging alternatives as Norway, the North African project, reinforcement of the British in the Middle East and even an expedition to Persia. As a result Eisenhower was set to prepare a survey of the strategic situation for Marshall to discuss with the Combined Chiefs of Staff. This survey[14] which was written on the day the Germans captured Rostov, suggested that nothing should be done that would interfere with Round-Up in 1943. If however by 15 September the situation was such that a 1943 Round-Up looked impracticable, then operations in North Africa should be undertaken before

[12] Papers I, No. 387
[13] Butcher, *Three Years with Eisenhower*, p. 24
[14] Papers I, No. 389

December 1942. This view was not completely in accord with Roosevelt's determination that American troops must be in action before the end of the year, nor with the British contention that Torch did not imply a break in the continuity of combined strategy. Nevertheless, the recommendation was accepted by the Combined Chiefs, but they did authorise combined planning for Torch to begin at once.

An exchange of messages between Hopkins, Roosevelt and Churchill showed that the President ignored his Joint Chiefs of Staff's proviso about Round-Up. He saw no reason why the withdrawal of a few troops for Torch in 1942 should affect Round-Up in 1943. As Commander-in-Chief he made the decision on 30 July that Torch should be undertaken at the earliest possible date.[15] In the meantime it had been agreed that Torch, whenever it took place, should be primarily an American operation since this would be likely to make it more acceptable to the French in North Africa. Apart from an assumed affinity with a sister Republic, the French were still bitter with Britain over their contribution in 1940, their attack on the French fleet, and their attempts to wrest the French Colonial Empire from allegiance to Vichy. The commander of the Allied forces was to be an American and as early as 25 July Marshall told Eisenhower that he would be responsible. Both Marshall and Eisenhower believed that Marshall would be the Supreme Commander for all Allied operations against Germany and that therefore preparations for Round-Up and Torch would come under the same head and Eisenhower would be the deputy for both. Neither had completely given up hope that Sledgehammer might yet be possible and Eisenhower continually refers to the importance of including within Round-Up preparations for Sledgehammer in case 'by good fortune we should get an unexpected opportunity to execute that operation under favourable circumstances.'[16] On 6 August Eisenhower was formally notified that Roosevelt had nominated him as Commander-in-Chief Allied Expeditionary Force. Even after this there was some confusion in Eisenhower's mind about his responsibilities. It was not until 15 August that it occurred to him that the British did not regard him as having any authority for war strategy or the cross-Channel operation, but recognised him only as the Allied Commander for Torch and the United States Commander in Britain. On 22 August the Combined Chiefs of Staff finally cleared up the matter by agreeing that a separate

[15] Matloff & Snell, *op. cit.*, p. 289
[16] Butcher, *op. cit.*, p. 27; Papers Nos. 393 and 399

6 *With MacArthur in the Pilhippines, 1939*

7 *Philippines, 1939*

8 *Third Army Training Camp, 1940 (Eisenhower in centre)*

planning staff for Round-Up would be instituted under a British officer. Eisenhower now found himself Allied Commander of an operation which Marshall by no means wholeheartedly supported. When it is remembered how completely Eisenhower looked to Marshall as the fountain of military inspiration and how disappointed he himself had been in the Torch decision, it might be imagined that he would regard his command with mixed feelings. The position was almost the exact opposite to what planning for Sledgehammer had been. There the Americans had been busy making plans which principally British forces would have to execute. Now Britain was taking the initiative in operations in which, for political reasons, the original landings must be American. It was believed that United States troops might land with French connivance, whereas British landings would almost certainly be opposed. Moreover, the main reason for Roosevelt's support of Torch stemmed from his determination that United States troops would be in action against the Germans before the end of 1942. Not only national but also inter-service conflicts had to be resolved. Here Eisenhower's views on command[17] were to stand him in good stead. He was strongly against what he regarded as the British 'Committee System' and was firm in the understanding that he was not only the Allied Commander but that all forces involved, whether land, sea or air, came under his orders. This might have involved him in great difficulties because at that time the British naval and air force commander had considerable active experience, especially in the Mediterranean. In particular, the Royal Navy would be taking a predominant part since it was only for the army that political factors demanded American initiative.

The early planning for Torch involved not only all the British service ministries and the United States War Department but also the shipping agencies, the foreign services and a whole host of government departments on each side of the Atlantic. Such a comprehensive array and so many conflicting interests could so easily have led to a fruitless search for an agreed plan, but now Eisenhower had been appointed Allied commander he was in authority and decisive action could begin. Eisenhower took Clark as his deputy and managed to extract from Marshall, as his Chief of Staff, Brigadier-General W. Bedell Smith, who was then serving as Secretary to the Combined Chiefs of Staff. With Clark as his deputy Eisenhower would be looking for a commander for the American Army committed to the operation. There is no doubt that Patton was in his mind

[17] See pp. 16 and 25-6

but he did not ask for him at once. Patton had written to Eisenhower soon after he arrived in Britain and had received the answer: 'It is entirely within the realm of possibility that I will need you sorely; and when that time comes I will have a battle with my diffidence over requesting the services of a man so much senior and so much more able than myself. As I have often told you, you are my idea of a battle commander, and if the fates decree that battles by big formations are to come either wholly or partially within my sphere of influence, I would certainly want you as the lead horse in the team.'[18]

Eisenhower lost no time in putting to the British Chiefs of Staff a very clear exposition of his views on the command organization required.[19] He suggested that he should have as his principal commanders a United States Army Commander, a British Army Commander (Alexander had already been nominated), an Allied Air Commander and an Allied Naval Commander. The American Army Commander would, as a matter of course, command the air forces in his support, and he believed that the British Army Commander should do the same. Eisenhower did not believe that naval action covering the widespread movement of shipping which was involved could come under him, but nevertheless he believed that Torch must be regarded as an amphibious operation from beginning to end and that there must be an Allied Naval Commander directly subordinate to him.

The Chiefs of Staff could not accept at once Eisenhower's views on naval and air command. Portal, the Chief of Air Staff, was opposed to a single allied air command and regarded air operations, like the naval covering operations, as coming within existing spheres of command. The British view was accepted although, as will be seen later, the air command arrangements did not work well and Eisenhower was forced back to his request for an Allied Air Commander. While the command question was still being debated Vice-Admiral Ramsay was appointed chief naval planner. Later it was decided that Cunningham, formerly Commander-in-Chief of the Mediterranean, must be placed in command of the Allied Naval Forces under Eisenhower. By this time Cunningham had made an outstanding reputation as a fighting commander in the Nelson tradition, and before 1942 was over was to be promoted Admiral of the Fleet. In Eisenhower's own words: 'He thought always in terms of attack, never of

[18] Papers I, No. 383
[19] Papers I, No. 411

defence. He was vigorous, hardy, intelligent and straightforward. In spite of his toughness, the degree of affection in which he was held by all grades and ranks of the British Navy, and, to a large extent, the other services, both British and American, was nothing short of remarkable. He was a real sea dog.'[20]

There is little doubt that Cunningham's relations with Eisenhower and their spontaneous reactions to each other were most important factors in the forging of Eisenhower the commander. The willingness of Cunningham to accept him fully and loyally was just what was necessary to establish confidence at the moment when Eisenhower faced for the first time his immense personal responsibility. Cunningham has written of the impression which Eisenhower made on him:

> I liked him at once. He struck me as being completely sincere, straightforward and very modest. In those early days I got the impression that he was not very sure of himself, but who would wonder at that? He was in supreme command of one of the greatest amphibious operations of all time, and was working in a strange country with an ally whose methods were largely unfamiliar. But as time went on he grew quickly in stature and it was not long before one recognised him as the really great man he is – forceful, able, direct and far seeing, with great charm of manner, and always with a rather naive wonder at attaining the high position in which he found himself. . . . We fast became firm friends. . . . From the very beginning he set Anglo-Saxon unity and friendship as his aim, and not only on the surface. He left nothing undone to advance it. The staffs were closely integrated, and it was not long before the British and American members ceased to look at each other like warring tom-cats and came to discover that the nationals of both countries had brains, ideas and drive.[21]

Eisenhower had more than a theoretical understanding of the problem of command and staff organization. He understood also human nature and the effect of national prejudice. He determined from the first that he would have a command and staff system devised for the tasks in hand which avoided divisions along national or service lines. Such a system was then a completely new idea, going far beyond what had existed in the last days of the First World War. Then Foch with a small personal staff, all French, worked entirely through national headquarters. Moreover, Foch had only armies to command so that he was spared inter-service differences, which are more difficult to resolve than national. Eisenhower set his face sternly

[20] *Crusade in Europe*, p. 99
[21] Quoted in Warner, *Cunningham of Hyndhope*, p. 186

against what he called 'the inevitable trend of the British towards "committee" rather than "single" command'. He also castigated any American commander who came short of his ideas of unity. In this vein he was to write, later, to Patton: 'The intelligent direction of opinion in our Army, so that there is created a spirit of partnership between ourselves and the British forces, is of real importance. Negative measures will not answer the purpose; without being extravagant and without blatant propaganda, we can produce the results desired by sound leadership and the exercise of good sense. . . . I expect you to respond to General Alexander's orders exactly as if they were issued by me.'[22] And again: 'I realise also that the great purpose of complete Allied teamwork must be achieved in this theatre and it is my conviction that this purpose will not be furthered by demanding the last pound of flesh for every error, when other measures should suffice. . . . When we have anything we feel compelled to report that smacks of criticism of another Service or of any collaborating agency, we must see that the matter is handled in a purely official manner and given in the nature of a confidential report to the next superior only. Better than this method is a friendly and personal conference with the man responsible.'[23]

One point on which all British officers who had personal experience of Eisenhower or who served on his staff emphatically agree is his tremendous emphasis on this singleness of purpose and swallowing of national or service prejudice or preferences in the execution of a common task. That and the personal loyalty that he himself from the first inspired are what those who served with him most remember. In the search for unity Cunningham was a most valuable ally. Lord Ampthill, who served on Cunningham's staff, wrote very much from the point of view of the Royal Navy:

> None of us British, and for that matter not many of the Americans, knew anything about 'Ike'. He was an unkown quantity. There was much (at the lower staff levels) friction between British and American officers. All the Americans knew A.B.C.'s wonderful fighting record in the Eastern Mediterranean, and really admired him and looked up to him. . . . It seemed to me that A.B.C. went out of his way to hoist 'Ike' into his proper position as Supreme Commander and that A.B.C. did as much or more than anyone else to give 'Ike' confidence, and also to blend the British and United States staffs into a reasonable smooth working Allied team.[24]

[22] Papers II, No. 865
[23] Papers II, No. 928
[24] Warner, op. cit., p. 189

In the making of Allied Force Headquarters into a truly single Allied inter-service headquarters, Eisenhower started on a task that was to continue throughout the war—and beyond. Its fulfilment was perhaps more than any other his special contribution to the practice of war. In commenting on an incident in which his precepts had not been followed, he explained his methods to Marshall:

> However, I never get really discouraged because I realise that the seeds for discord between ourselves and our British allies were sown, on our side, as far back as when we read our little red school history books. My method is to draw all these matters squarely into the open, discuss them frankly, and insist upon positive rather than negative action in furthering the purposes of Allied unity. I must say that Cunningham, Tedder and Alexander are able lieutenants in developing and executing this policy.[25]

The Allied decision to land in North Africa involved Eisenhower in a far more ambitious project than the purely American landing at Casablanca, which Churchill had first suggested to Roosevelt. Now the aim was to overrun Tunisia and to seize Bizerta before the Germans could forestall us, while at the same time Rommel's army was to be defeated in Tripolitania. Such an operation demanded landings within striking distance of Algiers and farther east if possible. Eisenhower was quick to see the problem and to support British plans for bold action inside the Mediterranean. He believed that Tunis was so great a prize that landings should be made at Bone, the farthest east at which fighters from Gibraltar could operate. The difficulty was that landings at Oran, Algiers and Bone would take up all the shipping and escorts that could be found and would leave nothing for a simultaneous landing at Casablanca. Marshall was strongly against such forward operations. He believed it would be madness to risk forces inside the Mediterranean without first securing an alternative line of communication along the railway, small capacity as it was, which ran from Casablanca through Oran and Algiers into Tunisia. The dangers to which shipping in the Mediterranean were subject had been fully demonstrated by the heavy losses of both naval and merchant ships which the effort to keep Malta supplied had involved. Besides the hazards of enemy submarine and air action and the unknown factor of French opposition, there was the danger of intervention from Spain. Gibralter was the only available area for land-based aircraft until airfields in North Africa could be occupied, and Spanish action could make it unusable. Another possibility was a

[25] Papers II, No. 927

German invasion of Spain to capture Gibraltar, although the political indications were that Germany would not enter Spain without an invitation. The American view was that a strong force landed near Casablanca would considerably lessen the possibility of Spanish intervention or connivance at German action.

The British realisation of the importance of Casablanca was tempered by the knowledge that at this season surf conditions made a landing impossible on four days out of five. They would therefore be happy to leave a Casablanca landing until after the establishment of forces inside the Mediterranean, or even to capture Casablanca from the landward side. The Americans however attached so much importance to Morocco that Marshall suggested that the Torch objectives should be limited to 'from Rio de Oro exclusive to Oran inclusive'. To this suggestion Eisenhower sent a strong telegram pointing out that such an operation would have all the disadvantages of violating French neutrality without the show of force which would make their acquiescence probable and that it would make the eventual capture of Tunisia unlikely. In summary Eisenhower said: 'broad strategic risks are equally great and under the new proposal we do not have a gambling chance to achieve a really worthwhile strategic purpose.'[26]

As might be expected Churchill kept a close watch on the progress of planning for his own chosen operation. He had, since Eisenhower's arrival in London, had him and Clark to luncheon at 10 Downing Street each Tuesday. As Churchill said, 'nothing but shop was ever discussed on any of these occasions.' As a result of a meeting at dinner on 25 August (Churchill had only arrived back from Cairo on Tuesday the 24th), Churchill decided to intervene once more with Roosevelt. He was very conscious that, unless the planning differences were resolved, Torch would no longer be effective either to help the Russians, then heavily engaged at Stalingrad, or to act in concert with the offensive about to be launched at El Alamein. In a telegram to Roosevelt, Churchill pointed out that Torch was political in its foundations; the aim must be to avoid a battle with the French, but if there was one, to win it. He wanted to give Eisenhower the task of attacking by a certain day, say 14 October, with what could be got ready rather than trying to arrange to begin when everything was ready. Such a directive would give Eisenhower the powers an Allied Commander-in-Chief should have. Churchill went on:

[26] Papers I, No. 448

In order to lighten the burden on the military commanders, I am of the opinion that you and I should lay down the political data and take this risk upon ourselves. In my view, it would be reasonable to assume (a) that Spain will not go to war with Britain and the United States on account of Torch; (b) that it will be at least two months before the Germans can force their way through Spain or procure some accommodation from her; (c) that the French resistance in North Africa will be largely token resistance, capable of being overcome by the suddenness and scale of attack, and that thereafter the North African French may actively help us under their own commanders; (d) that Vichy will not declare war on the United States and Great Britain; (e) that Hitler will put extreme pressure on Vichy, but that in October he will not have the forces available to overrun unoccupied France while at the same time we keep him pinned in the Pas de Calais, etc. All these may prove erroneous, in which case we will have to settle down to hard slogging. For this we have already been prepared, but a bold audacious bid for a bloodless victory at the outset may win a very great prize. Personally, I am prepared to take any amount of responsibility for running the political risks and being proved wrong about the political assumptions.[27]

Roosevelt showed himself more conscious of the real purpose and advantages of Torch than did the War Department, and within a week there was agreement between the two Chiefs of Staff Committees. There were to be three landings, Casablanca, Oran and Algiers. At the first two all the land forces were to be American; at Algiers the landings were to be made by American troops, but British forces were to be available for a dash for Tunisia and after the capitulation of Algiers might make landings east of that port. Much remained to be done but by 5 September Eisenhower was able to go ahead on a firm outline plan, a plan very much on the lines he himself had advocated.

Eisenhower's original straightforward command structure with Patton as United States Army commander, Alexander British Army commander and single Allied naval and air force commanders required considerable modification to fit in with the new plan. The landings at Casablanca and Oran provided no difficulty. Patton commanded the Western Task Force, in which all components, land, sea and air, were American. Major General Fredendall, who had succeeded Clark in command of II U.S. Corps, commanded the Centre Task Force consisting of American army and land-based aircraft supported by the Royal Navy including carrier-borne aircraft. The Eastern Task Force at Algiers posed a more difficult problem. The Eastern Assault Force was to be commanded by Major General

[27] Churchill, op. cit., IV, p. 474

Ryder, commander of 34th U.S. Infantry Division, but it was to be supported by the Royal Navy and the Royal Air Force, and immediately after the assault the Eastern Task Force under British command was to take over for the thrust into Tunisia. When Alexander had been appointed to command in the Middle East, Montgomery had been nominated as Commander First Army and Eastern Task Force. He in turn was required elsewhere. He had been sent to command the Eighth Army and Lieutenant General Anderson had taken his place. It was not these changes that caused the complications but the problem of command of the air forces. Instead of the simple American system favoured by Eisenhower, in which land-based air forces were an integral part of the army and came directly under the Task Force Commander, there was an independent air force, Eastern Air Command, under Air Marshal Welsh, in support of the operation. The object of this complication was to ensure that the air forces in the Mediterranean would not be restricted to particular operations but would be available for the air battle as a whole. To the same end the Americans had grouped their air forces as Twelfth Air Force under Brigadier-General Doolittle who reported direct to Eisenhower while Brigadier-General Cannon and Colonel Norstad came directly under the Western and Central Task Force commanders respectively. The division into task forces presented no such problem to the navies and with a commander-in-chief of the calibre and reputation of Cunningham it was likely that any difficulties would be quickly sorted out.

Eisenhower had more than problems of military command and tactical plans to fill his mind; the political problems of Torch were of overriding importance. We have already seen that Churchill was doing what he could to ease Eisenhower's burden in this sphere but nothing could alter the fact that the whole scope of the military operation would be affected by the degree of resistance or co-operation afforded by the French and by the reactions of Spain. Time was vital if the Allies were to anticipate the Germans in Tunisia, and the best way to gain time was to ensure the help of the French in Algeria. The British Foreign Office had long worked on the problem of enlisting the help and collaboration of the French throughout North Africa and one of their officials, Mr. W. H. Mack, was appointed to Eisenhower's headquarters to form a Political Affairs Section. The United States, who had never broken with Vichy, already had Mr. Robert Murphy as their chief diplomatic representative in French North Africa. Although the President wished to retain personal direction of political activities, he agreed that Murphy must work direct with Eisenhower and at a suitable moment would actually become a member of his staff. As in all command questions Eisenhower had strong views about his ultimate responsibility. In a personal signal to Marshall he said:

> As I am responsible for the success of the operations I feel that it is essential that final authority in all matters in that theatre rest in me, subject only to the combined Chiefs of Staff and the President, with Murphy as my operating executive and adviser for Civil Affairs. This is in accordance with my understanding of the President's intentions . . . and I believe the directive should clearly set forth this relationship. . . . There is a possibility that unless the directive is revised as indicated there may develop in the minds of the French officials, after my arrival, the idea that there is a division of authority between the American civil and military officials. I am sure that Murphy will agree with the foregoing and with the necessity of presenting the French with a clean cut and single authority.[28]

One of the worst of the political complications was the position of de Gaulle, recognised by the British Government as 'leader of all Free Frenchmen, wherever they may be, who rally to him in support of the Allied cause'. He was not so recognised by the United States government and he was regarded by many Frenchmen as a traitor. He had in fact already been condemned to death *in absentia*. Churchill hoped that de Gaulle would eventually be accepted by the French in North Africa[29] but he could not deny that it would be madness to land in North Africa with the apparent intention of substituting Free French rule for that of Vichy. If French co-operation were to be assured it must be under the guise that the Vichy government would have authorised it if they had been free agents. An essential requirement for the Allies was to find a man recognised throughout the French community as a patriot who would lead them to seize an opportunity for the liberation of France. Such a man would have to have the qualities of leadership and the standing which would impress both the high command and the whole body of French officers in North Africa, bound as they were by an oath of loyalty to Marshal Pétain.

Even before the final decision for Torch was taken Murphy had worked on the problem of finding the right leader. There appeared to him to be advantages in seeking such a leader in the existing structure of Vichy or its military establishment. Admiral Darlan, who was next in succession

[28] Papers I, No. 506
[29] Churchill, *op. cit.*, IV, p. 543

to Pétain, had late in 1941 confided to the United States Ambassador that he might wish to lead his countrymen back to the side of the Allies. General Juin, the Commander-in-Chief of the French Army in North Africa, had shown himself as determined in preparation against German invasion of Tunisia. General Noguès, Resident General of Morocco, had been an early advocate of continued French colonial adherence to the Allied cause. Nevertheless, all who had accepted Vichy were objects of Allied—and particularly British—distrust. The danger that a man like Darlan would double-cross the Allies was deeply felt and even with the others there was a danger that a leak of information would make surprise impossible. Fortuitously there appeared to be in unoccupied France just such a man as the Allies required. General Giraud, captured by the Germans in May 1940, had escaped and found his way back to southern France in April 1942. He had undertaken to support Pétain's authority but he had written an analysis of the causes of French defeat and was working for the day when Frenchmen might fight once more for their freedom. Murphy flew to Washington in September to get authority to bring in Giraud as French leader. Armed with this authority Murphy flew, under the disguise of Lieutenant Colonel McGowan, to discuss with Eisenhower the political plan. Eisenhower had far ranging discussions with Murphy at his country cottage and said of him: 'I have the utmost confidence in his judgment and discretion and I know that I will be able to work with him in perfect harmony.'[30] Murphy warned Eisenhower that Giraud's adherents in Africa clearly expected that Giraud would become Commander of the Allied Forces in French North Africa. Eisenhower was quick to show that French forces would require rearming by the Allies with modern equipment and that until they were in a position to defend North Africa they must co-operate fully with the Supreme Allied Commander. He felt he must be untrammelled in his conduct of operations to anticipate the Germans in the race for Bizerta. Another problem which worried Eisenhower was the notice which might be given to friendly commanders and officials in North Africa that invasion was necessary. Murphy had been authorised by Roosevelt to give at least 24 hours such notice. Eisenhower realised that more than this 24 hours would be necessary but insisted that no French leader should be told until invasion was imminent.

Giraud's home near Lyons was closely watched but he had means of

[30] Papers I, No. 506

communication with French patriots in Algiers and elsewhere. Of these the Allies were in touch with Major General Mast, commander in Algiers, and Major General Béthouart, commander in Casablanca. Mast was convinced that Giraud was the only man who could rally the French Army in North Africa and that he would prefer to work apart from Darlan. Mast suggested that a conference with Murphy and Eisenhower's representative to discuss specific military plans should take place at Cherchil (90 miles west of Algiers) on 21 October—only five days notice. Eisenhower, accompanied by Clark, had hurried discussions with Churchill and the Chiefs of Staff. It was concluded that Giraud should be regarded as 'our principal collaborator on the French side' and that he should be Governor-General in North Africa responsible for both civil and military affairs. Eisenhower's suggestion that Giraud should be requested to negotiate with Darlan and try to bring in the fleet from Toulon was agreed. Eisenhower decided to send Clark with four other officers[31] to meet Murphy and Mast at Cherchil.

There is little doubt that the initiative at this early stage for a possible approach to Darlan came from Eisenhower and was probably the result of talking the question over with Murphy and Clark. The question of the French fleet was important, but that Churchill should contemplate using the hated Admiral shows how much he trusted Eisenhower's judgment. It seems that already Eisenhower envisaged the possibility that Giraud might have to be thrown over in favour of Darlan. On 17 October he had telegraphed Marshall:

> As a possible formula affecting the delicate command situation, we are suggesting the following and will ask the British to comment. Initially the Allied expedition to be commanded exactly as now contemplated. Giraud to be recognised as our principal collaborator. . . . Giraud to be requested to make proper contacts with Darlan and to accept him as Commander-in-Chief of French military and/or naval forces in North Africa or in some similar position that will be attractive to Darlan. . . . I believe tentatively that, while we must decide as to which one of these individuals we should make our chief collaborator, we should at the same time attempt to secure the advantages accruing to us if both are absolutely honest in their proposals for assistance.[32]

Eisenhower then went on to discuss the problem of convincing the French that ultimately the entire command in North Africa would pass to them

---

[31] It is interesting that two of these, Lemnitzer and Wright became Supreme Allied Commanders in Europe and the Atlantic respectively, after the war.
[32] Papers I, No. 557

but not until such time as it could not interfere with the success of operations. If it were possible reasonably quickly to concentrate all the American contingents, the United States Fifth Army might be constituted with Clark as Commanding General. 'This would make it possible to designate either Giraud or Darlan as Deputy Allied Commander, which would give added assurance that we were honestly working towards the time when the French could take over.'[33]

Much has already been written about Clark's journey by air and submarine to Cherchil. The agreement reached there was that if Giraud agreed to come to North Africa he should be brought out by American submarine. He would be given a letter from the Allies setting forth their intentions. The provisional understanding was that France should be restored to her 1939 boundaries; that she should be accepted at once as an ally, and that supreme command in North Africa would pass to the French 'at the appropriate time'.[34] The French collaborators were not told how imminent the invasion was. By the time Clark got back to London the Western Task Force had already sailed and the others were about to do so. The terms on which Giraud would collaborate were not yet agreed and there was obviously a difference between his views about command on French soil and those which Eisenhower considered practicable. Nevertheless, Giraud accepted the summons to join Eisenhower, who on 5 November set up his advanced command post at Gibraltar in newly excavated quarters deep in the Rock. Eisenhower had with him Clark, Cunningham, the two major air commanders Doolittle and Welsh, Anderson and a number of liaison and staff officers.

As the first ships in the assault convoys were passing through the Straits of Gibraltar, Mast was sending out his warnings to Oran and Casablanca. At the same time Juin was taking measures to resist a possible German initiative in Tunisia. He was discussing with Murphy the possibility of Allied aid but warning him that should the Allies invade before the Axis did he would be bound to resist them. Murphy passed on the information but at that stage there could be no question of postponing the operation.

[33] Ibid.
[34] Howe, Northwest Africa, p. 82

4

The Race for Tunisia

The landings in North Africa took place as planned in the early hours of 8 November. Fears that loss of surprise might lead to disaster had prevented the Allies from taking their French collaborators fully into their confidence. Not even Mast and Béthouart were aware of the exact time and place of the landings. As a result there was a good deal of confusion and neither Casablanca nor Oran nor Algiers was taken without a fight. Nevertheless, at Algiers, Mast had made excellent arrangements and there only the effort to force an entry into the harbour had met with resistance. Fortuitously Darlan was present at Algiers, where he was visiting a sick son. All the more senior French commanders and officials, including Juin and Noguès, disregarded the broadcast that had been made in the name of Giraud and looked instead to Darlan for instructions. Darlan, at a meeting with Juin and Murphy, agreed to telegraph to Pétain for instructions. In the meantime Juin arrested Mast and other collaborators and released senior officers that Mast had arrested. For a time Murphy too was in French custody.

Roosevelt had sent a message to Pétain asking for his co-operation. In a series of vacillating decisions and messages Pétain sought for the best of both worlds. For the benefit of the Germans he denounced the invasion but to Darlan he accepted the necessity to bow to *force majeure* and secretly advised collaboration. The Germans were not deceived and moved into unoccupied France.

In the early days, while his plan was being put into effect, Eisenhower could do little but wait. As soon as reports of successful landings came in he decided to send Clark off to Algiers to establish advanced head-quarters there. Giraud had arrived at Gibraltar on 7 November and most of Eisenhower's energies since then had been devoted to efforts to bring him into the operation to the best advantage of the Allies. The meet-ing between the two of them explains why Giraud did not land on the first day to rally all Frenchmen. Giraud made it clear at once that he had not departed from his early conviction that he must command all the troops that fought in concert with the French on French soil. Eisenhower could not persuade him that the authority for his own command came from the Combined Chiefs of Staff and was not for him to bestow. Giraud was no more ready to accept the authority of the Combined Chiefs of Staff than the command of Eisenhower. In vain Eisenhower pointed out to Giraud that the greatest good he could do to the Allied cause was to ensure that their forces met with no resistance so that all their resources could be used against the common enemy and not against Frenchmen. Giraud had already given authority to Mack for the broadcast referred to above, but now he said he could not make any effort to ensure that the French did not resist. In his report to Marshall Eisenhower said:

> In my anxiety to keep Giraud with us, even though it is too late for him to assist us in the role in which we especially desired him, I conceded every point he made except only that I must remain directly responsible to the Combined Chiefs of Staff for operations of the Allied force until different arrangements could be made with the consent of the two governments. I even went so far as to state that I would support his ambition to command the forces here as quickly as he had completed the great civil and military organizational task in North Africa and he could place in the field an organized French force of any respectable size. . . . I carefully explained that his proposal would make me responsible to him on the one hand and on the other to the two governments, which are providing all the resources and dictating the major strategy. He seemed totally unable to grasp the point that I could not be responsible to two entirely separate agencies whose views, respecting immediate and primary objectives in the theatre, do not remotely agree.
>
> As a final word he stated that he would be a spectator in the affair. He would not interfere with our plans or operations but would not take part in them and would not authorize the use of his name in any way in connection therewith.
>
> My impression, shared by Clark and Cunningham, is that Giraud is playing for time and that he is determined, knowing that there will be some French resistance, not to lay himself open to the charge of being in any way responsible for the shedding of French blood. . . . If we are generally successful tonight we will not be surprised to find him more conciliatory tomorrow morning since it must be obvious to him that in every way we are trying to make him the big man of the region and give him a definite personal influence and leadership in winning the war. . . .[1]

Eisenhower was bitterly disappointed because he had counted on Giraud for effective assistance and believed it was in his power to give it. But he did not allow this disappointment to affect his plans, and the next day

[1] Papers II, No. 586

Giraud repented sufficiently to accept Eisenhower's recognition of him as Commander-in-Chief of all the French forces in the region and Governor of the area. He agreed thus to go to Algiers on exactly the same terms as Eisenhower had from the first proposed. Giraud and Clark left for Algiers, in separate aircraft, on the 9th. There Clark found that Darlan had already agreed to a local armistice and that his authority appeared much more acceptable to the French commanders than that of Giraud. The situation was not made easier by the natural impatience of Clark and all the American soldiers with the interplay of French personalities. This American military attitude, much criticised by Murphy, emphasises how wise and patient Eisenhower had been. Furious as he was, he had kept his temper and probably, deep down, he had realised the feelings of the French commanders who saw the first chance of effective action since their disastrous defeat of 1940. It is clear from Murphy's account[2] that all were looking for a course of action which would help the Allies but which would retain the sovereignty of France and the appearance of loyalty to her legal government. This became apparent when Giraud met Darlan, little as they otherwise had in common. Giraud had been shocked to find on his arrival in Algiers that he was regarded as a dissident. He had no intention of political intrigue and, without persuasion from anyone, he agreed that he should become Commander-in-Chief of the armed forces under Darlan as High Commissioner. As news of Darlan's armistice reached Oran and Casablanca, resistance in those areas gradually ceased. News on the 11th of the German invasion of southern France clinched the matter. In Tunisia, however, the problem was not so much one of calling off French resistance as of ensuring that they offered resistance to the Germans. Here the connivance of Vichy and the equivocation of the French leaders allowed the Germans to take their opportunity. On 9 November they seized an airfield near Tunis and on the 11th troops and tanks began to move in through Bizerta. Another blow to the Allies was that the most valuable prize that might have come to them from collaboration with Darlan—the French Fleet—was denied to them. Darlan sent advice rather than orders to Admiral Laborde at Toulon to sail for North Africa. Laborde hesitated until it was too late. Subsequently the German attempt to seize the fleet was thwarted by the scuttling of the ships on 27 November according to a prearranged French plan. Thus was lost to both sides the great prize of which Churchill had said to Eisenhower: 'If I could meet

[2] Murphy, *A Diplomat among Warriors*, Ch. 10

Darlan, much as I hate him, I would cheerfully crawl on my hands and knees for a mile if by doing so I could get him to bring that fleet of his into the circle of Allied forces.'[3]

The responsibilities bearing on Eisenhower were indeed heavy. He firmly supported the line which Clark was taking at Algiers, but the storm which was raised in Britain and America by the decision to use Darlan surprised even Churchill and Roosevelt. Their attempt to justify the decision as a 'temporary expedient' did nothing to confirm the French leaders in wholehearted support of the Allies. But the question of French leadership was only part of Eisenhower's problem. He had never lost sight of the fact that his primary aim was to get possession of Tunisia. For this purpose Anderson had landed on 9 November to take command of the primarily British Eastern Task Force. The title British First Army was more a forecast of future intentions than of present strength: little more than one infantry division was immediately available. It had been intended that, immediately after the capture of Algiers, parachute troops and seaborne commandos should land on successive days to seize Bone, Bizerta and Tunis. The German initiative and uncertainties about the French reaction caused the abandonment of this plan. Instead it was decided to occupy the port of Bougie and the airfield at Djidjelli, 40 miles beyond, and to move on to the Tunisian border while a second force occupied Bone and its airfield.

The execution of this plan began on 10 November and the next day Bugie was occupied by the leading brigade of 78th British Division. There were delays in capturing Djidjelli airfield but on the 12th commandos occupied Bone and a parachute detachment landed on the airfield. All these moves got a friendly French reception. Eisenhower saw that Anderson wanted all the assistance he could get and that the situation at Oran would make some United States troops available. As early as 9 November he sent Anderson a signal saying he was directing Fredendall to be ready to assist him. Eisenhower saw that the situation was touch and go and was quick to disabuse the Combined Chiefs of Staff of their idea that the Torch aims were achieved and that they could be thinking of other projects, such as the capture of Sardinia.[4]

On 13 November Eisenhower flew to Algiers for the day and saw Clark and all the French leaders. He impressed on Clark the necessity for

[3] *Crusade in Europe*, p. 116
[4] Papers II, No. 615

9 *Eisenhower, visiting the British Fleet during the North African Campaign, is seen here with Cunningham (left) and Admiral Wallis*

10 *Eisenhower with Alexander at the Tunis Victory Parade*

11 *With Giraud, driving to the Tunis Victory Parade*

12 *Eisenhower and Giraud*

forgetting the past friction and misunderstandings. He insisted that all should be as one in their effort and that there should be 'optimism, confidence, friendship to French and faith in them'. A similar instruction was sent to Patton at Casablanca. Patton was at that time much concerned that Béthouart and other French collaborators were still held under arrest by order of Noguès. Their release was achieved on 17 November.

By 16 November Anderson's force was close to the Tunisian border. British and American parachute drops had gained Souk el Arba, Tebessa and Gafsa, only 70 miles from the Gulf of Gabes. Another column had reached Tabarka on the coast road to Bizerta. It must be emphasised that these four places were captured by detachments of the strength of a battalion or less and that they were 60 to 80 miles from each other. The Germans were equally thin on the ground. They had two battalions at Bizerta and two at Tunis, which had flown in from Italy on 11 November. In these similar circumstances the two sides took diametrically opposite action. Anderson decided to pause to concentrate for an advance to Tunis. The Germans did not wait to concentrate but thrust out small detachments boldly along all the routes into Tunisia. They also seized the essential airfields and used fighters and dive bombers in close support of these detachments. The French now held the key to the situation; if they could resist the Germans the British would gain the initiative. The French outnumbered the Germans but it must be remembered that they were in no sense equipped as a modern army. They had no anti-tank or anti-aircraft weapons, no signals equipment and no motor transport. Units were manned by North Africans led by French officers and there were almost no trained staff officers. Not even adequate supplies of boots and clothing existed.

At this stage Eisenhower wrote his thoughts to Bedell Smith:

It is difficult to picture the situation in Tunisia because of the sixteen to eighteen French battalions (so called) in that region, I estimate that we may get a combat efficiency of about one battalion. The figure can easily go up if Giraud and Juin, who have gone down there, can actually galvanize the troops into serious effort. They will not be of any great use offensively but they could do a lot of protecting our flanks and establishments in the rear. To date, it is my estimate that the Germans have not gotten any particular ground strength in Tunis but he has gotten small armour units and considerable air. . . .

You cannot imagine just how much I would like to be down there in actual

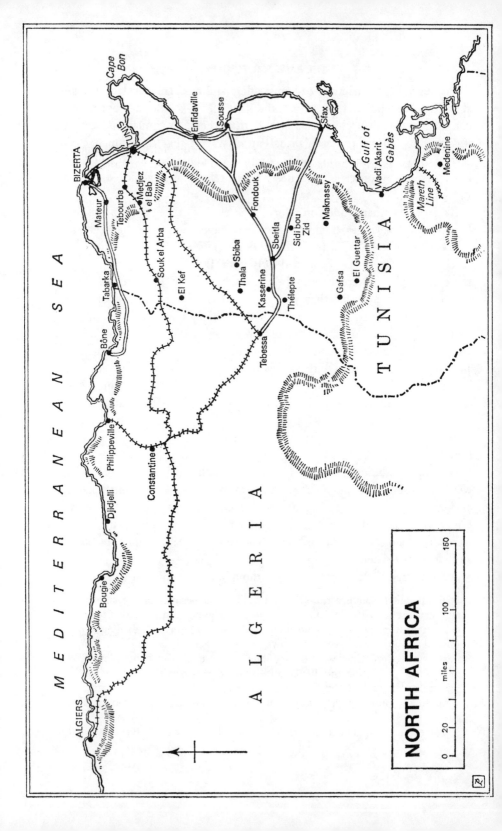

NORTH AFRICA

charge of the tactics of that operation. This does not imply any lack of confidence in Anderson; on the contrary, I think he is doing a grand job and almost carrying things forward on his own shoulders. It is merely that I get so impatient to get ahead that I want to be at the place where there is some chance to push a soldier a little faster or hurry up the unloading of a boat. You can see that this business of high command has certain drawbacks.[5]

The French were deceived by the German boldness and drew back to await the Allies. Even the arrival of leading elements of Allied troops, a British parachute battalion and an American field artillery battalion, failed to prevent the Germans, supported by dive bombers, from capturing the important bridge at Medjez el Bab, 35 miles west of Tunis. Similar German detachments struck west from Bizerta and also blocked the approaches from the Tripoli front at Suisse, Sfax and Gabes.

By 24 November the forward concentration of most of 78th Division and one armoured regiment was completed. One battalion of light tanks, the first of the American troops that Eisenhower had ordered forward from Oran, had also arrived. Some progress was made; the bridge at Medjez was recaptured and the advance continued through Tebourba to within 12 miles of Tunis. But the Germans had also been considerably reinforced and took advantage of their local air superiority to use dive-bombers most effectively. Anderson decided to consolidate his position and wait until the Allied fighter resources could be deployed. The position then reached was the closest the Allies got to Tunis until the final stages of the battle.

On 28 November Eisenhower, accompanied by Clark, went up to see Anderson and to visit the forward areas. The whole of one armoured combat command (about one third 1st U.S. Armoured Division) had now arrived in the forward area and, in addition, Patton had been ordered to send forward 25 of the latest medium tanks from Casablanca. Parts of 1st U.S. Infantry Division were also on the way forward and another division was deployed to protect the lines of communication. This piecemeal reinforcement of Anderson by American troops meant that they had to fight direct under British operational command. Eisenhower was content that this should be so and believed it was necessary to get forward to Anderson everything possible. As Eisenhower said, there was no lack of advice to the contrary or of warnings that the United States forces ought to be kept concentrated until they could be used intact. Clark was one of the most persistent exponents of this view. He said:

[5] Papers II, No. 631

As soon as I could, after American strength justified it, I raised objections to the Anderson arrangements, recommending that American forces should be withdrawn from his command and organized in a separate sector of the front under their own commander. Not only did I feel that American-trained commanders knew better how to get the best out of our men and their equipment, but I felt that Anderson was using them piecemeal, interspersed with British forces, and that they were suffering as a result.

Eisenhower, of course, had a tremendously difficult job in co-ordinating the Allied commands and keeping them working as a team. It often seemed to me that perhaps he overdid his efforts to avoid showing any partiality towards the Americans in his desire to be objective and promote harmony. But Allied success, he knew, depended on eliminating friction between the different parts of the team. He wanted to get U.S. formations under one command, but was willing to defer this action in order to capture Tunis before the bad weather set in. He was willing to gamble on the piecemeal employment of American troops under British command if in that way time would be saved and all of Tunisia could be occupied.[6]

The reluctance of the French, at any rate at the higher level, to serve under British command added strength to Clark's arguments. Despite such advice and difficulties Eisenhower remained staunch in his belief in integrated Allied command. He did not forget the way Anderson had, from the moment he set foot in Africa, responded to the bold orders he had received from himself, an American.[7] As American strength increased their Fifth Army was constituted under Clark but its role was the protection of rear areas, preparing for the possibility of intervention from Spanish territory and training for a future invasion of Europe. All American troops that could be got forward and maintained in Tunisia came under Anderson's command.

In his visit forward Eisenhower saw at first hand the difficulties which winter imposed, particularly the glutinous Tunisian mud. He also saw the effect of German local air superiority and this he determined to remedy. He saw that his two air commanders, Doolittle and Welsh, had to live from hand to mouth and had neither the resources nor the communications to deal with the air situation as a whole. He knew, as he had originally recommended, that he needed a single air commander-in-chief under him. Tedder, the Air Commander-in-Chief Middle East, had recently come to see Eisenhower and had much impressed him. He saw that Tedder had 'exactly the kind of experience and leadership' that was required in the

[6] Clark, *Calculated Risk*, p. 134
[7] *Crusade in Europe*, p. 130

present air situation. He therefore telegraphed to the Chiefs of Staff asking that Tedder should be lent to him for a fortnight or so to study the situation and give him 'the benefit of his great experience in this type of operation'. The Chiefs of Staff replied that they were anxious to help but that they doubted if Tedder could best be used in an advisory capacity. Instead they suggested that Tedder should be responsible for all air operations in North Africa. He would answer to Eisenhower for the Torch operations and, as before, to the Chiefs of Staff for Eighth Army and Middle East operations. Eisenhower answered that, although this might be an admirable long-term arrangement, it could not answer his immediate problem. He did not see how Tedder could serve two land force commanders in separate theatres with greatly differing tactical problems. He decided, therefore, to appoint Spaatz as his deputy for air operations. Difficulties of communications and staff complications prevented him, for the time being, appointing Spaatz as a commander, as he would have liked. In fact the Chiefs of Staff had only sent their answer after Portal had discussed the question with Tedder and the solution which Eisenhower rejected was Tedder's own suggestion.[8]

Anderson's pause to allow the air situation to be improved and his build-up to be continued did not give him the respite he wanted. The Germans too had been reinforced and their Commander-in-Chief, Kesselring, had visited them to demand further efforts. The Germans now had a number of the new Pz IV tanks with the long-barrelled 75 mm gun and also five Tiger tanks, mounting the 88 mm gun, which were for the first time being given their trials in battle. Kesselring had demanded the mounting of a counter-attack to recapture Tebourba and Medjez-el-Bab and the resultant converging thrusts caused the Allies to withdraw from Tebourba. Anderson was in favour of a longer withdrawal but Eisenhower specifically forbade him to give up Medjez-el-Bab. In the withdrawal the American Armoured Combat Command 'B' was reduced to about a quarter of its strength in tanks. Most of the losses were caused by tanks being bogged down in mud rather than from enemy action. These losses and the bad weather persuaded Anderson to put off his renewal of the offensive until Christmas Eve. He now had Vth British Corps forward, commanded by Allfrey and consisting of 6th Armoured and 78th Infantry Divisions and the American troops (Combat Command 'B' and 1st Infantry Division) and a number of French units under command. There

[8] Tedder, *With Prejudice*, p. 373

was a change in the German command, Colonel-General von Arnim having taken over what was now known as Fifth Panzer Army. Arnim had one panzer and one improvised infantry German division and one Italian division, totalling little more than half the fighting strength the Allies had forward.

During December Eisenhower found time to express his thoughts to two old friends. On the question of high command he wrote to Lieutenant-Colonel Hodgson, a West Point contemporary:

> High command, particularly Allied Command, in war carries with it a lot of things that were never included in our text books, in the Leavenworth course, or even in the War College investigation. I think sometimes that I am a cross between a one timer soldier, a pseudo-statesman, a jack-legged politician and a crooked diplomat. I walk a soapy tight rope in a rainstorm with a blazing furnace on one side and a pack of ravenous tigers on the other. If I get across, my greatest public reward would be a quiet little cottage on the side of a slow-moving stream where I can sit and fish for catfish with a bobber. In spite of this, I must admit the whole thing is intriguing and interesting and is forever presenting a new challenge that will have the power to make me come up charging.[9]

To Handy, his successor in the Plans Division, he gave a full résumé of all that had happened since he arrived in North Africa. In the course of his letter he said:

> As you know, the sketchy forces we were able to get inside the Tunisian border were not in sufficient strength to sweep the Germans out of the way; and the French in the critical corner of the region would not take a definite and prompt stand in our favour. . . .
>
> As quickly as I saw opposition building up in Tunisia, I realised that Anderson, with his own forces, was not going to be strong enough to seize Tunis; and so I immediately began combing the area to find everything that could move and be gotten up to him.[10]

Eisenhower went on to explain how Combat Team 'B' with its personnel carriers marched 700 miles. Other units went by train, and all were put piecemeal into the battle as they arrived in a desperate attempt to make the last dash into Tunis. On the air situation he said that his own airfields, often out of action through rain, were over a hundred miles away while the enemy had two all-weather airfields within 15 miles. He gave the Intelligence estimate of the strength of the enemy as 31,000 of whom

[9] Papers II, No. 688
[10] Papers II, No. 698

20,000 were Germans. He pointed out that the enemy were 'well supplied with tanks and they operate in close co-ordination with their stuka and fighter planes.' He mentioned also the identification of the new Tiger tank. He ended his letter:

> Of course, in a very definite sense, the problem from Algiers eastward was given to the British Army. But responsibility for the attainment of the objective is mine. Consequently, most of the American units sent forward to Anderson's support were ordered and started even before he asked for them. He himself has worked like a dog and, in my opinion, has done everything that was humanly possible to make the big gamble win.[11]

Eisenhower came forward for the Christmas Eve battle, but already the Allies had got into difficulties during their preliminary moves. Eisenhower visited Anderson, Allfrey and all the divisional and group commanders in the forward areas and found that in the mud it was impossible to move any type of vehicle off the road. Since that made manoeuvre impossible and prevented effective use of the Allied superiority in artillery, Eisenhower decided to call off the attack. The Germans had proved, as so often during the war, their superiority in using small forces to gain time and in disguising their weakness by bold local counter-attacks. The time thus gained was used to gather the forces which could regain the initiative or at least hold the ring. By his decision Eisenhower admitted that the Allies had lost the race for Tunisia. Separate battles in Tunisia and Tripoli would be necessary before the Allies could return to their master plan of crushing the Germans between the Torch forces and Montgomery's Eighth Army.

Eisenhower's mind now turned to the possibility of switching operations further south to the Tebessa area where the Americans had long had light forces dropped by parachute. Such a move would not only offer a chance of better weather conditions but would help him solve his command problem. Giraud had again insisted that the time had come for him to take over operational command in Tunisia. He refused to serve under Anderson or to allow French formations to do so. Eisenhower solved the problem temporarily by establishing his own advanced command post at Constantine so that he himself could co-ordinate the operations of British, French and American forces. The move forward of American troops from Oran and the change in area of operations gave the opportunity for the grouping of all the American troops under one command. Eisenhower

[11] *Ibid.*

toyed with the idea of bringing Clark forward and directing operations through First and Fifth Armies. He finally rejected this idea as too cumbersome and decided to have only an American corps which at first he kept directly under his own command. As all the troops had come forward from Fredendall's II Corps, he resisted the temptation to bring Patton to the battle and brought forward Fredendall. Eisenhower had had some doubts about Fredendall when he had first been appointed to his command. He was not one in whom Eisenhower had 'had instinctive confidence' but he grew in Eisenhower's estimation. After the landings at Oran Eisenhower wrote to Marshall: 'I bless the day you urged Fredendall upon me and cheerfully acknowledge that my earlier doubts of him were completely unfounded.'[12] The French command problem eased because Giraud's mind was turned to other things by the assassination of Darlan. Giraud became High Commissioner and command devolved on Juin. Juin belittled Giraud's fears that the French would not willingly serve under British command. Nevertheless Eisenhower retained the French under his own command and used them to hold the arc between Allfrey's corps in the north and Fredendall's at Tebessa. Juin was happy to work in with both corps and to put his troops under their command as the situation demanded.

Eisenhower had other things to think of besides the immediate battle and, although in Brigadier-General Truscott he had a most capable custodian at his advanced command post, the difficulty of trying to control the battle himself soon became apparent. For some time he had toyed with the idea of shifting the emphasis of operations towards Sfax rather than Tunis and so disrupting Rommel's communications. While planning for this operation was taking place, he was distracted first by the assassination of Darlan and then by the important Allied conference at Casablanca. Hopping between Casablanca, Algiers and Constantine, he found the pull between high strategy and the immediate battle intolerable. In addition the administrative difficulties of the thrust to Sfax were becoming apparent and he decided that for the time being II U.S. Corps on the southern flank should be held in reserve.

The assassination of Darlan on Christmas Eve had brought Eisenhower back to Algiers immediately after he had agreed with Anderson to call off the offensive. Eisenhower had not himself chosen Darlan—the French themselves had regarded him as the legitimate representative of the only

[12] Papers II, No. 606

French Government—but once the choice had been made he had accepted full responsibility for the choice. He had not wavered in his support of Darlan and had told Marshall that he was the source of all the help that the French had given and that all Frenchmen, including Giraud, had awaited his lead.[13]

Eisenhower expressed his personal feelings in a letter to Mme Darlan in which he said that he had lost a most valuable ally and supporter and that Darlan had died in the service of his country. The immediate task was the appointment of a successor and Eisenhower looked on that as a matter for the French themselves to be expressed through Darlan's Imperial Council. Noguès, probably the only acceptable rival, proposed Giraud and, as the Council unanimously approved, persuaded him to agree to become High Commissioner. Eisenhower confirmed the appointment. Roosevelt thought he had gone too far in doing so and believed that he ought to have regarded the Council's nomination only as a recommendation to the Allied Governments.[14] Eisenhower strongly resisted this view. He asked Marshall to make it clear that he was not in a position to deal with the French 'on the basis of giving orders and demanding compliance'. He went on to say that he regarded the question only from a military point of view and that his concern was to ensure that the French continue to co-operate actively.[15]

The removal of Darlan from the scene made it possible that the complication of Allied relationships with de Gaulle and the Free French might be resolved. Accordingly de Gaulle and Giraud were asked to meet at the conference which Churchill and Roosevelt were about to hold at Casablanca. This conference, which took place from 13 to 20 January, was not primarily concerned with North Africa but was a meeting of the two heads of government with their military advisers, to discuss the Allied strategy for 1943 and to decide the objectives and priorities. Eisenhower was ultimately responsible for the security and 'housekeeping' arrangements for the conference and he himself attended the first meeting of the Combined Chiefs of Staff and the plenary conference to report on the operations in Tunisia and his future intentions. Alexander was also there and he, Brooke and Eisenhower discussed the effect of the Tunisian and Tripoli operations on each other. Alexander made it clear that after the capture of Tripoli, which he expected by the end of January, Rommel

[13] Papers II, No. 683
[14] Howe, op. cit., p. 355
[15] Papers II, No. 760

might be free to turn against Eisenhower's southern flank. Brooke was emphatic that Eisenhower's plan to move towards Sfax was rash and that he must wait until the Eighth Army was within striking distance before moving in that direction. Brooke wrote in his diary: 'Eisenhower's previous plan was a real bad one, which could only result in the various attacks being defeated in detail. As a result of our talks a better plan was drawn up.'[16]

For Eisenhower there were two most important decisions at the conference. The first was a reorganization of command to take effect in February. As Montgomery approached Tunisia the Eighth Army was to come under Eisenhower's command. Alexander was then to become Eisenhower's deputy in place of Clark and, as Commander 18th Army Group, was to direct the operations of both First and Eighth Army. Cunningham was to remain Eisenhower's Naval Commander-in-Chief but was now designated Commander-in-Chief Mediterranean. Tedder was to have a similar position for the air forces. The other decision concerned the strategic objectives for 1943. After the destruction of the German forces in North Africa, Sicily was to be the first objective, with a view to getting complete control of the Mediterranean, undermining the German position in Southern Europe and bringing Turkey into the war on the side of the Allies. These were the tasks which would engage the forces under Eisenhower's command. The possibility of a major cross-Channel operation in 1943 was not discounted—Marshall pressed for it throughout the conference but it was agreed it could not take place until the autumn and then only if there were signs of Germany cracking.

Pleasing to Eisenhower as was the forthcoming unification of the battle for North Africa, particularly in the air, he had little time to think about future operations, becoming involved again in the immediate battle. After visiting Anderson he decided to transfer to his command all three national forces in the battle. Thus, broadly speaking, Anderson had a British, an American and a French corps under his command although there was some mixture of nationals in the corps from time to time. In particular, one Combat Command of 1st U.S. Armoured Division was retained in support of XIX French Corps. Juin agreed to the new command arrangements. On 26 January Eisenhower wrote a personal directive to Anderson covering the immediate tactical objectives and confirming the command arrangements. He drew Anderson's attention

[16] Bryant, *op. cit.*, I, p. 548

to the danger to his right flank and the necessity to protect the airfields near Tebessa. He advised him to keep 1st U.S. armoured division well concentrated with a view either to seizing an opportunity for advantage or to counter an enemy threat. A paragraph on command showed how sensitive Eisenhower was to the honour of France and the necessity for showing great understanding of Juin's effort to conserve French forces.[17] This care was especially important because most of the French units had been long in battle and needed relief for rest and refitting. Eisenhower saw Anderson again on 1 February and once more emphasised the necessity for keeping 1st U.S. Armoured Division well concentrated even if that meant pulling back the line and giving up Gafsa.

The Germans too were giving their minds to the possibilities of co-ordinating the action of the armies fighting in Tunisia and Tripoli. Their command system was complicated because of Hitler's desire to give the Italians the appearance of commanding operations in North Africa. Thus eventually Rommel's Africa Corps and the Fifth Panzer Army would both come nominally under General Ambrosio and the *Commando Supremo*. But all the German forces in Africa came under Kesselring, the Commander-in-Chief South and he kept a close watch on *Commando Supremo*. As early as November Rommel had thought of using all except a small delaying force to move quickly through Tripolitania in order to liquidate the American forces in Algeria before they had time to get established. That would give him the time and opportunity to prepare his counter-stroke against Montgomery. The Italians had not been willing to give up Tripoli so easily. Now Rommel saw his last chance of dealing with the two enemy armies separately. He could delay Montgomery on the Mareth Line and deliver a quick blow with all available armour against the Americans. That would gain him time for a counter-stroke against Montgomery. The trouble was that two out of the three German panzer divisions were under Arnim, who had different ideas of how the battle should be fought. Kesselring supported Rommel's plan but his intentions were slightly obscured in the orders from *Commando Supremo* to Rommel. Nevertheless a most effective counter-stroke was launched against Anderson's southern flank. First Arnim's two divisions overwhelmed the French garrison at the Faid Pass and proceeded to defeat in turn two out of three of the Combat Commands of 1st U.S. Armoured Division. Eisenhower approved Anderson's decision to retire from Gafsa and to

[17] Papers II, No. 791

hold a line covering the airfield at Thelepté and the Kasserine Pass and running across to Fondouk, where the Allied Intelligence believed the main enemy attack would come. At this stage Rommel, having found Gafsa unoccupied, took the leading part in the battle. He quickly captured Thelepté but the whole of the next day, 18 February, was wasted because Arnim had already committed 10th Panzer Division which was required by Rommel. Consequently, instead of the sweep round the flank to Tebessa which he would have preferred, Rommel then struck direct for the Kasserine Pass and up the road towards Thala and Le Kef. The Kasserine Pass was captured but Anderson had moved the remainder of 1st U.S. Armoured Division and a small detachment of 6th British Armoured Division south, and dogged resistance north-east of the pass and at Sbiba held the Germans for the first time. This action, and the day wasted by the Germans, saved the battle for the Allies. Anderson had sent the armoured brigade of 6 Armoured Division to II Corps, and Fredendall had time to organize a position with 1st U.S. Infantry Division and what remained of his armoured division to hold astride the roads leading to Tebessa and Thala. Rommel saw that he had lost his opportunity and must turn away to deal with the Eighth Army.

This was the first major battle fought under Eisenhower's command. He was not in direct control, because all the forces were committed to Anderson, but his was the responsibility. The gist of the instructions he gave to Anderson has already been given and he was wise enough not to breathe down Anderson's neck. He had, however, naturally a father feeling for Fredendall, whose relatively inexperienced American troops were bearing the brunt of attacks delivered by German commanders who were masters of their craft. Eisenhower was visiting forward units of II Corps just before the battle began and he was at the headquarters when the enemy struck. He was never far from Fredendall but careful to act in the knowledge that Fredendall was under Anderson's command. At one moment towards the end of the battle he did intervene; on the evening of 22 February he told Fredendall that the enemy attack was held and that he would take responsibility for any counter-attack launched with proper artillery support. Fredendall did not take his advice and—although Rommel was ready for his riposte—it is probable that Eisenhower was right.

Eisenhower considered that, apart from the inexperience of his troops, the major cause of the First Army difficulties was bad Intelligence. The Intelligence staff had clung to a preconceived idea that the enemy would make his main drive through Fondouk. This misconception had been the main cause of the failure to concentrate on the southern flank and the failure to counter-attack when the fleeting opportunity occurred. Reconnaissance reports from the forward units had shown that the enemy was not disposed for an attack through Fondouk, yet Intelligence had persisted in their view. Another cause was faulty dispositions in II Corps. Eisenhower admitted that this stemmed from the risks he himself had taken in the hope of quick success in Tunisia, but he considered Fredendall could have kept his formations more concentrated and occupied the forward defiles only with reconnaissance and delaying elements. For these reasons Eisenhower made two changes after the battle. The first was the replacement of his Chief of Intelligence, a British officer, by Brigadier Kenneth Strong, also British. Except for a brief interlude when Eisenhower left the Mediterranean to take over preparations for Overlord Strong remained as his chief Intelligence officer throughout the remainder of the war. The other was to bring up Patton from Casablanca to take over from Fredendall and this change caused Eisenhower much anxious thought. He recognised Fredendall as a good fighting commander but doubted if he had the gift of handling subordinates or was big enough to handle an American corps in an almost independent role. On 5 March he made the final decision. At the same time he suggested to Marshall that Fredendall's abilities and experience should not be lost to the army.[18] Fredendall returned to the United States where he became Deputy Commander, and later Commander, of Second Army. A few days after Patton assumed command, Eisenhower sent Bradley to him as Deputy Commander. In turn Bradley took over the corps from Patton in mid-April in order to free Patton for planning the Sicily operation.

Eisenhower had expected Alexander to arrive on 4 or 5 February to command the land operations but before the battle opened he had heard that he could not arrive until the 16th. In fact Alexander did not take over 18th Army Group until the 20th by which time there was little he could do to influence the battle. He had already spent two days with Eisenhower, who found that they 'saw the essentials of the situation eye to eye'. On the 21st Eisenhower addressed a personal message to Alexander[19] giving his long-term view of the battle. First he emphasised the necessity for the speediest possible action at Mareth in order to influence the First Army

[18] Papers II, Nos. 858, 861 & 865
[19] Papers II, No. 835

battle. Second, he urged the overriding importance of keeping the First Army intact even if ground had to be given up, but he considered the line covering Bone—Souk Ahras (on railway to south)—Constantine must be held at all costs for the sake of future operations. Happily the need for such a withdrawal never arose. The relationship between Eisenhower and Alexander was always excellent. Before the Casablanca conference Eisenhower had expressed himself as ready to serve under Alexander should it be the wish of the Combined Chiefs of Staff. The only occasion on which Eisenhower seems to have exerted pressure on Alexander was over the future of II Corps. Eisenhower was confident that under Patton the morale and efficiency of the corps would be brought to the highest pitch. Alexander was inclined to send the corps to the rear area for further training but Eisenhower insisted that the entire corps should be kept in being as an effective independent formation.

With the formation of 18th Army Group under Alexander's command Eisenhower had less direct control of the land battle and this is a suitable moment to review his handling of the campaign. He had certainly lost the race for Tunis. As he himself realised, it was lost by the decision not to make initial landings in the Mediterranean farther east than Algiers. The failure to risk a landing at Bone can be attributed to lack of shipping— there was only sufficient for three landings. This forced a choice between Casablanca and Bone and the demand for the more cautious plan came from Marshall and the War Department. They were even prepared to cut out Algiers but Eisenhower was adamant and was supported by the British Chiefs of Staff. However, the outline plan envisaged that immediately after the capture of Algiers parachute and commando landings should be made at Bone, Bizerta and Tunis, and Eisenhower must bear the responsibility for the decision not to execute that part of the plan. In the light of the uncertain attitude of the French and the German strength in the air it would have been a bold move. Nevertheless the risk was worth taking and was certainly no greater than the risk taken by the Germans in their entry into Tunisia. In the overland advance from Algiers Eisenhower certainly showed himself ready to take risks but time and space were already against him. It would be censorious to blame Eisenhower for his caution over the landings and then to criticise him for the risks he took with II Corps. Doubtless he created the situation which led to their difficulties but if the corps had been handled as he directed the risks would have been kept to a minimum.

In his conduct of the battle Eisenhower showed that understanding of air power which was evident throughout his exercise of command. Local military command of air forces and current United States army doctrine tended to dissipate the limited air resources. Eisenhower, who also had a Royal Air Force Contingent, brought his air commanders to see the air battle as a whole. Writing in retrospect General Norstad said: 'I may be somewhat prejudiced on the point since I was there at the time but I think history will support my own feeling that this action of Eisenhower early in 1943 created the U.S. Air Force in fact, if not in name.'[20]

In one respect at least the genius for high command was manifested in this period. Eisenhower always seemed able to decentralise and yet to keep his finger on all that was going on. His subordinates were able to see that they were expected to act, they were told what was in Eisenhower's mind, and they knew that he would not shirk his responsibility. Typical of this was the latitude he gave to Clark at Algiers, Patton at Casablanca and Anderson in Tunisia. Nor was he blind to the faults of his subordinates or diffident in pointing them out. He frequently warned Clark of the dangers of undue or premature publicity and guided his erstwhile senior, Patton, with a judicious blend of encouragement and restraint. With all the great matters that demanded his attention he never forgot to look at the problem of the fighting units with the eyes of the practical Regimental Officer. He was conscious that, in addition to his Allied responsibility, he had the task of launching the spearhead of a national army into battle for the first time and that what was learnt there would forge the steel of the army that was to come. His instructions to his senior commanders, sent also to the training armies at home, on the duties of officers, the meaning of discipline, vigilance in battle and training for battle were a model for the guidance of a young army. In this way and by his constant visits to forward units Eisenhower made it abundantly clear to all that he was their commander and personally bound up with their performance in battle. Naturally he took special care to gauge the qualities of all his generals and he personally dealt with all promotions to that rank. Cunningham was particularly impressed at his robust methods with his generals. He was invited to a dinner Eisenhower gave to 'a bunch of generals' just after the Kasserine battle. Eisenhower spoke to them in strong terms about the performance of American troops and indicated how shortcomings could be put right. He told Cunningham he was particularly glad to be able to say

[20] Letter to the Author, April 1971

what he thought in front of a British officer.[21] Eisenhower thus showed himself fully aware of the greenness of his troops but he quickly put an end to any loose talk about failure either in Allied or American circles. He had no doubt about the courage of the American soldier and his willingness to fight, and he would not tolerate such doubts in others.

On 11 February Eisenhower had been promoted to the temporary rank of General. This is normally the highest rank in the American Army, as 'General of the Army' is an honour only specially conferred. He was modest enough to remember that he was still only a Lieutenant Colonel in the Regular Army.

[21] Cunningham, *A Sailor's Odyssey*, p. 520

13 *Eisenhower and Clark visit McCreery, commanding the X British Corps in Italy*

14 *With Ramsay at the 21st Army Group Headquarters on D-Day*

5

Mediterranean Command I
The End in Tunisia and Planning for Sicily

Although Eisenhower had taken part in strategic discussions with Churchill and had kept up a constant correspondence on the subject with Marshall, he had had no direct say in the choice of Sicily as the next objective. He had given his views in the preliminary discussions at the Casablanca Conference, but the choice of Sicily had been almost inevitable because of the differences between the British and the American strategic outlook. By January 1943 it was accepted that no cross-Channel operation could be mounted before Spring 1944. Churchill and the British Chiefs of Staff were determined that the intervening period should be used to strike hard at the Axis and they believed that the armies in the Mediterranean area could be used effectively in Southern Europe in operations which would themselves facilitate the eventual landing in North-West Europe. Roosevelt was almost persuaded that this view was right but his Joint Chiefs of Staff, especially Marshall, greatly feared that any operation in Southern Europe would engage so much of the Allied strength that Round-Up would not be possible even in 1944. Moreover, they had a strong suspicion that even if this were not so the British would use Southern European operations as an excuse for avoiding an operation about which they had such doubts. This was unjust to Churchill and Brooke, both of whom knew that in order to win the war the Allies had to land in Western Europe. But they also knew that the one way they could lose the war was to make such a venture and fail. They believed that action in Southern Europe could weaken and distract Germany. In this way not only would success in Round-Up be more likely but succour to our Russian Allies would be afforded more quickly than otherwise possible. Neither Marshall nor Eisenhower was ever convinced that this was what Brooke genuinely believed.[1] In these circumstances it was not possible for the Combined Chiefs of Staff to get down to a straightforward study of the best way of

[1] *Crusade in Europe*, p. 185

15 *With Churchill at an inspection of American airborne troops, 23 March 1944*

tackling Southern Europe. There was however one point on which the Allies were fully agreed and that was the need for all possible shipping, so that Britain could exist and the great American armies could be brought across the Atlantic. With North Africa cleared of the enemy all that was necessary to re-open the Mediterranean was possession of Sicily. The use of the Mediterranean instead of the Cape Route would save the Allies about a million tons of shipping. On this basis Brooke was able to get the Americans to agree to an attack on Sicily.

There is little doubt that if the problem had been debated on the question of the best way to attack southern Europe, both the Chiefs of Staff and Eisenhower would have preferred Sardinia rather than Sicily.[2] Giraud also was in favour of such a course and hoped that from there French forces could go on to Corsica.

The new command arrangements and the strategic directive from the Casablanca Conference gave Eisenhower two main tasks: the final defeat of the Germans in Tunisia, and the planning and execution of operations to capture Sicily. For both tasks Alexander was to command the land battle. As we have seen, the first task posed no difficulty in the relationship between Eisenhower and Alexander. On the other hand, the second task brought out the ambivalent attitude of the British towards Allied command and inter-service command. The British had very much tended to lead at the Casablanca Conference and the instructions on Sicily had directed Alexander to work out the planning details in co-operation with Cunningham and Tedder. Alexander's own memoirs confirm this idea. He wrote: 'At the Casablanca Conference, January 1943, I was assigned to the operational command of "Husky"—the code-name for the invasion of Sicily.'[3] Eisenhower on the other hand was certain that as he had been designated Supreme Commander in the Mediterranean, Alexander, Cunningham and Tedder were equal commanders under him and that inter-service planning would be a question for his command and not for co-ordination. Eisenhower took the strongest exception to what he considered to be a muddling of the command procedure. He did not regard it as a deliberate attempt to bypass him and he knew there would be no difficulties between himself and the three British commanders, but he saw it as an example of British inability to understand the principle of unity of command. In a message to

[2] Papers II, No. 1091 and *Crusade in Europe*, p. 176. The author discusses the strategic problem more fully in his *British Generalship in Twentieth Century*, Ch. 10
[3] Alexander, *Memoirs*, p. 105

Marshall he made it clear that he would go ahead on the understanding that although all the commanders were British he would fulfil his responsibilities as Supreme Commander. Alexander as the Task Force Commander would control the tactical details of the operation and would have considerable latitude in organizing his forces—himself using the principle of unified command. But there would remain many broad problems which must be dealt with by the three Commanders-in-Chief under Eisenhower's own direction.[4] To this end the planning staff for the Sicily operation was set up as part of Supreme Allied Headquarters operations staff—G3 in American parlance.

To turn now to the battle in Tunisia. Eisenhower was content to leave this to Alexander in all respects except one. He remained the watch-dog of the American Army and ensured that II Corps was given a proper place in the battle and the opportunity to prove itself the capable fighting force he knew it to be. He continued too to keep close personal touch with the corps; Patton, and when he left Bradley, were always conscious of his support and received a stream of advice.

Rommel's projected stroke against Eighth Army had been held at Medenine and from that moment Rommel decided that it would be madness for the Axis to try to stay in Africa. He flew to persuade Hitler and Mussolini to accept this view. Alexander's plan was to deliver a converging attack on what had been Rommel's Army, now commanded by the Italian General Messe, with the German Bayerlin as his Chief of Staff. Montgomery was to turn the Mareth Line while Patton was to move to Gafsa in the rather limited role of drawing off the enemy. Eisenhower had ideas about how the final battle should be conducted and on 23 March he wrote to Alexander 'in the confidence that nothing I say will be taken by you as unjustified interference in your special province'. He was surprised that Patton's seizure of El Guettar (beyond Gafsa) had evoked so little reaction from the enemy. He had great hopes that aggressive action by II Corps would prevent a substantial portion of the enemy finding its way back to a final bridgehead in the Bizera—Sousse area. He impressed on Alexander the necessity for making a real effort to use II Corps right up to the end of the campaign. He said:

I would consider it unfortunate if the development of the campaign were such that participation by American troops, in an American sector, was deliberately eliminated as the crisis of the campaign approaches. I believe that our units

[4] Papers II, No. 811

are learning fast. Their morale, technique and physical condition improve daily, and the idea of U.S. British partnership that is so essential to the final winning of the war, constantly grows in strength. The only unused reserves are now training in the United States. The morale and tactical effectiveness of these troops are things of the utmost importance to us. . . . I expect you, sooner or later, to be a battle commander of far more troops than we now have in this particular theatre. I want, here, to keep large U.S. formations learning, through experience, the lessons that must be carried home to those training units. . . .

I am convinced that when the time arrives for the final attacks, the II Corps will be a real asset and one capable of delivering sturdy and effective blows, unless of course, it should become badly depleted in the meantime. It will be just as bold and aggressive as you tell it to be.[5]

At the very moment that Eisenhower was writing, Patton, who had already been unleashed by Alexander, was using his 1st Armoured Division to force the pass near Maknassy in a bid to cut the coast road. It was an attack which Patton said must succeed. It did not succeed and Patton relieved the divisional commander. A well-handled German force, including two panzer divisions, held off the American attack. First Italian Army successively escaped encirclement by the Eighth Army at Mareth and Wadi Akarit and was able to make its way north through the corridor thus held open. Attacks by First Army further north at Fondouk also failed to close the gap so that by 10 April both Axis armies were united under Arnim, covering an arc from Bizerta to Enfidaville.

During all this phase First Army and II U.S. Corps had some hard fighting and inflicted very heavy casualties on the enemy. On a visit to their front on 26 March Eisenhower saw what he described as 'a lovely sight'—27 completely destroyed German tanks in one spot, including three of the big Tiger tanks with the 88 mm gun. Yet the Press seemed incapable of realising that anyone except the Eighth Army deserved praise. Both the First Army and the Americans suffered from this attitude. The United States press, ignorant of the limited role Alexander had at first given II Corps, was full of stories that Patton ought to have thrust through to cut off the enemy during the Mareth battle. Then in the Fondouk battle there was considerable criticism of the part played by 34th (U.S.) Infantry Division. This division was temporarily under command of Crocker's IX British Corps, working directly under Alexander's orders, to intercept and destroy retreating Axis forces. Far from being action against disorganized retreating forces the corps came up against a flanking position

[5] Papers II, No. 906

strongly held by German troops of the Afrika Korps. Ryder, the 34th Divisional Commander expressed misgivings about the corps plan, which committed him to attack across ground open to the front and dominated by a commanding feature on the northern flank. He did not succeed in getting Crocker to change his plan. Ryder, remembering Eisenhower's injunction that orders from a British commander were to be accepted as his own, complied with the instructions and decided to attack so that he was on the objective before dawn. The night attack, hastily mounted, went wrong and the subsequent attack in daylight, supported by tanks, failed. There were considerable mutual recriminations, Crocker blaming 34th Division for faulty execution and all responsible American commanders believing that Crocker had been prodigal of American men and material. Eisenhower and Alexander suppressed the recriminations and 34th Division showed itself determined to prove its mettle and improve its technique. The press, especially in the United States, magnified the story and presented it as an American failure which spoilt an opportunity to trap the Germans. Eisenhower was furious. He knew that his own Public Relations officers and censors were at fault, and he determined to put that right. He held a Press Conference on 17 April. In his investigation of the report which had been sent home he was appalled to find that his censor had sent the report back unexpurgated because of one of his own rules. He had given stringent orders that 'no personal criticism of me or of my actions is ever to be censored. The fool censor extended this to include troop units, though how he reasoned that one out is beyond me.'[6]

Eisenhower spent 14 and 15 April with Alexander and Anderson discussing the plans for the final battle in Tunisia. Eisenhower again insisted that II Corps must be given a real task and used with all its own four divisions. He emphasised how important it was for American opinion at home to realise that American troops were playing a substantial part in operations and not merely acting as suppliers of equipment to the British. American disenchantment could lead them to turn their eyes towards Japan and away from the strategy of beating Hitler first. Alexander readily took the point and for this reason decided that the main attack should be made in the north with First Army, and that Eighth Army should be relegated to a secondary role of exerting pressure on Enfidaville. At first Alexander intended to put II Corps again under First Army but at Eisenhower's insistence they were given instead the independent role

[6] Papers II, No. 946

of capturing Bizerta. This involved a complicated movement and supply problem because the corps would first have to move round to the north of First Army. Eisenhower considered the logistic burden and risk justified and in fact the move was carried out without a hitch.

It was at this stage that Eisenhower pulled out Patton to get on with the Sicily planning and replaced him by Bradley. He had every confidence in Bradley and a week or so before the change had written: 'Patton is in good fettle and it is a real pleasure to see what he has accomplished in a very short time. Bradley is equally on the job. What a godsend it was to me to get that man!'[7] Although he had seen Patton and Bradley only a few days before the hand over, Eisenhower set down in a letter to Bradley his thoughts on command of II Corps:

> The coming phase of the operations is of special significance to the American forces involved. To date, the 1st and 9th Division, particularly the former, have established themselves as sound fighting units. ... On the other hand the 1st Armoured and 34th Infantry have been subjected to quite severe criticism. Even though some of this criticism has been unjust and disregardful of the difficulties encountered, there is no blinking the fact that we have had certain disappointments with these organizations. In view of the excellence of the material we have, the last thing we should do is to entertain any thought that they cannot rapidly become first class fighting units. ... Beyond all this, the experience of the British Army in its early days in the desert, was in some instances, far more unfortunate than has been our own.
>   ... the one way to establish the battle-worthiness of our units is to see that the facts speak for themselves. In other words, it is strictly up to us.
>   I realize that the sector you have been given is not well suited for sustained and heavy attacks; the character of the country and the paucity of communications make your task a difficult one. But we must overcome these difficulties and prove to the world that the four American Divisions now on the front can perform in a way that will at least do full credit to the material we have and the quality of our leadership.[8]

Eisenhower went on to discuss the sector in which Bradley would be working and the way that armoured units could best be used. He also pointed out that Alexander and Anderson saw the problem of the use of American troops exactly as he himself did and that Bradley could rely upon their unwavering support and sympathetic attitude. He finished his letter: 'You must be tough with your immediate subordinates and they must be equally tough with their respective subordinates. ... We have reached the point where troops *must* secure objectives assigned by

[7] Papers II, No. 899
[8] Papers II, No. 947

commanders and, where necessary, we must direct leaders to get out and *lead and to secure the necessary results.'*

Alexander's plan for the final battle was that Anderson with his two British and one French corps, reinforced by 1st Armoured Division from Eighth Army, should make the main advance into the Tunisian plain to seize Tunis. II Corps remained under Alexander's command but Anderson was responsible for co-ordinating its action in the attack on his left flank and issuing the necessary orders direct. The Germans launched a spoiling attack on the night of 20 April but suffered heavy casualties and did not prevent the Allied attack going in on 22 April as planned. In hard fighting up to the 30th the corps of all three nations gave a good account of themselves and it is interesting that 34th U.S. Division earned special commendation in Anderson's despatches. By these attacks the Axis forces were pressed back to a precarious position with no depth, covering Bizerta and Tunis. In the south they were holding strongly against Montgomery's attacks near Enfidaville. On 30 April Alexander decided, therefore, to transfer two more divisions, 7th Armoured and 4th Indian, from Montgomery to Anderson. In the resolute final thrust IX Corps captured Tunis on 7 May and the same day II Corps captured Bizerta. Eisenhower's hopes and his faith in Bradley and his men were by this last success fully vindicated. There now remained only a vigorous pursuit and rounding up and on 12 May Arnim surrendered. In his final despatch Anderson said of the forces that had fought under his command:

> Right throughout the campaign we were all of us, in varying degree, thrown into intimate touch with the armies of our American and French allies, usually under conditions of stress and danger demanding instant decision and the closest collaboration. I say without hesitation that the mutual goodwill, tolerance, understanding, and above all the confidence which each of us had in the other was quite remarkable.
>
> I count myself indeed fortunate to have had under my orders such loyal and gallant men as General Koeltz and the soldiers of the French 19 Corps: while always my relations with United States commanders and men have been entirely frank, cordial and understanding. I owe much to General Eisenhower for his valiant (*sic*) wisdom and encouragement, and to those of his commanders who served under me with such loyal friendship.[9]

All this time that Eisenhower had been so concerned with the growing pains of the American Army he had also been pressing on with the planning and mounting of Operation Husky, the invasion of Sicily. It will

[9] Anderson, *op. cit.*, p. 5462

readily be appreciated that the difficulty of such planning was that the three land force commanders principally concerned, Alexander, Montgomery and Patton, were fully engaged in operations against the enemy. Plans can be worked out by planning staffs but the results of their labours can have no life or validity until they are accepted and the finishing touches are put to them by the commanders who will have the responsibility for executing them. As Eisenhower knew well the product of a planning staff, particularly an inter-service staff, will nearly always be a compromise, counting every hazard and playing for safety.

Despite their great responsibilities Cunningham and Tedder were less closely engaged in the battle of the moment so that they were able to give priority to Husky, the greatest combined operation yet envisaged. Planning at Eisenhower's headquarters had begun in February under Major General Gairdner, a British officer who was also Alexander's representative. Gairdner had free access to Eisenhower, Cunningham and Tedder but Alexander, Montgomery and Patton could only occasionally be consulted. Both Montgomery and Patton appointed representatives to deal with Husky planning. There were further complications because some forces were being provided from outside Africa. An assault-trained division was coming specially loaded in convoy from the United States, and the opportunity was also being taken to get the Canadians into action by providing an infantry division and an armoured brigade to be mounted in Britain. The result of the planners' work was that a plan acceptable to Cunningham and Tedder and considered by all to be administratively sound was produced in early March. On the 13th Eisenhower discussed this plan with his three Commanders-in-Chief, Alexander, Cunningham and Tedder, and accepted it. The plan involved three widely separated attacks. Eighth Army was to land in the south-east corner from Gela to Augusta and to secure the airfield complex of Ponte Olivia and the port of Syracuse, while Patton's Seventh Army was to land in the south-west and capture the Castelventrano airfields. Two days later in fresh landings Montgomery was to capture Catania, and Patton Palermo. Airborne troops and commandos were to be used to assist the landings. This plan had the advantage of well separated convoy areas, the early capture of all the airfields and the securing of three good ports from which the force could be maintained. Both Eisenhower and Alexander had some misgivings about the plan because of the magnitude of the task given to Montgomery, who had to capture Gela, Syracuse and Catania and the three most important airfields

SOUTHERN ITALY AND SICILY

xxxxxxxxxxxx Gustav Line
R19 Roads

0   20   100 miles

Rimini
Pisa
Leghorn
Rome
CORSICA
Naples
SARDINIA
Cagliari
Tunis

Terni
Viterbo
R16
GRAN SASSO
Rieti
Pescara
R3
R17
R2
Tiber
Casoli
ROME
Pescina
Sangro
R1
Frascati
Trigno
Ostia
Velletri
Frosinone
Biferno
A D R I A T I C
Cassino
Campobasso
GARGANO PENINSULA
S E A
Anzio
R7
Liri
R17
R16
Foggia
Terracina
Garigliano
R6
Vinchiatura
R90
Gaeta
Volturno
GULF OF GAETA
Caserta
Benevento
Bari
Capua
Ofanto
Avellino
Altamura
NAPLES
Capri
Potenza
Sorrento
Salerno
R94
Brindisi
GULF OF SALERNO
Taranto
R18
R19
GULF OF TARANTO
T Y R R H E N I A N
Castrovillari
S E A
C A L A B R I A
R106
Crotone
Catanzaro
I O N I A N
Messina
Gioia
S E A
Palermo
Bagnara
Reggio
R113
Castel-vetrano
R120
R114
Mt. Etna
R121
Enna
Catania
R115
R112
Gerbini
Ponte
Olivia
R124
Augusta
Licata
Gela
Syracuse
PANTELLERIA
R115
Pachino

at Ponte Olivia, Pachino and Gerbini. Nevertheless, on the assumption
the enemy was not likely to have more than two German divisions plus the
Italian garrison, both considered the plan feasible. Not so Montgomery;
he considered that the tasks were too dispersed for the five divisions (four
assault and one reserve) for which he was allotted shipping. He proposed
either that the Gela landing should be abandoned or that he should be
given another division. The first alternative would uncover the Ponte
Olivia airfield and was unthinkable to Tedder, who was strongly supported
by Cunningham. For the second alternative the difficulty was shipping,
but this was overcome by increased use of Malta and an additional division
was provided. However by this time Montgomery was able to give his
undivided attention to the plan and he was not satisfied even with this
additional division. He demanded that his initial landing should be
confined to the area from the Pachino peninsula to Syracuse. Eisenhower
at this stage kept out of the discussion; the task to be given to a subordinate army commander was one for Alexander. Alexander seems not
to have looked at the problem as one in which he was fighting a battle
with two armies under his command but rather as one in which he would
have to accept Montgomery's views because Montgomery was the one who
would have to fight the battle. But again Cunningham and Tedder could
not accept a plan which required all the ships carrying Eighth Army to
move in a restricted area while the enemy was free to use some 13 airfields
in the vicinity.[10] Alexander then decided to recast the whole plan. He
would abandon the attack in the south-west and the early attempt to
capture Palermo. This would enable him to use Seventh and Eighth
Army side-by-side in an assault landing from Licata to Syracuse. It was
hoped that Catania would quickly be captured and opportunity given for
a thrust to Messina. The whole of the western half of the island would thus
be isolated and an opportunity taken later to capture Palermo.

    Eisenhower called a conference at Algiers for 2 May to discuss the plan.
Alexander could not get there—he was still heavily involved in the
Tunisian battle—but Montgomery came to expound his views. The
plan for a concentrated landing and attack accorded with Eisenhower's
own first thoughts about the conquest of Sicily. He believed that the
operation stood or fell by what happened in the south-east of the island.
Administrative risks were involved, especially for the Americans, who
would have to be maintained almost entirely across the beaches. The

---

[10] Tedder, *op. cit.*, p. 433; Cunningham, *op. cit.*, p. 536

advent of a new American vehicle, the DUCKW, a $2\frac{1}{2}$ ton amphibious lorry, was relied on to minimise this difficulty. Eisenhower himself accepted the plan and the next day at a staff conference attended by Cunningham and Tedder he ironed out the inter-service and administrative difficulties. Cunningham would have preferred the earlier plan with more room to deploy his ships but he accepted the change. Tedder's requirements for dealing with the airfields had been met, except for Castelventrano and he agreed that that airfield must be neutralised by the air forces. This led to a decision to capture Pantelleria, a rocky island 75 miles south of Castelventrano, which was used by the Italian Air Force. Eisenhower firmly believed that this island could be taken at slight cost. Cunningham agreed and Tedder and Spaatz also became enthusiastic about the project. Their belief was founded on the fact that most Italians were looking for any good excuse to surrender. They were right; the garrison surrendered on 11 June after a six-day air bombardment, even before the assault troops reached the shore.

On 12 May the Combined Chiefs of Staff approved the new plan. Eisenhower had certainly acted more as arbitrator and judge than as initiator in the tortuous course of planning. But there was one way in which he made a major contribution: once the decision was taken he bent his efforts to ensure that all three services and both nations worked in full accord towards victory. In this direction his influence with Patton was dominant. In all the earlier plans Patton had an independent task. Now his role, important as it was, seemed more like that of protecting Eighth Army's flank. As Alexander said:

> The administrative risk was unevenly divided and almost the whole of it would fall on the Seventh Army. In other ways also it might well seem that the American troops were being given the tougher and less spectacular tasks; their beaches were more exposed than the Eighth Army's and on some of them there were awkward sand bars, they would have only one small port for maintenance and Eighth Army would have the glory of capturing the more obviously attractive objectives of Catania and Messina, names which would bulk larger in press headlines than Gela or Licata or the obscure townships of central Sicily.[11]

Patton's staff and Admiral Hewitt, his opposite number, were very sore about the change[12] but whatever feelings Patton himself may have had, he

[11] Alexander, Despatches
[12] Cunningham, *op. cit.*, p. 538

had been left unmistakeably certain of Eisenhower's views on Allied command. He accepted the change in plan loyally and without complaint and he saw that his subordinates did so too.

The planning date for Husky suggested at the Casablanca Conference had been for the most suitable moon conditions in July. In February the Combined Chiefs of Staff had said that if possible the operation should be expedited to June. In April Eisenhower reported that the preparations, assembly of landing craft and training would not be ready for a June date but that there was no reason why he should not be ready for July. He chose 10 July when the moon would be in the second quarter, so offering light in the early part of the night for parachute landings and darkness after midnight for the naval approach. These decisions were straightforward but in a different way the date and nature of the attack on Sicily caused Eisenhower some concern. As early as January Marshall had put into Eisenhower's mind the possibility of an immediate follow-up from North Africa to Sicily. In an act of exploitation the enemy could well be caught unawares and all the tedious preparations for a full-scale attack against an enemy that had been given time would be avoided. Behind Marshall's suggestion lay the feeling of the War Department that the Americans had been shuffled away from the Round-Up conception by skilful British manoeuvring. A quick dash for Sicily would end the Mediterranean adventure before too much harm was done and the Allies could get down to their proper preparations for the cross-Channel operation. Although Eisenhower was intrigued with Marshall's suggestion he had moved away from the idea that Round-Up was to be lightly undertaken. Writing to Handy after Casablanca he had said: 'Round-Up, in its original conception, could not possibly be staged before August of 1944, because our original conceptions of the strength required were too low.'[13] Then in April he wrote to Marshall: 'I have never wavered in my belief that the Round-Up conception is a correct one, but the time and assets required for building up a successful operation in that direction are such that we could not possibly undertake it while attempting, simultaneously, to keep the forces now in or coming into this theatre operating usefully.[14] Nevertheless Eisenhower saw the advantages of quick exploitation from Tunis and he frequently discussed the possibility with Alexander, Cunningham and Tedder. On 3 May he cabled to Marshall:

[13] Papers II, No. 796
[14] Papers II, No. 949

All of us are exceedingly anxious to be in position to take advantage of a sudden crumbling of the hostile resistance in Tunisia which would, we believe, have temporarily a devastating effect on Italian morale. We are constantly finding ways and means of following up on an exploitation basis, but I must admit that the prospects do not look too bright. It is clearly obvious that we could well afford to strike with only a portion of the strength that will be necessary after we give the Axis an additional number of weeks to prepare defences. In fact, I would be entirely ready to take the risk of capturing the important southeastern airfields with no greater strength than that necessary to hang on to a bridgehead while all of the later strength, now allocated to a formal Husky, would be brought along to exploit the initial success.[15]

Nevertheless in the end Eisenhower rejected the idea and on 11 May he informed the Combined Chiefs of Staff that he had decided to carry out the full-scale Husky in July. His reason was that he had only enough assault craft for one division immediately available. He considered it would be useless to attack with less than two divisions in the assault and a reserve division assault loaded. Instead he had decided to use his divisional lift to enable him to capture Pantelleria.

The healthy respect which Eisenhower had acquired for the fighting qualities of the German Army brought him nearer to the British strategic outlook but it also got him into trouble with Churchill and the Chiefs of Staff over the assessment, referred to above, that Husky would only succeed if not more than two German divisions were in Sicily at the time of assault. This looked as if he considered that the operation should be called off if more German divisions were put in. Churchill, who had been angry with Eisenhower for rejecting the June date for Husky, commented caustically that his statement contrasted strangely with his previous confidence about invading France across the Channel. Churchill wondered how, if the presence of more than two German divisions was held to be decisive against the million men then in North Africa, the war could be carried on. He thought that the operation must be entrusted to someone who believed in it and trusted that the Chiefs of Staff would not accept 'these pusillanimous and defeatist doctrines from whoever they came'. The British sent these views on to Washington and in more guarded terms they were passed on to Eisenhower. In reply to Washington and to London Eisenhower said: 'Operation Husky will be prosecuted with all the means at our disposal. While we believe it our duty to give our considered and agreed opinion of relative changes under conditions as stated in our

[15] Papers II, No. 968

previous messages, there is no thought here except to carry out our orders to the utmost limit of our ability.'[16]

Before the invasion of Sicily was begun, Churchill and Roosevelt had met again, this time in Washington for conference Trident. At last it was agreed that the target date for the cross-Channel operation, henceforward known as Overlord, should be May 1944, but in addition plans were discussed for the exploitation of success in Sicily and knocking Italy out of the war. Thus, having completed plans for the capture of Sicily, Eisenhower was rightly charged with working on subsequent operations in the Mediterranean. After Trident Churchill, accompanied by Brooke and Marshall, visited Eisenhower and had meetings attended by all the senior commanders. At meetings on 29 May and again on 3 June, Alexander stated that 'securing a bridgehead on the Italian mainland should be considered as a part of Husky'. He pointed out that once we had a hold on the airfields in south-east Sicily it should be possible to cross into the Toe of Italy 'which was the very windpipe of Husky'. It did not appear likely that the Toe would be so strongly held as to require restaged operations. All these views were passed on by Eisenhower to Patton[17] but nevertheless operations for the Toe of Italy were planned as part of the exploitation and not as an integral part of Husky. Kesselring and Hube, who successfully extricated the German corps from Sicily found it incomprehensible that nothing was done to cut them off in the Toe. There is no doubt that operations for this purpose should have been mounted in Africa as soon as the situation was firm in south-east Sicily. There would have been difficulties because of competition for landing craft with administrative requirements. But it was an essential of the Sicily operation and Eisenhower, as the Supreme Commander, must bear the responsibility that it was not done.

[16] Papers II, No. 942
[17] Papers II, No. 1038

6

Mediterranean Command II
Sicily and Italy

In early April Eisenhower's mind began to turn to possibilities that might arise out of the Sicily operations. On the 19th he sent his tentative views to Marshall. He saw the advantage of the quick capture of Sardinia and possibly Corsica with a view to future operations against the thinly defended west coast of Italy. The chief advantage of occupying Italy seemed to him to be the use of extensive airbases from which the Rumanian oilfields and other targets in central Europe could be attacked. But he saw too the disadvantage of transferring from Germany to the Allies the responsibility for the maintenance of Italy, where coal supply especially was a formidable problem. He also mentioned the possibility of action in the Eastern Mediterranean which might bring Turkey into the war and facilitate an attack on Germany from that direction.[1]

As Eisenhower pointed out, such decisions on policy were at that time more the concern of Washington and London than of his headquarters, and the Prime Minister and the President were already making arrangements to meet and discuss them. The resultant conference, Trident, took place in Washington from 12 to 25 May. Here the United States staff was much better prepared to argue its case than it had been at Casablanca and there was a closer accord between Roosevelt and his military advisers. American efforts were directed towards ensuring that a firm decision was taken to mount Round-Up in spring 1944 and that it should have first priority. Churchill was more concerned to ensure that opportunities in 1943 were not lost. He and the Chiefs of Staff believed that the Mediterranean would offer such opportunities in the autumn and winter of 1943, which might be decisive. Operations there would certainly be more effective in paving the way for successful cross-Channel operations in 1944 than would the transfer of Allied troops back from the Mediterranean to the United Kingdom. The collapse of Italy would lead to the

[1] Papers II, No. 949

withdrawal of German forces from the eastern front to garrison southern Europe and the Balkans, and would be the only way to ease the pressure on Russia in 1943 and early 1944. Marshall summed up the difference between the Joint Chiefs of Staff attitude and the British thus: '. . . our attitude is to the effect that Mediterranean operations are highly speculative as far as ending the war is concerned. On the other hand, the British feel that Mediterranean operations will result in a demoralization and break-up of the Axis.'[2]

As usual the debate turned on whether Mediterranean operations would facilitate a 1944 Round-Up or draw away the forces necessary for its execution. The availability of landing craft was a paramount factor and until the cross-Channel operation was planned in more detail the real picture could not be seen. To that end a special planning staff had already been set up and was known as COSSAC—the suggestion being that its head should be Chief of Staff Supreme Allied Commander. In the end the Trident decisions on the war in the West were: the cross-Channel operation, henceforth referred to as Overlord, was to be 'first charge' on Allied resources with a planning date of 1 May 1944; a combined bomber offensive would be mounted in the United Kingdom to disrupt 'the German military, industrial and economic system' and undermine German morale, and operations in the Mediterranean were to be directed to eliminating Italy from the war. Planning for this last task was to be Eisenhower's responsibility but the final decision was to rest with the Combined Chiefs of Staff. The conference agreed that seven battle-experienced divisions, four United States and three British, should move back from the Mediterranean in November to participate in Overlord and that Eisenhower's own operations should be planned on the availability of 27 divisions, including those required for garrisons.[3]

Thus, as a result of Trident, Eisenhower was given two tasks in exploitation of Husky: to eliminate Italy from the war and to contain the maximum number of German forces. At the end of June he sent to the Combined Chiefs of Staff the result of his first studies based on the assumption that Sicily had been captured but that Italian resistance had not collapsed. He discounted the possibility of an amphibious attack against the Heel of Italy because of unsuitable weather, inadequate air cover and shortage of landing craft. He saw himself thus left with the

[2] Quoted Matloff, *Strategic Planning*, 1943-4, p. 151
[3] *Ibid.*, pp. 133-4

16 *Talking to the Press in Normandy*

17 *With Montgomery and Tedder in Normandy*

18 *At Montgomery's HQ in Normandy.* Left to right: *Air Vice-Marshal Broadhurst, Brigadier de Guingand and in the background, Lieutenant-General Horrocks*

alternative either of landing on both sides of the Toe of Italy or of the capture of Sardinia. He said that he could not yet decide between the two because the answer would depend upon the morale of the Italian forces and the extent to which the Germans had reinforced them. He was satisfied that it would be unsound to commit the necessary six divisions to the mainland unless the situation were such as to make possible quick occupation of the Heel and exploitation to Naples. In such circumstances it would be better to go to Sardinia. The limiting factor to exploitation was that all landing craft would be tied up in maintenance over beaches of the forces in Sicily and that landing craft would have to be withdrawn 30 days before the next assault could be mounted. For this reason Eisenhower's time forecasts were very cautious. If an assault were required at Crotone as well as at Reggio it could only take place after an interval of 30 days whereas the attack on Sardinia could hardly take place before 1 October.[4] Tedder who had not seen the signal before its despatch strongly disagreed with the implied preference for the capture of Sardinia. He believed that the advantages of a hold on 'even a hundred miles or so of the Italian mainland would far outweigh any which might arise from the capture of Sardinia'.[5]

The result of these first planning studies and Eisenhower's cautious reaction explain, although they do not altogether excuse, the failure to include the planning of the landing in the Toe of Italy as part of the battle for Sicily. It must not be doubted that the difficulties would have been very real. The withdrawal of landing craft from the task of supplying troops over the beaches would have involved improvisation and serious administrative risks. All the assault-trained divisions except one were involved in the initial series of landings in Sicily and there were no landing craft for training further divisions. The attainment of air superiority over the Toe of Italy would not have been easy. Nevertheless, certainly with the advantage of hindsight, it looks as if the difficulties would have been less and the results more rewarding than efforts to cut off the enemy at Messina. In short, if the landing in the Toe had been regarded as an integral part of the Sicily campaign, the battle would have been fought differently and the difficulties overcome.

It must not be imagined that as the time for Husky approached Eisenhower was left free to concentrate on that operation and its exploitation. Politics is an essential element of strategy and the very purpose of the

[4] Papers II, No. 1088
[5] Tedder, *op. cit.*, p. 454

command arrangements in the Mediterranean was that a Supreme Commander should be available not only to direct and co-ordinate the three Commanders-in-Chief but to gather together the political and military strands in the theatre. Eisenhower had extremely good relationships with his two principal political advisers, Murphy the American, and Macmillan the British. Both have expressed their high regard for him. With two such advisers Eisenhower was, in theory at any rate, left with considerable freedom of action. He was, moreover, subject to the Combined Chiefs of Staff who would interpret for him the decisions of the two governments. On the other hand, with two heads of governments so closely concerned with the conduct of the war as were Roosevelt and Churchill, and with the facilities which modern communications give, it was not to be expected that Eisenhower would be left in peace to run his own show. Although the problem of fighting a campaign on French soil was happily over, that of political control of French North Africa was by no means settled.

In the aura of the victory in Tunisia British efforts to draw de Gaulle and Giraud together had had some success. De Gaulle had come out to Algiers in June and progress was made in forming a French Committee of National Liberation with the two generals as joint presidents. After a few meetings, however, de Gaulle had withdrawn because of opposition to him on military matters. The quarrel was about control of the army. Giraud was no politician but he wanted to remain head of the army unfettered by political control, and he felt himself in a strong position because of the arrangements he had made with the Americans for the re-equipping of the French forces. De Gaulle saw himself as the legitimate successor of the defeated French Government so that in him must rest the command of the French forces, not only in North Africa, but wherever they showed themselves free of Vichy. He looked to the making of a new French Army; Giraud, he thought, would only reconstitute the old defeated army.

In this complicated situation it was Eisenhower who had to try to find a workable solution—one which would give him a secure base, available ports and communications and an efficient French contingent. Murphy and Macmillan worked well together but they were the representatives of heads of government who looked at the problem in entirely different ways. When Roosevelt learnt of de Gaulle's resignation he saw it as an opportunity to get rid of him altogether and signalled Eisenhower to that effect. Churchill thought quite differently. He and all the Cabinet, as well as Macmillan, believed that a break with de Gaulle at that time would be fatal. Churchill's only fear was that his efforts to prevent it would cause a rift between the British and French governments. For this reason Churchill was inclined to follow Roosevelt's lead and he concurred in instructions sent by Roosevelt that Eisenhower was not to allow de Gaulle any control over military affairs in North Africa, nor in West Africa, which was also in Eisenhower's theatre.

In Algiers Macmillan had no doubt that de Gaulle was right to try to ensure proper ministerial control over the army. Eisenhower too was beginning to see that Giraud was not handling the situation well and had no proper idea of the sphere of Commander-in-Chief. Eisenhower decided that he would see de Gaulle and Giraud together. Despite a series of instructions from Roosevelt directing the line he was to take, Eisenhower sent a firm telegram to the President saying that he thought it best to confine himself to stating his minimum requirements affecting command of the French forces in North Africa. He would make it clear that they must remain under command of Giraud. By thus confining the issue there could be no question of seeming to interfere with French administration or sovereignty. If de Gaulle still wanted to break with the Allies his position would be indefensible. Eisenhower believed that all the other questions could be solved by the French themselves and Macmillan strongly agreed with him. They put their trust in two members of the French Committee, Jean Monnet and General Catroux, both of whom had been largely uncommitted to de Gaulle and—most important of all— neither of whom had the taint of collaboration with Vichy.

Eisenhower saw the two generals on 19 July; no one else was present except Bedell Smith. Eisenhower succeeded in making quite clear the enormous Allied military commitment and the necessity for security of the base and communications. Nothing he said made even de Gaulle fear that he was impinging on French sovereignty. It was the first time he had had serious official dealings with de Gaulle and they impressed each other. After the meeting, the Allied requirements were put in writing for the two generals and for members of the French Committee. For the present Giraud was left as Commander-in-Chief and he had to have effective control of the forces and of those civilian facilities—docks, railways, etc.—necessary for the Allied forces. This was not the last crisis. Soon afterwards there was another over Admiral Boisson, Governor

General of French West Africa. De Gaulle with bitter memories of the Free French rebuff at Dakar was determined to get rid of him. Both Churchill and Roosevelt had promised he would not be punished for having co-operated with Vichy. Roosevelt sent Eisenhower instructions to demand Boisson's retention. In the event Boisson resigned and, despite conflicting telegrams sent by Giraud first accepting and then refusing the resignation, Eisenhower did not intervene. He did not join issue with Roosevelt but the inference from his message to Roosevelt[6] is that Boisson's resignation offered a happy way out and that all that was necessary was to ensure that the replacement nominated by the French Committees should be trustworthy from Eisenhower's point of view. So the matter fizzled out, and General Boisboissel, who had already worked well with the Allies was appointed by Giraud.

Soon after the Boisson affair Giraud left for Washington. Roosevelt had invited him in the hope that his reception at the White House would increase his standing with the Free French. He returned at the end of July full of confidence that all American material support was promised to him personally. But in his absence de Gaulle had not been idle and he had ready for him three proposals from which he might choose. Giraud could be Commander-in-Chief with de Gaulle as Minister of Defence, and each as joint President; Giraud could be joint President but as Commander-in-Chief he would come under a civilian Minister of Defence, or Giraud could be Minister of Defence and Commander-in-Chief but no longer joint President. Giraud, confident of American support, refused all three and threatened to resign. This time the Allies did not intervene and the French Committee worked out a compromise accepted by both generals. Giraud was to remain Commander-in-Chief and joint President on the understanding that if he took over any active operational command he would cease to be part of the Government. Murphy thought that Giraud had been tricked out of everything, but to Macmillan the solution was a wise compromise as it confined Giraud's attention to military matters and left the political field to de Gaulle.

In the long political wrangle there are unmistakable signs of Eisenhower's growth in stature. They were manifest in his ability to see what was militarily important, to keep clear of political matters that did not affect Allied security, to trust his own judgment and to stand firm in what he believed to be essential. Eisenhower's attitude to Roosevelt was no less

[6] Papers II, No. 1074

firm than his attitude to de Gaulle. He knew Roosevelt's views and he naturally wanted to keep in line, but he saw that Roosevelt had a false idea of the extent to which French affairs could be directed. He was not afraid to tell Roosevelt that the political questions could best be left to the French themselves and that dictatorial action would certainly create antagonism. Unquestionably, however, Eisenhower did overestimate the effect of Allied influence and the ability of the other members of the French Committee to manage de Gaulle. For instance, Allied support of Boisson and Peyrouton did not prevent de Gaulle from later action to imprison them. Nor did their support prevent him from removing Giraud, and this was by no means a bad thing. Nevertheless there is little doubt that Eisenhower's firmness in restricting action to military necessity saved Roosevelt from undermining the whole future of Allied relations with the Free French. Churchill saw these dangers, especially because he was ardently worked on by Macmillan, but it is very unlikely that Roosevelt could have been deterred from precipitate action if it had not been for Eisenhower's wise handling of the situation in Algiers.[7]

During June there had been for Eisenhower a happy interlude when King George VI came out to visit the British troops in North Africa. On the day he arrived he arranged a dinner party to which Eisenhower was invited and after dinner he invested Eisenhower as Knight Grand Cross Commander of the Most Honourable Order of the Bath. The award had been announced on 25 May.

It will be realised that the controversies just described, which Eisenhower called 'the local political mess', were raging during the months of June and July which was also the period of final preparations for the assault on Sicily, the actual assault, and an important phase in the planning for exploitation. Eisenhower's ability to decentralise and his absolute confidence in Alexander ensured that there was no interference with the operation and that when decisions were required he could give his whole mind to them. He was less concerned now to father too closely the American contingent. The American II Corps had finally shown its fighting worth in Tunisia and now, still under Bradley, formed part of a United States Army which made up almost half Alexander's force. Patton as Army Commander could be trusted to look after American interests

[7] Murphy, op. cit., pp. 225–231; Macmillan, The Blast of War, pp. 325–361; Churchill, op. cit., V, pp. 154–161; de Gaulle, Unity, pp. 118–124; Papers II Nos. 1054, 1057–8, 1064–5, 1068–70, 1073–4, 1087, 1130

and to see that his army played its full part. The course of operations proved that this trust was not misplaced.

Although Eisenhower was prepared to leave the execution of Husky in Alexander's capable hands he certainly showed no inclination to shirk his responsibilities as Supreme Commander. A few days before the landing Eisenhower left Algiers and its political problems to take up his Command Post in Malta. Malta had been selected because of the excellent existing naval communications. Cunningham and Alexander were there and Eisenhower would have liked to have Tedder too. Tedder felt he must be where he could exercise the necessary close control over his subordinate commanders with direct communications to the squadrons. This was not possible from Malta so he remained at La Marsa near Tunis and sent a deputy to be with Eisenhower. The landing was due to take place in the early hours of 10 July, and on the day before, the wind blew strongly from the west. It looked as if conditions for landing, especially on the American beaches and for the air drops, would be almost impossible. There were plenty of meteorologists to give advice, and Cunningham with all his experience of the Mediterranean was there, but the decision whether to go or not to go was Eisenhower's responsibility alone. Postponement at this late stage would certainly involve confusion and loss of surprise and might mean disaster, but the same might befall a landing in well-nigh impossible weather conditions. As the last moment for decision arrived there were forecasts of slight improvement and Eisenhower gave the decision to go ahead. As predicted, a little before midnight the wind dropped and the heavy seas gradually subsided to a strong swell. The weather certainly contributed to the difficulties on the American beaches, and caused heavy losses among the gliderborne troops and confusion among the parachutists. But perhaps even more important, the landing under conditions which the enemy considered unsuitable meant that the landings came as a complete surprise.

Operation Husky was the greatest combined operation in history up to that date. In fact in the number of assault divisions, seven, it exceeded the five assault divisions to be used in the future Overlord. However, Eisenhower hardly intervened in the battle once it was launched so that little need be said here except that the conquest of the island was achieved in less than six weeks. The Germans eventually employed a corps of three and a half divisions, under Hube, and this corps, showing its mettle in country well suited to defence, escaped more or less intact across the

Straits of Messina. Before considering that escape, it is worth looking at the enemy's conduct of the defence of the island in the light of plans which Eisenhower considered and approved. There was a difference of opinion between Guzzoni, the Italian commander in Sicily, and Kesselring who had sent two German divisions to the island. Guzzoni was in favour of keeping his four mobile Italian and the two German divisions as a central reserve for a large-scale counter-attack when the area of landings had been identified. Kesselring believed that the mobile divisions should be well forward to support the beach troops and destroy any landing before it had time to get established. Kesselring's policy required a degree of dispersion between possible landing areas in east and west, and Kesselring had his way. Thus the dispositions actually taken up were far more suitable to deal with the series of Allied landings originally contemplated from Catania to Palermo than they were to deal with the actual concentration of landings in the south-east. Patton's Seventh Army would certainly have fared far worse if the whole six enemy mobile divisions had been concentrated—as Guzzoni wanted—south of Enna.

Eisenhower's non-interference in the land battle is all the more significant because there was a fairly sharp difference between Patton and Montgomery's view of their respective roles. There is no doubt that Montgomery regarded himself as carrying out the main task, with Patton in a supporting role on his left flank. An early incident in which Montgomery asked for and got the use of Route 124, previously allotted to Bradley's corps, is indicative of Montgomery's attitude. It is also strange that Alexander's headquarters allowed the change without ascertaining that it would cause—as it did—considerable frustration, delay and counter moves by Bradley's corps. Then later the idea that Patton should strike across to Palermo and so eventually thrust to Messina from the west came from Patton and not from Alexander—although Alexander gladly acquiesced. All of this shows that Eisenhower was right in believing that Patton was well able to look after local American interests and that Eisenhower had succeeded in making clear to Patton that he was to regard Alexander's orders as his own.

The failure to prevent the escape of Hube's corps is in a different category. The main reason for the failure has already been dealt with.[8] In the light of the fact that there was no landing in Calabria, the prevention of Hube's escape was a matter for the three services in combination and therefore Eisenhower's responsibility. The Straits of Messina were heavily defended by enemy coastal and anti-aircraft batteries. Action by light naval craft and tactical aircraft by day would therefore involve heavy casualties. It was believed nevertheless that evacuation could be prevented by day and that the enemy would make his main effort by night. Sufficient heavy bombers were available to keep up bombardment of possible embarkation points by night but it was not considered necessary to call off the strategic bombing programme against Italy to do the same by day. In the event, air action so interfered with the German efforts to embark by night that they made the attempt by day and succeeded. Tedder's mind had already turned to the process of softening up the Italian mainland[9] and Eisenhower should have made it clear that there could be no greater contribution to the future battle for Italy than the destruction of the German divisions in Sicily.

Much has already been written about the incident during the Sicily Campaign when Patton abused one soldier and slapped another because he thought they were malingerers. Suffice it here to say that Eisenhower handled this deplorable situation in the best possible way. He did not spare Patton but he did understand the feelings that had moved him. It might well have been the end of Patton's active military career and Eisenhower knew what a tragedy that would be for the American Army. In addition to his personal reprimand[10] he demanded that Patton should apologise to the hospital and to the men concerned. He also required Patton to see the officers and representative groups of the men of his divisions to say that he had acted on impulse and that no reflection on the fighting spirit of his army was intended. Eisenhower also handled the publicity side. He saw the press representatives, told them what had happened and his own action. He told them he hoped nothing would be done to hamper the war effort, but the use they made of the information was left to their own judgment and no pressure was put upon them to suppress the story. The press representatives responded to Eisenhower's explanation and the story did not appear in the newspapers until November, more than three months after the incident. Marshall was not told about the incident until September.[11]

Before Marshall had been told of the Patton incident Eisenhower had sent him a letter discussing the qualities of his senior commanders.

[9] Tedder, *op. cit.*, p. 457
[10] Papers II, No. 1190
[11] Papers III, Nos. 1416, 1448, 1396–7; *Crusade*, pp. 198–201

Eisenhower foresaw that because of their experience some of them would be taken from him to prepare for Overlord. His summary of their qualities and limitations, read in the light of their subsequent performance, shows Eisenhower to be a sound judge of character: Patton, the brilliant and aggressive fighting commander with the impulsive nature that would always cause his superiors some concern; Bradley, the man who always ran true to form and who had a thorough understanding of modern battle as well as the ability to get on with his associates, British as well as American; Clark, the best organizer and trainer of troops that Eisenhower had met—rightly or wrongly Eisenhower thought he had suppressed his undue love of publicity. At the same time Eisenhower did not hesitate to tell Marshall his views of British commanders. Obviously thinking of Marshall as the Supreme Commander for Overlord he advised him to take Alexander as his principal subordinate. He added: 'I would be perfectly content to accept Montgomery in Alexander's present place because during these months I have learnt to know him very well, feel that I have his personal equation, and have no lack of confidence in my ability to handle him.'[12] This letter crossed a signal from Marshall in which he said he wanted Bradley to command the American Army preparing for Overlord, a decision with which Eisenhower gladly concurred.

The fact that Clark and not Patton commanded the American troops involved on the Italian mainland was nothing to do with the slapping incident. Eisenhower saw Patton, Clark and Bradley as his three most capable commanders, all proven in battle and available to be used according to the needs of the moment. He regarded Clark as 'the ablest and most experienced commander we have in planning amphibious operations'. This, added to the fact that Patton and Bradley were fully committed in Sicily, made Clark the obvious choice for the forthcoming operations. He and the Fifty Army staff were available for this very purpose. Patton was destined to go with Bradley to Overlord, though Bradley was there the commander and Patton the subordinate, the reverse of the situation in Sicily.

While the Sicily Campaign was at its height there was exciting news from Italy. Before breakfast on 25 July Eisenhower heard of the fall of Mussolini. Badoglio, who had been appointed by the King as head of the government, had stated that the war would continue, but Eisenhower saw the possibilities and was full of plans for exploiting the situation. He sent

[12] Papers II, No. 1205

at once for Macmillan in order to draft messages to London and Washington to get authority for a declaration to the Italian people and possible terms on which the Italian Government might be invited to capitulate. Eisenhower knew that the Italians were largely at the mercy of the Germans, and that if advantage were to be taken of the situation the Allies must act quickly without trying to negotiate complicated terms. He believed that an immediate approach to the King with acceptable military terms would give the Italians the opportunity to surrender before the Germans had time to act. Churchill and Roosevelt did not look at the matter in quite the same way. They were both averse to allowing Eisenhower to address a propaganda declaration to the Italian people or to discuss armistice terms with the Italian Government. Nevertheless, in the end they did see that a military approach was necessary and that political, economic and financial matters must be left for later discussion. Roosevelt was disinclined to move far from his principle of unconditional surrender, which he had managed to get accepted at the Casablanca Conference. Churchill was more liberal and was willing to deal with any non-Fascist Italian Government that would help in the overthrow of Germany. Nevertheless, both governments ultimately approved the broadcast to the Italian people proposed by Eisenhower and altered his wording only in one or two details.[13]

Eisenhower felt that the terms for the Italians should depend upon the time at which they were offered. If the Allied invasion of the mainland had already begun, an armistice must involve the surrender of all German forces in contact with the Allies. Before an invasion he believed it would be foolish to expect the Italians to turn against the Germans. For them to do so would be an act of treachery and would certainly not get the Italians peace, which was at that time their sole interest. Eisenhower believed firmly that the terms of peace should be such as could be broadcast immediately to the Italian people. They should present 'such a promise of peace under honourable conditions that no Italian government could remain in power if it refused to request an armistice.'[14] In an exchange of messages with Churchill, Eisenhower found himself in close agreement with the Prime Minister on all points save one. Churchill had referred to the fury of the Italian people, Eisenhower believed that there was no fury left save that of desperation. They were tired and sick of the war and

13 Papers II, No. 1139
14 Papers II, No. 1139

only wanted peace. Consequently Eisenhower confined his demands to immediate evacuation of the whole peninsula by all German forces. He added: 'If the terms of the armistice should present to the Italian population only an immediate choice as to partners in the war, we must not forget that they are under daily domination by the hostile troops they see in their midst. Consequently the incentive to surrender will not be the same as if the whole population is given the promise of peace.'[15] Macmillan tells how at this time telegrams, all private, personal and most immediate, poured in upon Eisenhower. They came from the Combined Chiefs of Staff, his official masters; from Marshall, his immediate superior; from Churchill, and from Roosevelt. In addition there was a flood of such messages sent through Macmillan and Murphy from the Foreign Office and the State Department. Naturally many of the messages were conflicting or even contradictory.

In the midst of this turmoil Eisenhower had a meeting, previously arranged, with all his commanders to discuss plans for operations on the mainland of Italy. Planning had progressed since the days of the original choice between Sardinia and the Toe of Italy. Now Sardinia and Corsica were handed over as Giraud's responsibility to be seized as resources became available and circumstances allowed. Eisenhower intended that Alexander's forces should concentrate on the conquest of southern Italy. There was a host of plans in combination and alternative but the favourite was an operation by Eighth Army across the Straits while Clark's Fifth Army attacked the Heel. The Heel operation, a landing between Taranto and Bari, offered a favourable bridgehead from which action could be taken to seize the important airfield area of Foggia and possibly advance overland to Naples. Now the likelihood of an Italian capitulation demanded bolder action. Naples and Rome were the desirable prizes but even Naples was outside effective range for fighter cover from Sicily. The Bay of Salerno, south of Naples, was just within fighter cover and a landing there was planned under the code-name Avalanche. Eisenhower did not feel, however, that he could be sure he would not have to stage a combined operation to ensure a footing in Calabria. He therefore decided to keep in being plan Buttress for a landing on the north-west coast of Calabria. Buttress would be either alternative or supplementary to Avalanche. The British X Corps would carry out Buttress, but if the operation were not necessary, then X Corps would

[15] Papers II, No. 1140

form part of Clark's Fifth Army for Avalanche. One of the circumstances which Eisenhower saw would make Buttress unnecessary was that Montgomery should be in a position to make a direct crossing of the Straits of Messina—this indeed is what did happen. Eisenhower was prepared to launch Avalanche even if the Germans remained in strength in southern Italy, but if they staged a rapid withdrawal then he intended to try a rush operation to seize Naples with one division plus an airborne division.

Plan Avalanche received the ready support of the Combined Chiefs of Staff. Even before the fall of Mussolini, Marshall had suggested an amphibious assault on Naples as the quickest way of ending the Italian adventure.[16] Churchill characteristically welcomed any bold venture and the Chiefs of Staff had urged their American colleagues to make available the landing craft and naval forces, including carriers. The Joint Chiefs of Staff were adamant, however, and insisted that the Italian Campaign should be completed without any increase in the forces already earmarked. Marshall was confident that Eisenhower had sufficient forces to capture Naples and Foggia and stabilise the situation on that line. On the other hand, Eisenhower considered that he had neither sufficient strength in the air nor enough landing craft for such a major operation and he had preferred the less ambitious route through the Toe and Heel. Even now, when the apparent imminence of the Italian collapse made him favour the bolder course, he required a pause between the conquest of Sicily and the launching of Avalanche. Both Eisenhower and Alexander estimated that the Sicily operation would be completed by mid-August and so 7 September was fixed as the planning date for Avalanche. One of the divisions and certain other units and some equipment required by Clark for Salerno were engaged in Sicily. There was, however, a proviso that, if the Germans showed signs of a rapid withdrawal from southern Italy, a direct assault on Naples should be carried out as a rush operation using one division and one airborne division.

The first Italian approach to the Allies came while the Sicilian Campaign was drawing to a close and just as Churchill and the Chiefs of Staff were preparing to leave for Quadrant, the Allied Conference held in Quebec. On 18 August Eisenhower was directed by the Combined Chiefs of Staff to send two officers, one British and one American, to Lisbon to talk to General Castellano who had been authorised by Badoglio to speak

[16] Matloff, *op. cit.*, pp. 157–8

on his behalf. Bedell Smith, the Chief of Staff, and Strong, the head of Intelligence, left at once for Lisbon. The Italians were required to announce their surrender immediately; to send their navy, merchant ships and aircraft to Allied territory; and to resist and hamper the Germans as far as possible. The Italians showed no willingness to accept such terms. They were looking for a new alliance rather than a capitulation and, moreover, they were looking for adequate protection by Allied forces against anything the Germans might try to do. In the meantime they were trying to play off the Allies against the Germans as well as vice versa. In the light of the difficulty with which Eisenhower was scraping together four or five divisions (including only three assault divisions) for the Salerno attack, it is laughable to think that the Italians were looking for a landing by 15 divisions as far north as Leghorn. Although Eisenhower was empowered to accept the Italian surrender he was not authorised to modify the terms in any essential respect. Most important of all, he was not allowed to disclose the Allied plans. Perhaps, in view of the differences between these plans and the Italian expectations, this was just as well. Castellano was not authorised to accept the terms offered and so he had to return by devious and secret means to present them to Badoglio. He was given until 30 August to reply. There was then a series of comings and goings and several secret meetings which need not concern us here.[17] On 30 August word was heard from Castellano that he was coming to Sicily, where he arrived the next day.

In the meantime the Germans were certainly not deceived; they knew as well as the Allies that the Italians were looking for an opportunity to change sides. On 6 August the Italian Chief of Staff of the Armed Forces, Ambrosio, and the Foreign Minister had met Keitel and Ribbentrop, their opposite numbers. Ambrosio had requested the return of Italian divisions forming part of the Axis garrisons in southern France and the Balkans. Keitel not only refused but set on foot the plans the Germans already had for moving German divisions into Italy. By 17 August, the day Hube's corps left Sicily, the Germans had 17 divisions in Italy. By 30 August, four days before the Italian surrender was agreed, the final German plan was complete. Rommel with Army Group 'B' was to retain the German hold on northern Italy. Kesselring, Commander-in-Chief South was responsible south of the Pisa-Rimini line. He had a corps

[17] They are fully dealt with in Macmillan, *op. cit.*, pp. 378–88, and Strong, *Intelligence at the Top*, pp. 111–15

commander responsible for each of the probable Allied landing areas, Calabria, Naples and Rome. The Germans intended to co-operate with the Italians as far as possible but, if Italy defected, their troops were to be disarmed, by force if necessary, and then offered the choice of joining German units or going home. The German Navy was to take over the Italian fleet and the Air Force all Italian aircraft and major airfields.

Eisenhower's feelings during the protracted negotiations may be imagined. It is true that in Alexander, Cunningham and Tedder he had three Commanders-in-Chief capable of dealing with all operational matters, and that the negotiations he had to carry on with the Italians were confined by his political masters to accepting a military surrender. Yet he had the heavy responsibility of deciding the extent to which the scope and timing of the operations might be altered to take the greatest advantage from the Italian willingness to change sides. The time factor was especially important. Both the British and American Chiefs of Staff regarded the forthcoming operations as a walk-over but Eisenhower knew that, because of the small number of divisions he could lift, the Salerno operation was a gamble. It was important to get the Italian surrender arranged before Avalanche was launched. There were nothing like the same risks attached to Montgomery's operations across the Straits of Messina into Calabria and there was considerable advantage in getting this well under way before Avalanche. Montgomery was accordingly authorised to cross on 3 September. Even this was ten days later than Eisenhower had hoped. Time was necessary not only to get Eighth Army up the difficult route towards Salerno but also to get landing craft used by them back for Avalanche.

Castellano had arrived in Sicily not with authority to surrender but with the information that the situation had now completely changed. For their own part the Italians were willing to accept the terms but the Germans now had such a stranglehold on Italy that the Italian Government was no longer a free agent. They required to know where and in what strength the Allies intended to land. Bedell Smith pointed out that the Allies would neither disclose nor change their plans and that the best hope for Italy was to co-operate with the Allies. Protracted resistance would make Italy a battlefield and involve the destruction of the country by bombing. Castellano was thereupon persuaded to return to Rome to get permission to sign the instrument of surrender. On Castellano's return Eisenhower still left Bedell Smith and Strong to deal with the negotiations. At first Castellano said that although the Italian Government accepted the terms he had no authority to sign anything. It was then thought politic to arrange for Alexander, whose headquarters was at hand, to make a formal call on Castellano to express his satisfaction that negotiations had been completed. When Castellano had to confess that this was not so, Alexander was able to impress on him the deplorable consequences for Italy of their continuing to resist. Bedell Smith then completed the negotiations and on 3 September, a few hours after Montgomery had crossed the Straits of Messina, Castellano received permission from his government to sign the instrument of surrender. Bedell Smith had had the task of persuading the Italians not only of the consequences of failure to capitulate but also of convincing them that the Allied action would be effective and would ensure the safety of Italy. This he succeeded in doing. In the light of what the Allies achieved Castellano considered that he had been tricked into misleading his government.[18] Certainly in the outcome Italy was spared little by her surrender and suffered just as much as if she had continued as part of the Axis. Eisenhower, and on his behalf Bedell Smith, did however act in good faith and they believed that the course offered to Italy was the best in all the circumstances.

One of the consequences of the Italian surrender was that the Allies were able to get information about the dispositions of the Italian and German forces. Eisenhower had no intention of departing from the main Avalanche plan but he felt that some subsidiary operation might be possible. Rome was not only a desirable objective for the Allies, but it was to the advantage of the Italians to have an Allied force there. The Italians had six divisions in the capital and this appeared ample to safeguard the airfields. It was therefore arranged that an American airborne division should land in Rome on the day the Italian surrender was announced. Eisenhower arranged with Badoglio that this announcement should be made by each of them simultaneously on the evening of 8 September. The Italians were not told that Eisenhower's reason for selecting this date was that the landing at Salerno was to take place that same night, a few hours after the proposed announcement.

The proposed airborne landing in Rome caused Eisenhower some concern. 82nd Airborne Division had originally been allotted to Clark as part of his reserve for Avalanche. If the Italians did not play their proper part in securing the landing places, the division might well be destroyed.

[18] Strong, *op. cit.*, p. 115

Accordingly, Brigadier-General Maxwell Taylor, the artillery commander of the division,[19] and another officer, were sent in secret to Rome with instructions to send a code-word if the landing seemed impracticable.

There was one other important change in Allied plans as a result of the surrender. Eisenhower had given up his plan for an assault on the Heel in favour of Avalanche—there were no resources for both. Now it seemed improvident not to take advantage of the surrender to secure the magnificent harbour and port of Taranto. Only one division was available—1st British Airborne—and there were no aircraft, merchant shipping or landing craft to move them. The close accord of Eisenhower and Cunningham solved the problem. Once Cunningham knew that the Italian fleet was committed to surrender he was willing to take the risk of treachery and the certain hazard of minefields to sail part of his battle fleet direct into the harbour. It was agreed that the cruisers should carry in the division on the day after the surrender was announced.[20]

As 8 September approached Badoglio became alarmed at the possibility that the Germans might take over Rome and assume the government of Italy by force. The Italian commander in Rome knew that his troops, short of ammunition and of vehicles and largely dispirited, would be no match for Student's Parachute Corps. They had no confidence that one American airborne division, even if it landed safely, could redress the balance. At noon on 8 September, the very day on which the announcement was to be made, Badoglio sent a message to Algiers saying that he could no longer accept an armistice. Eisenhower had left Algiers for his advanced headquarters near Bizerta, and in his absence Bedell Smith not only sent on the message to Bizerta but also sent it to the Combined Chiefs of Staff. Eisenhower was furious, not only with Badoglio but also with Bedell Smith for asking the Combined Chiefs for instructions. He thought it a matter which he was capable of dealing with himself.

Even if Eisenhower had been disposed to do so, there was no question of holding up Avalanche at this stage. He did not wait for the reply from the Combined Chiefs of Staff to Bedell Smith's cable, but immediately sent a short message to Badoglio telling him that he intended to broadcast the surrender message at the time planned. He made it clear that if Badoglio failed in his part the consequences for Italy would be serious and

---

[19] Later to give distinguished service as commander 101st Airborne Division, in command in Korea and as Chief of Staff of the Army

[20] *Crusade in Europe*, p. 208; Cunningham, *op. cit.*, pp. 563–4

19 *Eisenhower at a British Corps headquarters*

20 *Talking to men of the 8th US Division in France*

21 *Eisenhower and Bradley visit Heuber, commanding the 1st US Division in Normandy*

22 *Eisenhower visiting the Southern Group of Armies. Devers on the left, Major-General Brooks on the right and Lieutenant-General Patch in background*

he would also publish to the world a full record of the affair.[21] Although Eisenhower would not tolerate any delay in the announcement, nor any change in Avalanche, he did decide to postpone and possibly cancel the airborne landing in Rome. Maxwell Taylor had sent the code-word indicating that the situation in Rome was not propitious. Eisenhower was not confident that the postponement message would get through to 82nd Airborne Division in time so he sent Lemnitzer, then serving as Alexander's Deputy Chief of Staff, by air to the division, Lemnitzer arrived as the first aircraft were actually circling into their formation. Strong, who is seldom critical of Eisenhower, suggests that he was wrong to cancel the Rome flight. It was a risk but it might have done much to frustrate the enemy reaction to Avalanche. None of the information sent by Badoglio showed that the situation was in any way different from what had been expected. Maxwell Taylor on his return from Rome agreed with Strong that the situation in Rome was exactly what he had been told before departure. It was the Italian display of cold feet that had caused him to send his message. As soon as he had received the information Strong had gone to Eisenhower to point out that there was no change in the situation that had been previously known, but Eisenhower had already given the decision to cancel the operation. Eisenhower did not regret his decision because he did not believe he was justified in going against the advice of a commander whom he trusted, who had seen the situation at first hand.[22] That was his attitude at the time, but writing after the war he said: 'At the last moment either the fright of the Italian Government or the movement of German reserves as alleged by the Italians—I have never known which—forced the cancellation of the project.'[23] In that statement perhaps lies the indication that although he was determined to force his will upon the Italians, he was reluctant to take risks against the Germans, even when so much might have been gained.

As Eisenhower was making his broadcast, the convoy carrying Clark's force to Salerno was already on its way and in the early hours of 9 September the landing was accomplished. Of Hube's corps two divisions were north of Naples and only one, 16 Panzer, was in the Salerno area. But this was a first-class division, experienced in Poland, in France and in Russia, and with the highest morale. The Allied convoy had been sighted south of

[21] Papers III, No. 1244
[22] Strong, *op. cit.*, pp. 117–18
[23] *Crusade in Europe*, p. 202

Capri and the Germans were fully prepared—the Italians were already disarmed—as the assault waves approached. The Germans now bent every effort to destroy Clark's Fifth Army before the Eighth Army came within reach. It was the kind of operation in which the Germans were particularly skilful. Montgomery's advance was delayed more by demolitions and the difficult route than by fighting and the whole weight of the five divisions of the German Tenth Army was brought to bear against Clark. It was touch and go but in the nine days battle the Fifth Army held on and by the time the Eighth Army arrived the Germans had realized that they could not destroy the beachhead.

Eisenhower, naturally, had no part in the tactical battle for Salerno. It was Clark's battle fought under the direct command of Alexander. Eisenhower's part was in seeing that everything possible was provided to ensure success. Eisenhower had already seen that his ability to influence the battle would depend upon the use of his strategic air forces. In July he had pointed out to the Combined Chiefs of Staff that if the strategic air force could be doubled he could 'practically paralyse the German air effort in southern Italy and almost immobilize his ground units'. He asked that four groups of 'Flying Fortresses' should be sent from England. He also asked that three groups of medium bombers, which had been sent temporarily to the Mediterranean for operations against southern Germany and Austria, should be left with him until Avalanche was over. Neither of these requests was granted because of the priority given to the combined bomber offensive against Germany. A request for four medium bomber groups from England was similarly turned down. Two days after the landing Eisenhower in a letter to Wedemeyer said: 'I would give my next year's pay for two or three extra heavy groups right this minute.' On 15 September Eisenhower again put clearly to the Combined Chiefs of Staff that the only way of intervening in the critical situation was by air forces. He asked again for the four medium groups that had experience of Italy and also asked that heavy bomber forces from the United Kingdom should act against the German communications in northern Italy. This time both requests were granted.

For the movement of the army, too, Eisenhower was kept short of what could have been made available. In August he had asked the Combined Chiefs of Staff for the loan of landing ships for tanks, which were on their way through the Mediterranean *en route* to India; 'even for one trip' they would be useful. This request had been refused. After the landing had begun the decision had been reversed but the ships were loaded with steel rails and had to be unloaded before they could be used. By this time 82nd Airborne Division, now released from the Rome commitment, had been landed from the air on the beaches and the landing ships were used to take in 3rd (U.S.) Division.

At Taranto all had gone according to plan, and after 1st Airborne Division were established the port was used to receive 8th Indian Division which Eisenhower had persuaded Middle East Command to make available. Eisenhower wanted to go up to see Clark on 14 September but he made way for Alexander to do so and went two days later. Alexander had been impressed by Clark's handling of a very difficult situation and by McCreery, the British corps commander, but most unfavourably impressed by that of the United States corps commander. On arrival Eisenhower saw the situation for himself and immediately sent orders for Major General Lucas to take over the corps.

By the beginning of October the Allies had captured the port of Naples and the airfields of Foggia. Alexander was now firmly established in Italy with Montgomery on the Adriatic flank and Clark in the west. The Germans had withdrawn from Sardinia and Corsica and both islands had been occupied by French forces under Giraud. A firm foothold had been established in Europe and Eisenhower may be said to have succeeded in an essential part of the role given to him at the Trident Conference. Italy had not been completely eliminated from the war but the present situation in which she was half in the Axis and half in the Allied camp had considerable disadvantages for the Germans. The Germans were beginning to accept the necessity for a forward policy in Italy. Kesselring was the principal advocate of such a policy and now he was recommending a determined defence south of Rome. Although Rommel was using his influence for a withdrawal to the formidable mountain barrier from Pisa to Rimini—or even to the Alps—Hitler was turning to Kesselring's view. Thus Eisenhower's second, and in the British view more important, role, that of containing the maximum number of German formations, was certainly being accomplished. This success had been achieved without interfering with the plans for the withdrawal of the seven divisions to prepare for Overlord. Of these divisions only two, 7th (British) Armoured and 82nd (U.S.) Airborne, had been in action on the mainland, and both were released in November.

It may be asked whether in this exploitation phase Eisenhower was too cautious. Certainly enormous effort was put into Montgomery's laborious advance up the Boot of Italy. On the other hand nothing was lost by this advance; if it had not taken place not a man more could have been used at Salerno. Availability of landing craft was always the limiting factor. Eisenhower can be congratulated on having got so many men ashore at Taranto, and later at Bari, before he knew how the Salerno landing would go. Only in his decision not to land an airborne division at Rome can Eisenhower be said to have been too cautious. That criticism may be tempered by the thought that had the landings been attempted the division might well have been lost, but such is an inescapable risk of war. It is unthinkable that Kesselring or Rommel in similar circumstances would not have taken the risk.

Kesselring, himself an airman as well as an experienced soldier, believes that Eisenhower was wrong to have landed so far south as Salerno. It would have been a bold decision to have landed outside effective fighter cover and, judged by what actually happened at Salerno, an attempt further north would have involved unjustifiable risks and might well have led to disaster. There is little doubt that an advance further up the coast would have had to wait for the establishment of fighter bases in Sardinia, and the bomber resources refused to Eisenhower would have had to be provided. All this would have meant time and was in no way consistent with the efforts to take advantage of the Italian surrender.

A last criticism of this phase of the campaign came from Montgomery. He believed that the subsequent difficulties in Italy stemmed from a failure to decide in the first place how the campaign was to be conducted. In his own words: 'The basic trouble was that we became involved in a major campaign lacking a predetermined master plan.'[24] Montgomery does not lay the responsibility for that failure at any particular door. As the Supreme Commander, Eisenhower must bear some share of the blame but there were mitigating circumstances. In the first place he was never allowed to look at the Italian campaign as a whole because the Combined Chiefs of Staff could not decide how far they wanted to go in Italy. In the second place, the Italian offer to change sides, coming at the moment it did, complicated rather than simplified Eisenhower's problem. He was closely controlled on the conditions of surrender, and the real opportunity to benefit from the surrender demanded a larger amphibious lift than he had. As events turned out, Eisenhower's strategic direction enabled Alexander

[24] Montgomery, *Memoirs*, p. 199

to establish an army of some 14 divisions from Naples to Foggia and that was the moment when the lack of a master plan was felt. Whether this plan should have been made by Eisenhower or by Alexander, whose land campaign it was, is a moot point. That neither did so until November can be attributed to the lack of decision on the part of the Combined Chiefs of Staff, a matter which is discussed in the next chapter.

7

The Strategic Debate

All the time that Eisenhower was engaged in the Sicily Campaign and the preparations for the invasion of Italy, the strategic debate that had been only partially settled in Trident had continued in Washington and in London. After the conference there was no doubt that the cross-Channel operation, as its name Overlord suggested, had priority and must take place in about May 1944. It was also clear that in the meantime opportunity would be taken to exploit success in the Mediterranean, to knock Italy out of the war and to contain German forces in southern Europe. What was not decided was the extent to which operations in Italy should go, and when operations there, so far from containing German strength, would dissipate Allied resources necessary for Overlord. There was a strong body of opinion which held that the Allies might get so entangled in Italy that Overlord would be compromised. Either there would be a slow and costly advance which would call for constant reinforcement, or there would be such success that the British would suggest that Germany should be tackled from the south rather than from the west. Marshall wanted 'a short Italian campaign with limited objectives—air bases to supplement the Combined Bomber Offensive against southern Germany, and enough action to tie down German strength.'[1] Possibly this aim could be achieved by firm possession of Naples and Foggia; certainly it was not necessary to go beyond Rome. The British saw the campaign rather as one of opportunity. Rome must be captured and then advantage could be taken of the resulting situation to fight and contain the Germans so that success in Overlord would be facilitated. Possibly the British Foreign Office was conscious of the political advantages of operations in Greece and Jugo-Slavia but Churchill, wide ranging as his ideas always were, never advocated more than the support of guerrilla and raiding activities in the Balkans. Certainly Brooke was quite clear that the Italian Campaign was secondary to Overlord, but he was confident that active prosecution of a campaign in Italy was a valuable and in fact a necessary prelude to Overlord.

[1] Matloff, *op. cit.*, p. 162

The division of opinion was not altogether along British-American lines. Strong as American military opinion had been against Mediterranean adventures, as they progressed opinions began to turn. Such a turn of opinion may even have been born from a sense of frustration—a feeling that the cross-Channel operation was so constantly put on one side that the effort might as well go on where it had started. After the successful landings in Sicily, Major General Hull, Chief of the European Theatre Group of the Operations Division, had written:

> Although from the very beginning of this war, I have felt that the logical plan for the defeat of Germany was to strike at her across the channel by the most direct route, our commitments to the Mediterranean have led me to the belief that we should now reverse our decision and put our resources into the exploitation of our Mediterranean operations.[2]

Doubts were somewhat removed by the progress of the combined planners (COSSAC), who in July completed their outline plan for Overlord. Marshall was in no doubt that this plan ought to be discussed at the forthcoming meeting at Quebec between Churchill, Roosevelt and the Combined Chiefs of Staff (Quadrant), and that the British should be asked for a firm commitment to it for 1944. Roosevelt agreed with Marshall on the necessity for Overlord and promised that he would not support any British suggestions that might be put forward for operations in the Balkans. But Roosevelt thought that, as always, the planners were too conservative and saw too many difficulties. He considered that more could be done in the Mediterranean without compromising Overlord. He therefore proposed that seven fresh divisions should be sent to Eisenhower to replace the battle-experienced divisions being transferred to Britain for Overlord. Roosevelt believed this would enable Eisenhower to secure a position north of Rome and, with the possession of Sardinia and Corsica, pose a serious threat to southern France. Marshall did not think that the move of the seven divisions to the Mediterranean could be made in time to be of use without affecting the build-up for Overlord. Stimson, the Secretary of War, was even more bitterly opposed to the reinforcement of the Mediterranean. He was obsessed with the idea that Churchill and Eden were intent upon a Balkan adventure and that the British nursed a theory that Germany could be defeated by 'a series of attritions in the Mediterranean and the Balkans'.[3]

[2] Quoted Matloff, *op. cit.*, p. 165
[3] Matloff, *op. cit.*, p. 214

In the context of his discussion with Roosevelt, Marshall asked Eisenhower for his views on his ability to carry out his existing role and to pose a threat to southern France without increase in his planned forces. Eisenhower sent a cautious and reasoned reply of which the gist was that he could do both and that his potential depended less on getting additional divisions than on landing craft and ships and on his existing divisions being kept up to strength in men and equipment.[4] It must be remembered that this answer was sent on 12 August, as the Sicily operations were drawing to a close and before the first Italian overtures to the Allies or the German move into Italy. In the light of this date Eisenhower's message can be seen to be a far-sighted and realistic forecast of the Italian campaign as it was to develop. He pointed to the many indications of the German intention to reinforce Italy and to the uncertainty of the extent to which the Italians would assist them or would resist the Allies. The early part of the campaign would be a race for Naples and Foggia, and Eisenhower's ability to capture Rome and hold a line to the north would depend on German reactions. But if the Allies did capture Rome, Eisenhower doubted the possibility of stopping there. There could be no question of an Allied army in central Italy and a German force in the north with a no-man's land between them. The two armies would obviously be in contact and the Allies would attempt to destroy the German force or, if the Germans were strongly reinforced, they would have to fight to prevent their eviction from Italy. Eisenhower was not sure that if the Germans reacted strongly his present force (24 divisions) would be sufficient to gain and hold a position in the Naples-Rome area. However, if the Allies did succeed in establishing themselves in northern Italy, then ten divisions would be sufficient for defence and some six or more divisions (depending upon wastage and maintenance) would be available for offensive operations against southern France.

Armed with Eisenhower's views, Marshall was able to persuade Roosevelt that no reinforcement of the Mediterranean theatre was necessary. Marshall then felt that the Joint Chiefs of Staff had the President behind them in their plans for Europe. One other important aspect of these discussions, preliminary to Quadrant, was to have an important bearing on Eisenhower's career. That was the determination that the cross-Channel operation should be carried out under American command. Hitherto it had seemed that the British would take a preponderant part in the operation

4 Papers II, No. 1181

and would provide the Allied commander. But the Americans suspected that neither Churchill nor Brooke was wholeheartedly behind the operation, and that suspicion and a more realistic appreciation of the size of forces that would be necessary for Overlord caused a change of view. The extent of American suspicion, unjustified as it was, can be measured by the fact that during the discussions between Roosevelt and the Joint Chiefs the question was mooted whether, if the British insisted on postponing Overlord indefinitely, the United States should abandon the operation or carry it out alone. The President thought the British would make the necessary bases available; Marshall did not believe that the operation could be carried out without the 15 British divisions available on the spot.[5] Stimson was the first to set out for the President good reasons why Overlord should have an American commander. Stimson was not thinking of Eisenhower but of Marshall. He wrote of him to Roosevelt:

> I believe that he is the man who most surely can now by his character and skill furnish the military leadership which is necessary to bring our two nations together in confident joint action in this great operation. No one knows better than I the loss in the problems of organization and world-wide strategy centred in Washington which such a solution would cause, but I see no other alternative to which we can turn in the great effort which confronts us.[6]

Roosevelt said that Stimson had come to a conclusion he himself had already reached. Roosevelt furthermore stated there must be a preponderance of United States forces in Overlord from the first day in order to justify an American commander,[7] and from this time forward President, Secretary of War and Joint Chiefs of Staff were of one mind. The Americans got their way at the Quadrant Conference and there Churchill agreed that an American should become the commander for Overlord. Churchill's agreement was facilitated by the American acceptance of Mountbatten as Supreme Commander in the newly created South-East Asia Command. Churchill's understanding was that Marshall would command Overlord and would be replaced by Eisenhower, and that Eisenhower would be replaced in the Mediterranean Command by Alexander.

The Quadrant Conference (14-24 August) was in some degree a battle between Marshall and Brooke. Marshall was determined to get a decision whether a 1944 Overlord was to get overriding priority or a Mediterranean strategy was to be adopted. Brooke did not see that there was this conflicting

[5] Matloff, *op. cit.*, pp. 213-14
[6] Quoted, *ibid.*, p. 214
[7] *Ibid.*, p. 216

choice. He and the Chiefs of Staff agreed that Overlord was to be the major Allied offensive of 1944. But he saw that an active Mediterranean strategy would contribute materially to success in Overlord. He believed that the aim of the Allied operations in Italy should be to create a favourable situation for Overlord by containing the maximum number of German divisions and by air action from Italian bases to reduce German fighter forces. On this understanding he questioned the wisdom of withdrawing the seven divisions from the Mediterranean. Marshall did not believe that this indirect version of priority for Overlord was enough. He believed that unless Overlord was given overriding priority the operation might never be launched and he looked to Roosevelt, who was not present at the first three days of the conference, to clinch the argument.

When Churchill and Roosevelt joined the conference for the plenary sessions the issue became less clear-cut. Churchill said that none of the past objections to Sledgehammer applied to Overlord. Discussion then went on to point to the necessity for strengthening the initial assault force for Overlord and the means by which the Allies could take advantage of the impending surrender of Italy. The discussion on how far to go in Italy was inconclusive. Churchill said he was not committed to an advance beyond the line Pisa-Ancona but all were in favour of taking possession of Italian airfields as far north as possible in order to extend the range of the Combined Bomber Offensive. Similarly tentative views were expressed about the possibility of assisting Overlord by operations in southern France. Churchill showed his skill in phraseology by suggesting 'air nourished guerrilla warfare' in southern France.

No one suggested that any Anglo-American forces should be committed to offensive operations in the Balkans. Roosevelt did suggest that the Greek and Jugo-Slav divisions equipped by the Allies might be used to follow up the Germans if they decided to withdraw from south-east Europe to the line of the Danube. Churchill supported him with the suggestion that commando forces could operate in support of guerrilla activity. Marshall did not get the support he wanted from Roosevelt in forcing the issue of 'overriding priority'. Thus Marshall and his planners were left with their fears that resources necessary for Overlord would be drained away, as a consequence of which they resolved to restrict Mediterranean operations. The British were left resisting any strait-jacket which would jeopardise Mediterranean operations; operations that they now saw as all the more important to pave the way for Overlord.

The conference then went on to discuss matters outside the scope of this book. In the end the guidance left for Eisenhower was that the Combined Chiefs of Staff were agreed on their plans for Italy: first the elimination of Italy and the establishment of air bases in the Rome area and if possible further north; second the seizure of Sardinia and Corsica; third the maintenance of constant pressure on German forces in northern Italy and the creation of conditions favourable to the eventual entry of Allied forces, including French forces, into southern France.[8] It is easy to see how valuable such guidance would have been to Eisenhower if it had been given in May 1943 or even earlier. It was less valuable in August 1943 when Eisenhower had already pointed his first steps in a more cautious direction and when he was living from hand to mouth in the course of the negotiations for the Italian surrender. Even more unfortunate than the timing of the decisions was the failure to allot to Eisenhower sufficient air forces, shipping and landing craft to carry out his role quickly and effectively. As early as 24 July Brooke had written in his diary: 'Marshall absolutely fails to realize the strategic treasures that lie at our feet in the Mediterranean and hankers after cross-Channel operations. He admits that our object must be to eliminate Italy and yet is always afraid of facing the consequences of doing so. . . .'[9] Writing about these controversies in retrospect Brooke said:

> Our strategy had now become a delicate matter of balancing. Our aim must be to draw as many divisions as possible from the French Channel and to retain them in southern Europe as long as possible. . . .
> When arguing with Marshall I could never get him fully to appreciate the very close connection that existed between the various German fronts. For him they might have been separate wars, a Russian war on the one side, a Mediterranean war on the other and a cross-Channel war to be started as soon as possible.[10]

The result of Marshall's attitude was that nothing was allowed for Mediterranean operations that had not previously been earmarked for them—even the bomber squadrons and the landing craft that were within reach of Eisenhower were denied him until too late.

Only in one direction did Churchill show any determination for Allied intervention in the Balkans beyond the provision of supplies and assistance to guerrilla activities. That was in the desire to take advantage of the

[8] *Ibid.*, p. 228
[9] Bryant, *op. cit.*, I, p. 673
[10] *Ibid.*, p. 684

Italian surrender to secure for the Allies the Dodecanese Islands, especially Rhodes, which were garrisoned by the Italians. These islands were not in Eisenhower's command but within the sphere of Wilson, Commander-in-Chief Middle East, a wholly British command. He had already provided for Eisenhower all the divisions he had over and above what he considered necessary for essential internal security tasks. Wilson did however use one infantry brigade and some long-range fighters to get small garrisons into Cos, Leros and Samos. As in Italy the Italians showed themselves unwilling to fight the Germans, who reacted strongly and recaptured the islands. Rhodes was the key to the retention of all the islands and its capture from the Germans would require a properly mounted operation with landing craft and air support which were beyond Wilson's resources. In October Churchill asked Eisenhower to provide the necessary resources and when Eisenhower refused on the grounds that he had needs of a higher priority for all he could get, Churchill tried to press Roosevelt to overrule him. The Joint Chiefs of Staff had already decided to leave the decision to Eisenhower, and Roosevelt refused to intervene. There is no doubt that Churchill's demands, small though they were, did much to increase American suspicion of British ambitions in the eastern Mediterranean. Although aware of the opportunities, Brooke did not support Churchill in his importunity. He wrote in his diary: 'He has worked himself into a frenzy of excitement about the Rhodes attack, has magnified its importance so that he can no longer see anything else and has set his heart on capturing this one island even at the expense of endangering his relations with the President and the Americans and the future of the Italian campaign. ... He is placing himself, quite unnecessarily, in a false position. The Americans are already desperately suspicious of him, and this will make matters worse.'[11]

The American suspicions of British designs in the eastern Mediterranean bedevilled the discussion of the Allied command arrangements that became necessary as the time approached for Overlord. The British looked for the appointment of a Supreme Allied Commander for Overlord and they considered that the present division of command in the Mediterranean was now illogical. They therefore pressed for a single Mediterranean command. The Americans regarded this proposal as an artifice to involve the Allies in operations in the Balkans. They would agree to a single command in the Mediterranean only as part of a new command organization

[11] *Ibid.*, II, p. 51

which would put all operations against Germany under a single commander. They obviously saw Marshall as this commander and he would have under him two subordinate commanders, one for the cross-Channel operation and one for the Mediterranean. The American view was that control by the Combined Chiefs of Staff, subject as it must be to political pressure, was 'suitable for evolving strategy but not for conducting operations'.[12] The British had a more realistic view of the relationship of politics to strategy and of the machinery of command. They did not believe it possible that one man could direct the whole British and American effort against Germany.

Another aspect of command arrangements concerned the control of air operations. Arnold, Commanding General United States Army Air Forces, had for some time been pressing for the unification of British and American air commands. He believed that the air war against Germany could be intensified by co-ordinated use of bases in the United Kingdom and Italy and if possible also in Russia. He believed it was wasteful to vest control of part of the strategic air forces in theatre commands. Eisenhower heard of Arnold's proposal and did not like it at all. In a note which was used by Bedell Smith to discuss the question with the Joint Chiefs of Staff, Eisenhower said that the idea of transferring control of part of his air forces to London was intolerable. He did not believe in remote control of air forces, whose operations depended so much on day to day matters like weather over airfields and target and fuel and bomb supplies. He believed that the co-ordination of air attack against Germany could be better achieved by directing his attention to the targets that were to be hit. He was confident that such targets would be dealt with effectively. Arnold's proposal for a unified air command was as strenuously opposed by the Chiefs of Staff in London.

The whole question of command arrangements was so closely bound up with future strategy for the war against Germany that it was decided to leave all these questions to be settled at the next major Allied conference, Sextant, which was due to take place in Cairo in November. The Sextant Conference was of special importance because the western Allies prepared for the first time to meet Stalin and his military advisers in formal conference to discuss plans for 1944. American fears that Russia might make a separate peace with Germany had not entirely disappeared but now there were no grounds for them and indeed by the autumn of 1943 Stalin was

[12] Matloff, *op. cit.*, p. 271

confident of the ability of the Allies to finish off Germany quickly. It would be necessary therefore for the British and Americans to go to the forthcoming conference with the Russians at Tehran with very definite ideas about what they were going to do in 1944. The Americans had a new fear that the Russians might consider Overlord too distant an operation to meet the present situation and might insist that something be done quickly in the Mediterranean theatre to draw off German strength from the eastern front. Russian views might thus strengthen the British case for a Balkan adventure and so undermine Overlord.[13]

The Americans had already won the tussle for an American commander for Overlord, and now Churchill was eagerly waiting for confirmation of the appointment of Marshall. Roosevelt was not so sure that he could afford to lose Marshall as his principal military adviser. Marshall was too personally involved to take the initiative in resolving the question, but he instructed Handy, chief of the operations division, and Arnold to bring together all the problems on command for the war against Germany and to get a Joint Chiefs of Staff paper to the President for his decision.[14] The recommendation put to Roosevelt was that Marshall should be the commander of all British-American operations in Europe and the Mediterranean area. He should also remain Chief of Staff but his place in the Joint Chiefs of Staff and the Combined Chiefs of Staff would be taken by an Assistant Chief of Staff, who was not nominated. Under Marshall would be an American commander for Overlord and a British commander for the Mediterranean. Marshall's view was that Eisenhower should be the former and Alexander the latter. Roosevelt was not in a position to give a final decision before he had consulted the British but he liked the proposal. Neither he nor anyone in the War Department could easily accept the idea of Marshall being removed from Washington to be 'just another theatre commander', and this solution seemed to offer the best of both worlds. Marshall would not only have a directing voice in the strategy but would be responsible for its execution. The British, to whom the matter was put at Sextant, saw the matter very differently. The Chiefs of Staff pointed out that a Supreme Commander for the war against Germany would either have to take to himself all the functions of the Combined Chiefs of Staff and the business of consultation with governments, or else become a figurehead concerned with comparatively minor and strictly military

[13] Matloff, *op. cit.*, pp. 303–6
[14] *Ibid.*, p. 276

questions. He would 'thus be an extra and unnecessary link in the chain of command'.[15] The Americans therefore dropped their suggestion and Roosevelt once more postponed his decision about the Supreme Commander for Overlord.

On the way to Cairo for Sextant, Roosevelt had been met by Eisenhower at Oran and been taken by him to Tunis and had toured the battlefields there. Roosevelt had discussed the command problem with Eisenhower and had spoken of the possibility of Marshall becoming Supreme Commander and of Eisenhower replacing him in Washington. At the same time Roosevelt had expressed his dread at the thought of losing Marshall from Washington. King too had spoken of his own opposition to breaking up the Joint Chiefs of Staff which he considered a winning team. He added that his fears were lessened because of the probability that Eisenhower would replace Marshall.

The Sextant Conference straddled the conference with Stalin at Tehran. Before going to Tehran the Anglo-American discussions were surprisingly indeterminate. There was agreement that Overlord remained first priority. The Americans were inclined to regard the target date of 1 May as inviolable, whilst the British thought that a month's delay or so would be acceptable to allow operations in Italy. Churchill's programme was Rome in January, Rhodes in February, and then the opening up of the Aegean subject to a successful approach to Turkey. Eisenhower supported the idea of harassing operations in the Aegean but because of the forces required in Italy he did not think that effective action there could be taken until operations in Italy reached the Po. Indeed, with their present resources in Italy Eisenhower did not think that the Allies could do more than reach and hold a line north of Rome. At this stage the Americans accepted the British view about the Mediterranean provided that there were no major operations in the Balkans nor any diversion of troops to Turkey at the expense of agreed operations elsewhere.

The Tehran Conference took place from 28 November to 1 December. The British and Americans agreed that the military discussion would largely depend upon the outcome of the political discussion between the Heads of State. In these discussions, which dealt with the entry of Russia into the war against Japan as well as questions which affect us here, Roosevelt gave a broad survey of the war from the American point of view. He dealt not only with Overlord but put dispassionately the various

[15] Chiefs of Staff Paper quoted in Ehrman, V, p. 169–72

possibilities in the Mediterranean and their repercussions on Overlord. He emphasised that availability of landing craft was a limiting factor in what the western Allies could do. Stalin answered with his strong support for Overlord and added that it should be supported by an invasion of southern France. He said that Soviet experience over the past two years had shown that a large offensive from only one direction seldom succeeded. It was necessary to launch simultaneous converging attacks. Churchill put forward his plea for operations in the Italian and Mediterranean theatre, which would help Russia without delaying Overlord more than a month or two. Stalin was not to be moved from his opinion. He was against diversionary operations in the Mediterranean and believed the Allies should be prepared to remain on the defensive in Italy. He had given up hope of Turkey entering the war. Both the British and Americans were surprised that there was no immediate call for help in south-eastern Europe; Roosevelt sided with Stalin rather than with Churchill and the course of the subsequent military discussions was set.

Stalin was surprised that the commander for Overlord had not yet been chosen, and said that unless a decision was soon made the operation would come to nothing. Churchill promised that the choice would be made within a fortnight. The final military agreement was that Overlord would be launched during May in conjunction with a supporting operation against southern France (Anvil). In Italy the advance would be continued to the Pisa–Rimini line. No operations would be undertaken in the eastern Mediterranean unless Turkey were prepared to enter the war. Anvil was to be launched at the same time as Overlord in as great strength as availability of landing craft allowed. As has been indicated,[16] Anvil had already been discussed between Marshall and Eisenhower and it had been accepted at Quadrant, but the Combined Chiefs of Staff had not come to Tehran prepared to discuss it. Stalin's insistence on the import-ance of the operation had caught the British and the Americans by surprise and they accepted the commitment in the vague hope that the landing craft and other resources could be provided.

After the Tehran Conference the British and Americans returned to Cairo to tie up the loose ends. Once more they confirmed that Overlord and Anvil were to be the supreme operations for 1944 and that they were to be carried out during May. Planning for Anvil was to be carried out by the Supreme Commander Mediterranean in consultation with COSSAC

16 See pp. 108–109

23 *With the Southern Group of Armies.* Clockwise from the left: *Lt.-Col. Lodge, Bradley, Devers, de Lattre de Tassigny and Montsabert, commanding the II French Corps*

24 *Eisenhower decorates Spaatz with the Oak Leaf cluster to the Distinguished Service Medal*

25 *Relaxing during a visit to troops in Belgium*

on the basis of an assault force of at least two divisions. At last Roosevelt made his decision on a commander for Overlord. Eisenhower was to be the man; Marshall was to remain in Washington. On his return journey to the United States, Roosevelt stopped at Tunis to tell Eisenhower personally of his decision.

Eighteen months after Eisenhower had first set foot in Britain, an unknown staff officer from the United States War Department, he was chosen by the President and accepted by the British Prime Minister and Chiefs of Staff as commander of the decisive Allied operation of the war against Germany. The story that has been unfolded has told how Eisenhower grew in stature, how he rose to each occasion and how well his character fitted him for his so varied tasks. There was a certain amount of luck in his selection. The Supreme Commander had to be an American because the time had come when the American forces would be preponderant, although most of the experience of command in the field had gone to British generals. Eisenhower's selection for command of the American forces in the United Kingdom had come not from experience in the field but because he was Marshall's man and went to prepare a place for him as the probable Supreme Commander. From his position in the United Kingdom it followed naturally that Eisenhower should command in North Africa. There he had to deal with those who were among the best of the British commanders. The willingness of men like Cunningham, Alexander and Tedder to serve under him, when it might so easily have been the other way round, established Eisenhower's self-confidence and standing without in any way undermining his humility or his generous nature. The political complexities of his task in North Africa, and his happy relationship with Macmillan, kept Eisenhower in constant direct communication with Roosevelt and Churchill and showed both of them the man he was.

There was one aspect of Eisenhower's rise to the position of Supreme Commander which certainly owed nothing to luck. That was his attitude to inter-service and Allied command. From the first he had seen the necessity for an integrated effort and for sinking national and services' interests in a common system. He had illuminated the extra dimension involved in Allied command and had shown his ability to steer the forces entrusted to him to the single purpose of defeating the enemy.

26 *Eisenhower and Bradley examine a flying-bomb site*

8

The First Anvil Controversy

When the story of the battle for Italy was broken off to allow digression into the strategic debate, the Allied armies had just captured Naples and Foggia. Now that the Allies were firmly established on the mainland of Italy the campaign became much more the concern of Alexander, the force commander, and its subsequent course carries his imprint rather than that of Eisenhower. But it was to Eisenhower that Alexander had to look for the military resources that he required, for resolving the still remaining political problems of relations with the Badoglio Government and the military government of Italy, and for the interpretation of the directives of the Combined Chiefs of Staff. In this last requirement it must be confessed that the time lost in the circumstances described in the last chapter was never regained. At the beginning of October Eisenhower was talking of getting forward to the Po Valley, but success depended upon acting quickly while the Germans were still in doubt about whether to fight for Rome and central Italy. Alexander had as many divisions as he could maintain in action but his opportunity of forestalling German defensive plans lay in his ability to carry out a series of amphibious hooks. Small forces would suffice on the Adriatic flank but in the west at least a divisional lift was necessary and a parachute brigade was required in support. Eisenhower seemed reluctant to press the Combined Chiefs of Staff to make sufficient landing craft available and it was not until 25 October that he put forward Alexander's outline plan and stated categorically that more landing craft would be required. This request was repeated on 4 November, when Eisenhower expressed his belief in Alexander's plans and stated his own determination to establish his forces north of Rome.[1]

Just at the time when Eisenhower was pressing for the resources that Alexander needed, Hitler was making up his mind whether to accept the advice of Rommel or of Kesselring. Kesselring wanted to stand south of Rome; Rommel wanted to withdraw to the Apennine bastion north of Florence or even to the Alps. Hitler came down on the side of Kesselring.

[1] Papers III, Nos. 1360 & 1373

He had been impressed by the way Kesselring had handled the withdrawal from Sicily and the problems raised by the defection of Italy but, perhaps more important, he believed that to withdraw north of Rome would lay open to the Allies the whole of Greece and Jugo-Slavia. By the time Alexander was ready for his advance on Rome, Kesselring too was ready, in country admirably suited for defence, to fight in his 'Winter' or 'Bernhardt Line' from the River Garigliano across to the Sangro. Behind this line he was preparing the strong bastion of the Gustav line running along the high ground north of the Garigliano, through Cassino and through the mountains across to the Adriatic coast south of Pescara.

Eisenhower's attitude to operations in Italy at this stage can only be understood if it is remembered that he regarded them solely in the light of their effect on Overlord. He looked at them in this way without any knowledge that he would be the chosen commander for Overlord but in the hope that, rather than being called back to Washington, he would be allowed to remain in command in the Mediterranean. Nevertheless, he regarded himself as the agent of Marshall and was reluctant to ask for anything which he thought necessary in the preparation of Overlord. Undoubtedly Eisenhower was right in looking on the Italian campaign as subordinate to Overlord. That was the way Brooke looked at it too, but it was not for Eisenhower to forestall judgment of the priorities by hesitating to ask for that which was necessary for his own campaign. Indeed Eisenhower himself eventually came to that conclusion and on 4 November he wrote to the Combined Chiefs of Staff: 'Naturally I do not wish to interfere with the preparations for Overlord but I have felt it my duty to lay before you my requirements, leaving you to judge of priorities.'[2] His attitude to the campaign at this stage may be judged by his earlier review of the situation on 2 October—this was made for Bedell Smith to discuss with Marshall in Washington—and his signals to the Combined Chiefs of Staff on 9 and 25 October. The tenor of Eisenhower's thoughts was to do what he could with what he had got, to ask for nothing and to ensure that what could be spared was offered to Overlord. In this last respect it was experienced commanders that he thought he could offer. He asked Bedell Smith to impress on Marshall that he would need 'in his new job . . . a top air man who is thoroughly schooled in all the phases of strategic bombing and more particularly *in the job of supporting ground armies in the field.*' For this reason Eisenhower recommended that Marshall

[2] Papers III, No. 1373

should insist on getting Tedder, although he admitted it would be a bitter
blow to lose him. Eisenhower also wanted Marshall to know that in Patton
he could have a man particularly well suited to be an 'assault Army
Commander'. He believed that the best contribution that the armies in
Italy could make to Overlord would be to get firmly established in the
Po Valley. From there threats could be developed to southern France and
towards Trieste. Such threats would do more than anything else to draw
off reserves from the Overlord landings.[3] However, Eisenhower was
quick to see that his thoughts about the Po Valley were unduly optimistic.
On 9 October, less than a week after Hitler had made his decision that
Kesselring should fight south of Rome, he gave a very accurate assessment
of German intentions. It is interesting that Eisenhower was using his
arguments to show that the Allies should not be diverted towards the
Aegean, whereas Hitler had made his decision because he feared that the
Allies were intent on operations in that very area.[4]

While the Cairo and Tehran Conferences were going on Butcher urged
Eisenhower to put his thoughts on paper and to record what he had said to
the Combined Chiefs of Staff. This Eisenhower did in a diary entry for
6 December, the day before Roosevelt told him he was going to command
Overlord. He still believed that the proper objective for the Italian
Campaign was the Po Valley from where the Allies could threaten 'the
whole German structure in the Balkans, in France and in the Reich itself'.
But he believed that the attainment of this objective by early spring 1944
would require more resources than he had and that their provision would
delay Overlord for from two to three months. On the assumption that he
would have to do with what he had, he believed he must be content with
securing a line covering Rome and that thenceforward his attitude would
be generally defensive, unless there was a considerable weakening of
German forces.[5] In this entry there is no mention of an attack on southern
France but Eisenhower had already sent a report on this subject to the
Combined Chiefs of Staff on 29 October. In the light of his subsequent
views it is significant that on the whole his attitude to this operation was
lukewarm. He looked only to a small-scale operation by one division and
suggested that a threat might be of more assistance to Overlord than an
actual landing. A threat could suggest the possibility of large-scale

[3] Papers III, No. 1310
[4] Papers III, No. 1328; Ehrman, V, p. 68
[5] Papers III, No. 1408

operations whereas an actual landing would soon disclose its weakness.[6]

In fixing the date for Eisenhower to give up the Mediterranean command and to become Supreme Commander for Overlord, Roosevelt desired that Eisenhower should first have the glory of the capture of Rome. He therefore suggested 1 January 1944 or as soon after as Eisenhower thought fit. Whilst deeply appreciating this thought, Eisenhower believed that an indeterminate date would be a mistake. It was agreed therefore that Eisenhower should confer with Wilson to hand over the unified Mediterranean command in the last days of December and should leave Tunis a few days later. On the eve of his new command Eisenhower naturally looked to the appointments which American officers should fill both in his old and in his new theatre. He began his first letter on the subject to Marshall by telling him that of all the appointments 'this was the one I least expected, since I had assumed that the decision was firm that you were to take that job on personally'. He first toyed with the idea of Clark as United States theatre commander under Wilson but rejected the idea and suggested instead Devers from United States command in the United Kingdom. His reason was that he wanted Clark to stay in command of Fifth Army until Rome was captured and after that thought he should be brought back to Africa to take over the Seventh Army from Patton. That was the army that would have to undertake Anvil and he thought this the type of operation for which Clark had a particular skill. Incidentally in thinking of a successor for Clark, either if he became theatre commander or when he replaced Patton, Eisenhower nominated Lucas, who was subsequently to come to grief for his handling of the Anzio operations.

Eisenhower considered also the Allied structure of his new command, and his first thoughts were a very accurate forecast of what actually happened. He saw the need for a single land force commander until such time as two *separate* tactical air forces became necessary. This commander would presumably be British and, if he could get him, he hoped it would be Alexander (a few days later he said Alexander or Montgomery); whoever it was would subsequently become the British Army Group Commander, but before that time he would command one British and one American army for the assault. Bradley was to be the American Army Commander and he too would subsequently get an army group in which Patton would be one of his army commanders. Tedder would be Eisen-

[6] Papers III, No. 1369

hower's chief airman, and Spaatz would control the strategic air forces. Marshall's reaction to Eisenhower's suggestions was a fear that his idea of bringing back so many commanders from the Mediterranean and replacing them by commanders from the United Kingdom would create difficulties for Wilson. This led to a discussion whether Bedell Smith might be left in the Mediterranean Command, which Churchill much desired, but Eisenhower was insistent that Bedell Smith should be his chief of staff in the new appointment. Wilson would want his own senior staff officers and Eisenhower pointed out that the appointment of a British chief of staff, Morgan, would have complications because the British did not use a single chief of staff but separated the control of the general staff from that of the administrative staff. There was a friendly exchange of letters between Eisenhower and Morgan in which Morgan put himself completely at Eisenhower's disposal and Eisenhower said he would not make up his mind until he saw how the change-over went. Eisenhower told Morgan that he had spoken to the C.I.G.S. and that whatever happened there would be an important job for him, possibly as corps commander. In the event Bedell Smith remained as Eisenhower's Chief of Staff and Morgan became the Deputy Chief of Staff.

When the final decisions were made there were few changes from Eisenhower's original suggestions. Tedder was not appointed to command the air forces but became Eisenhower's Deputy Supreme Commander, and Air Chief Marshal Leigh-Mallory was given the command. This was a decision not altogether to Eisenhower's liking and, as will be seen, one which caused considerable controversy in the planning of air operations. The choice between Alexander and Montgomery was a difficult one and eventually went to the War Cabinet for decision. Montgomery had a unique reputation which inspired confidence throughout the British Army and his name counted among the Americans too. An additional consideration was that it would hardly be wise at this stage to take Alexander away from the Italian operations. So the choice fell on Montgomery, a solution entirely acceptable to Eisenhower. Cunningham had already become First Sea Lord and Ramsay, who had worked with Eisenhower in the early days in North Africa, was appointed Naval Commander-in-Chief.

On Christmas Eve Eisenhower, who was in Italy for a visit to the forward troops, heard Roosevelt broadcast the announcement of his appointment as Supreme Allied Commander Allied Expeditionary Force. On

Christmas Day he returned to Tunis for a conference with Churchill, Wilson and Alexander. Alexander, who had been strongly supported by Brooke, was at last bringing to a head his plans for an amphibious hook to Anzio, which was an essential part of his bid for Rome. Eisenhower did not want to intervene in an operation which could not take place until after he had given up command. Moreover, he was not optimistic about Anzio because he knew that only two divisions could be used in the assault and he believed that several strong divisions would have to be ashore to achieve significant results. He took part in the discussions, therefore, chiefly to consider the possible effect on Overlord. In this role he lent his support to the retention of the necessary craft in the Mediterranean, even though this might mean the delay of Overlord from the beginning to the end of May.

The Combined Chiefs of Staff were committed by the discussions at Tehran to launch Overlord in May but already it seemed certain that a stronger assault force than originally envisaged would be necessary. This would mean that the operation could not be launched at the beginning of May so that moon and tide requirements would make the first suitable date early June. Eisenhower believed that this later date would allow Alexander to complete his operation and still get the craft back in time to prepare for Overlord.

Eisenhower was anxious to get to London to take over his new command but Marshall insisted that he should come back to the United States for consultation with Roosevelt and the Joint Chiefs of Staff, and for a few days leave. Eisenhower gave Montgomery, who was already in London, full authority to act in his name for all Overlord matters during this short period of absence. On New Year's Eve Eisenhower left Tunis for Washington and on 14 January 1944 he arrived in London. Montgomery and Bedell Smith had already carried out a full examination of the COSSAC plan. Their conclusions were the same as had struck Eisenhower when he first heard the plan. In late 1943 Morgan had sent an American staff officer, Brigadier-General Chambers, to expound the plan to Eisenhower. Eisenhower, who at that time had no idea that he was to command Overlord, gave his personal opinion that the assault was on too narrow a front. Five or six divisions were required rather than three. Without such strength it would be impossible to obtain an adequate bridgehead quickly and to retain the initiative. Morgan is not to be blamed for the inadequacy of the force envisaged for the assault. He had been instructed by the Combined

Chiefs of Staff to draw up a plan which included an assault with three divisions because this was the maximum force for which shipping and assault craft could be provided. Although the Americans gave the war against Germany priority over the war against Japan, so far as naval matters went, the priority worked in a rather rigid way. The resources considered essential for the war against Germany were allotted and anything else was taken up for the war against Japan. Any addition to the original allotment required a fierce struggle with Admiral King in the Joint Chiefs of Staff. From an Allied point of view matters were made worse because, although much of the invention and pioneering work in landing craft had been done by the British, almost all the production was American. As Eisenhower wrote in his diary on 7 February: 'The fighting in the Pacific is absorbing far too much of our limited resources in landing craft during this *critical* phase of the European War. . . . We are fighting two wars at once—which is wrong—so far as I can see from my own limited viewpoint.'[7] Eisenhower saw that his first efforts must be directed to making the Combined Chiefs of Staff increase the assault force to five divisions. His first demand to this effect was made on 23 January.

As landing craft was the limiting factor, the question of increasing the Overlord assault force was closely bound up with Anvil, the landing in southern France. Eisenhower's attitude to Anvil suffered a series of changes, not altogether inexplicable. As has been seen, in October 1943 his reaction to the plan had been lukewarm, and he had thought the forces in Italy could best assist Overlord by getting forward into the Po Valley. That was before the operation received the support and fervent advocacy of Stalin at Tehran at a time when the capture of Rome seemed imminent. At the time of handing over command in the Mediterranean, Eisenhower was more favourably inclined to Anvil and believed that if there were a conflict for resources between Anvil and the Anzio landing, Anvil should be favoured. After Eisenhower had taken over in London controversy over Anvil began to take shape as an Anglo-American tussle. COSSAC had already made it clear that the choice was between Anvil and an increase in the Overlord assault and had recommended that Anvil be scrapped. The British who had studied Anvil in more detail had come to the conclusion that Overlord and Anvil were not closely intertwined because 500 miles, much of it rugged country, separated the two landings. Such long-distance effect on Overlord as could be exerted by Anvil could be more

[7] Papers III, No. 1536

economically effected by operations in Italy. The Americans still believed in Anvil, especially because it would give them Marseilles and Toulon. Without the use of the French Mediterranean ports some eight or nine divisions might be lost because of inadequate port facilities in north-west Europe and Italy.

Eisenhower had already made his own views clear to his staff, to Marshall and to the Combined Chiefs of Staff. When Montgomery and Bedell Smith had examined the COSSAC plan they had been prepared to see Anvil reduced to a threat in order to find the craft to strengthen the Overlord assault. This accorded with Eisenhower's views of October 1943 but now he did not agree. He believed that greater efforts to increase the amphibious lift, including resort to the use of some unarmoured craft in all except the assault waves, would make both operations possible. Only if the Overlord assault could not be broadened in any other way would he recommend to the Combined Chiefs of Staff the abandonment of Anvil.[8] To the Combined Chiefs of Staff he said on 29 January:

> Overlord and Anvil must be viewed as one whole. If sufficient forces could be made available the ideal would be a five divisional Overlord and a three divisional Anvil or, at worst, a two divisional Anvil. If insufficient forces are available for this, however, I am driven to the conclusion that we should adopt a five divisional Overlord and a one divisional Anvil, the latter being maintained as a threat until enemy weakness justifies its active employment. This solution should be adopted only as a last resort and after all other means and alternatives have failed to provide the necessary strength by the end of May for a five divisional Overlord and a two divisional Anvil.[9]

On 6 February Eisenhower asked Marshall for his support in getting the Anvil question resolved. He wanted to be quite sure that he and Marshall were working on the same lines because only then could the best results be achieved. He still wanted to work for a five divisional assault for Overlord by the end of May combined with a strong Anvil. Some doubts were, however, creeping into Eisenhower's mind. In Italy the Anzio landing had gained a footing but had petered out and it looked as if Kesselring had the battle for Rome well in hand. Eisenhower foresaw that it might be impossible to disentangle the forces necessary for a strong Anvil. He wondered whether the drain on the enemy of the fighting in Italy might compensate for the loss of Anvil.[10] In his reply Marshall

[8] Papers III, Nos. 1369 & 1473
[9] Papers III, No. 1497
[10] Papers III, No. 1531

commented on the reversal of position of the British and Americans, now it seemed that the Chiefs of Staff were all for concentrating on Overlord and the Joint Chiefs looked for Mediterranean operations. He was also somewhat perturbed that Eisenhower was so close to the Chiefs of Staff and subject to direct influence from them. He wondered if Eisenhower was suffering from localitis (sic).[11] Churchill was as anxious as Eisenhower to get a decision and suggested a Combined Chiefs of Staff meeting in London to resolve the question. The Joint Chiefs of Staff were at this time much involved with Pacific operations and, despite Marshall's earlier doubts, on 11 February they delegated to Eisenhower authority to decide the question in consultation with the Chiefs of Staff.

Eisenhower was subjected to heavy and conflicting pressures. We have seen that Marshall was confident that there were sufficient landing craft in the west for Overlord and Anvil, and he also believed that there were sufficient American and French troops in Italy and North Africa to mount Anvil without serious effect on operations in Italy. On 21 February Montgomery wrote to Eisenhower: 'I recommend very strongly that we now throw the whole weight of our opinion against Anvil. Let us have two really good campaigns—one in Italy and one in Overlord.[12] Brooke was certain that Anvil was not possible if sufficient divisions were to be retained in Italy to maintain the offensive. He believed that Marshall neither understood the necessity for a strengthened Overlord nor the realities of the Italian campaign. On 22 February he wrote in his diary: 'Eisenhower sees the situation a little more clearly, but he is too frightened of disagreeing with Marshall to be able to express his views freely.'[13] This was not just to Eisenhower. He was stung by Marshall's suggestion of 'localitis' and answered in what he himself described as his most defensive telegram to Marshall since he became a theatre commander. He did not, however, weaken in any way his opinion that the strengthening of Overlord was more important than Anvil. Moreover on 22 February, the very day of Brooke's diary entry, Eisenhower made a decision acceptable both to Brooke and to Marshall, as well as to Churchill and to Roosevelt. In this decision he showed himself conscious of the relative importance not only of the operations for which he himself was responsible but also of the Italian campaign. First he agreed to the transfer of sufficient landing

---

[11] Harrison, *Cross-Channel Attack*, pp. 168–9; Pogue, *The Supreme Command*, p. 113
[12] Montgomery, *op. cit.*, p. 221; Letter quoted in Matloff, *op. cit.*, p. 420
[13] Bryant, *op. cit.*, II, p. 152

craft from the Mediterranean to the Overlord assault; second, he agreed that the Italian operations should have priority over all the other operations in the Mediterranean, and last he insisted that planning and preparations should be continued for Anvil in case it should later be found possible or necessary. He also recommended that all the arrangements should be reviewed on 20 March—ten days before the craft were due to leave the Mediterranean—and that if it was then decided that Anvil could not be mounted (presumably because of the situation in Italy) then additional landing craft should be withdrawn from the Mediterranean for use in Overlord. In any case sufficient craft for one division would be left for use in Italy.

For the moment the argument was over. It may be asked why Eisenhower, who made such wise decisions about strengthening the Overlord assault and maintaining the pressure in Italy, did not see that the logical corollary was the cancellation of Anvil. Cancellation was what the British wanted and what they hoped would follow from Eisenhower's decision. It seemed to them evident that if Anvil could not be carried out as part of the main invasion of France it should not be carried out at all. What could be achieved by a postponed Anvil could almost certainly be achieved more economically by other means. They no doubt realised that if Eisenhower had accepted the cancellation of Anvil, the agreement of Roosevelt and the Joint Chiefs of Staff would not have been forthcoming. However, there was more in Eisenhower's compromise than a desire to please his masters in Washington. The decision was typical of the man. He liked to keep his options open. He saw the need for a landing in Normandy in overwhelming strength but he knew that the establishment of the beachhead alone would not be enough to win the battle for France. In the south of France the Resistance Movement was at its strongest and, working in conjunction with a small Allied landing, it could be a serious drain on German resources. Then the south of France was the logical area for entry of the French forces which had been constituted in Africa for the very purpose of participating in the liberation of France. There was also the value of the southern ports for the entry of United States divisions in North Africa which could not be maintained in Italy, and for the entry of further forces direct from the United States without cramming the bottleneck of British ports. All these were arguments to be used again when the controversy was renewed.

By 20 March when the review was due, Eisenhower had hardened against Anvil. He saw that the situation in Italy, where the Third Battle of Cassino was then at its full fury, would not allow the withdrawal of troops. His recommendation, which coincided with that of Wilson, was that the present conception of Anvil of a two divisional assault building up to ten divisions should be abandoned. Instead Eisenhower suggested that Wilson should be directed to ensure that the forces in the Mediterranean should 'constantly look for every expedient, including threat and feint, to contain the maximum possible enemy forces away from the Overlord landings. Eisenhower coupled his recommendation to the Combined Chiefs of Staff with a request for more landing craft for Overlord. He had been content with numbers barely sufficient only so long as he was sure of a simultaneous and effective Anvil; now he required 'to strengthen Overlord and to increase the flexibility of the build-up during the early critical days'.[14] The Chiefs of Staff strongly supported Eisenhower's recommendations. But the Joint Chiefs of Staff, while agreeing to most of the recommendations, preferred to postpone rather than cancel Anvil. They asked for a new target date of 10 July.[15]

[14] Papers III, No. 1595
[15] Ehrman, V, p. 247

9

Problems of the Strategic Air Forces

The role of the strategic air forces in the defeat of Germany had been defined at Casablanca in January 1943. The Combined Bomber Offensive, known as Pointblank, was intended to create the opportunity for the later military invasion of the Continent. Pointblank was under the strategic direction of Portal, the British Chief of the Air Staff, but in its execution the two commanders, Air Chief Marshal Harris of British Bomber Command and Major General Eaker, United States Eighth Air Force, each had almost complete autonomy. There was a considerable difference in the strategic and tactical views of the two: Eaker believed in daylight attacks against selective targets, but Harris did not believe it was possible to pin-point and destroy individual targets and so favoured area bombardment by night attacks. The British Air Staff eventually came down on the side of Eaker because the difference was really one of attitude to air superiority over the Continent. The same degree of air superiority that was required for the American daylight attacks would also be necessary to make Overlord possible. There was then general agreement that the aims of Pointblank should be first to gain and maintain air superiority over western Europe and then to destroy Germany's military and industrial capacity. It was believed that in the process the morale of the German nation would be destroyed and so the launching of Overlord facilitated. Indeed many of the senior air force commanders went further. Harris believed that concentration on the Bomber Offensive would win the war and that all that was required from the armies was a lightly armed force more in the nature of police than soldiers.[1] Spaatz, who at Eisenhower's instigation had changed places with Eaker, and who had then been given command of all the United States strategic air forces in Britain and the Mediterranean, had similar views. He believed that if only they could get another 20 or 30 clear days the strategic air forces could finish off the war on their own.[2] How unrealistic this view was may be judged by the

[1] Webster & Frankland, *The Strategic Air Offensive against Germany*, Vol. III, p. 10
[2] Tedder, *op. cit.*, p. 509

effectiveness with which the German Army fought throughout 1944 and up to the crossing of the Rhine in 1945, and by the evidence throughout this time of continued industrial production.

Eisenhower knew the tremendous power of the Allied air weapon and he knew that, properly used, it could be a decisive factor in the coming operation. But he also knew that the war could not be won by air action alone. His strength as Supreme Allied Commander came from the vision that the mighty invasion being prepared was a single venture to which the resources of the two nations, sea, land and air, must be primarily directed. From the first he had hoped that, under him, Tedder would command all air operations in support of Overlord, and that for this purpose he would have at his disposal not only the tactical air forces but also the resources of Bomber Command and the United States Strategic Air Force in the United Kingdom. Thus for the period of the invasion Pointblank would be absorbed into the Overlord plans. The British took a much more limited view of Eisenhower's responsibilities for air operations and thought he should have control only of the tactical air forces, that is to say those concerned with the immediate protection and support of the landings and subsequent land operations. It was for this reason that Leigh-Mallory, whose whole experience had been with fighters, had been appointed Air Commander-in-Chief, while Tedder was given the more general responsibilities of being Eisenhower's Deputy. Churchill felt that there could be no question of handing over to Eisenhower control of the British Fighter, Bomber and Coastal Commands because all the forces had much wider spheres of action than the support of Overlord. Similarly, both Harris and Spaatz made it clear that they were not prepared to accept direction from Leigh-Mallory, an officer whose experience lay in a sphere of air operations far different from their own. On the other hand Eisenhower felt so strongly that he must have control of air operations during Overlord that he told Churchill that unless the question could be satisfactorily settled he would 'simply have to go home'.[3]

Churchill, as so often, thought he could expose a solution in one of his dramatic phrases. He suggested that Tedder should be 'the Aviation Lobe of Eisenhower's brain', empowered to issue orders in Eisenhower's name to Harris, Spaatz and Sholto Douglas (Coastal Command) for any employment of their forces which the Combined Chiefs of Staff had sanctioned.

---

[3] Butcher, *op. cit.*, p. 417

To this end Eisenhower would submit his plans to the Combined Chiefs of Staff who would do their best to meet his requirements and specify what air forces should be placed at his disposal and for how long.[4] Churchill did not see any difficulty. Despite his approval of the appointment, he did not regard Leigh-Mallory as the Air Commander-in-Chief and asked Eisenhower: 'Why did we give you Tedder?' to which Eisenhower made the simple and pertinent reply 'Why?'[5] Eisenhower was not happy at the restriction in his power of command and the suggestion that he should submit his detailed plans to the Combined Chiefs of Staff. In this view he had the support of Arnold and the other American Chiefs of Staff—indeed, they were even less inclined than Eisenhower to accept a compromise.

However, in early March an agreement was reached between Portal and Tedder which Eisenhower regarded as exactly what he wanted. Eisenhower (as the direct agent of the Combined Chiefs of Staff for Overlord) and Portal (as their executive for Pointblank) were together to approve the air programme for Overlord. The whole of the air operations in support of Overlord thus agreed would be under the supervision of Tedder. These arrangements would continue until such time as the progress of operations on the Continent made a change in control desirable. The Joint Chiefs of Staff objected to the arrangement because of the word 'supervision' instead of command, but eventually accepted the word 'direction'. Eisenhower would certainly have preferred the word 'command', but he saw that he had got what was necessary for the effective conduct of the invasion. On 9 March he wrote a directive to Tedder which, although it was never formally promulgated, expressed the Portal-Tedder agreement and was used by Tedder, Leigh-Mallory, Spaatz and other air commanders as a definition of what Eisenhower wanted. The directive emphasised that the needs of the commander of 21st Army Group, who was controlling the assault and the operations in the beachhead, would be paramount in the critical days of the assault and the establishment of the beachhead. He must, therefore, state what he hoped for from air action. The operations of Pointblank and Overlord in this period must be completely integrated and this integration would most clearly be shown in the common aim—the destruction of the German Air Force.[6]

[4] Tedder, *op. cit.*, pp. 510–11
[5] Papers III, No. 1577
[6] Papers III, No. 1584

It is only too easy to fall into the error of thinking that these arguments about command of air operations were academic or inspired by selfish seeking for authority. That is not so. The difficulties arose because of conflicting views held passionately by men who believed they had the key to victory over the Germans. Eisenhower was at his best. He had a true understanding of the meaning of air power and its place in military operations. The differences in the two schools of thought come out clearly in the preparatory phase for Overlord. The architects of the strategic bomber offensive were disciples of Douhet, who soon after the First World War had expounded the theory that air forces could by themselves win wars. They believed that the best contribution they could make to Overlord in the preparatory stages was to intensify the attacks on German industry, in particular those against aircraft production and oil resources. Eisenhower and Tedder both believed that such a policy could have only long-term results and that the tactical air forces alone could not create and maintain the situation in which a landing was possible and the German Army was deprived of the ability to manoeuvre and to use its reserve forces at the decisive time and place of the battle.

Eisenhower saw the necessities of the air battle clearly. He knew he must have a single commander of the invasion forces (Montgomery) working closely with a single commander of the tactical air forces (Leigh-Mallory) acting solely on his demands. This would take up the whole of the resources of tactical air forces and the task of sealing off the battle-field, of providing a bombing pattern as part of the deception plan, and of destruction of the air forces on the more distant airfields must fall to the strategic air forces. In the preparatory phase the strategic air forces would be required to destroy the communications system on which the German Army depended. The welding together of so comprehensive a plan—one on which the whole safety of Overlord depended—could hardly be entrusted to a committee, however single-minded its members might be. And that they were not likely to be single-minded had been shown by the views that Harris and Spaatz had already expressed. Beyond doubt, Eisenhower was right in insisting that the plan for the whole of the air operations should be the responsibility of one air commander directly subordinate to him.

From the beginning Eisenhower had wanted Tedder to discharge this responsibility, albeit as his Air Commander-in-Chief and not as his Deputy. It was the British who had wanted Tedder to fill the more general

27 *With Patton and Bradley in Belgium during the Ardennes campaign*

28 *Eisenhower and Ritchie, commanding the XII British Corps*

29 *With Crerar, Simpson, Dempsey* (back row), *Montgomery and Bradley during the Rhineland battles*

and advisory role rather than a purely executive one. In the end Eisenhower's firm and steadfast resolve to be guided by his own judgment was completely justified. It was the final arrangement between Tedder and Portal which allowed Eisenhower to seize the substance and neglect the shadow. Having insisted throughout on the full measure of control necessary for the vital phase of Overlord, he ultimately got his way because he was not so small-minded as to insist on the particular title he wanted or the words in which Tedder's power to command were disguised. If further evidence of the importance of the question is needed, it may be found in the fact that this is the sole occasion on which Eisenhower felt so strongly about the issues that he was ready to relinquish his command rather than to accept a compromise on essentials.[7]

The part which air forces would play in the invasion had its controversies on the other side too. The Germans knew now that the invasion must come in 1944; the only question was exactly when and where. Rundstedt was Commander-in-Chief West, and under him Rommel with Army Group 'B' was responsible from the Loire to the Low Countries. Rundstedt's greatest experience had been in the victorious German campaigns in Poland in 1939 and France in 1940, in both of which the Germans had overwhelming air superiority. He had not fully grasped the meaning of the changed air situation and he still had classical views on defence. He believed that minimum forces should be used in defence of the beaches and that the maximum defence forward should be what was necessary to prevent the Allies getting possession of a port. In this way the area of Allied effort could be identified before it became dangerous, and then by the use of reserves which had been centrally placed the invasion forces could be destroyed. Rommel was less orthodox and had recent experience of fighting in the face of growing Allied air power. He believed that one division on 'D' Day would be worth three a few days later. The battle would have to be fought for the beaches and reserves must be close at hand. If they were not, then air action would prevent their getting to the battle in time. The Germans never fully resolved this conflict of opinion. As will be seen in subsequent chapters it was this failure as well as the effective use of Allied air power in the preparation and execution of Overlord which were the decisive factors in the battle for Normandy.

[7] Papers III, No. 1601

10

The Launching of Overlord

The matters which caused Eisenhower most trouble, as he himself testified,[1] were those on which only the Combined Chiefs of Staff could make the final decision. Principal among such subjects were the command of air forces and the resources to be allotted to Overlord and Anvil. These have been dealt with in the preceding chapters. Eisenhower felt much happier in handling those more purely military questions in which the decision was his own responsibility: the training, the plan of attack, the deception plan and the tactical and administrative expedients for facilitating the landing. In these matters Eisenhower had a sound basis on which to work. He acknowledged the debt which he owed to Morgan and the COSSAC staff for their comprehensive study and preliminary plans. He also owed much to Paget for his enlightened and realistic training of the British Home Forces, and for many practical experiments in the technique of landing. From the moment of his arrival in Britain in June 1942 Eisenhower had been impressed and attracted by the original mind of Mountbatten and now he was to reap the harvest of the work that had been done at Combined Operations Headquarters.

Morgan's plan had embraced a landing by three divisions and two airborne divisions on a 25 mile front from the River Orne to the estuary of the Vire. Morgan and his senior planners would have liked greater weight in the assault but doubted the wisdom of extending the frontage.[2] As has been seen Eisenhower was in no doubt that the size of the assault force and the frontage of the landings must both be increased. The plan he finally approved had five divisions and three airborne divisions on a 50-mile front from Cabourg (east of the Orne) to Quineville on the east face of the Cherbourg peninsula. Montgomery, as commander of the forces designed to establish the beachhead, developed this plan with his fellow commanders-in-chief, Ramsay and Leigh-Mallory.

[1] Papers III, No. 1601
[2] Harrison, *op. cit.*, p. 166

Eisenhower was much exercised about the best use of airborne troops in the early stages of Overlord. As early as February 1943, in Algiers, Marshall had sown in his mind the idea that the field of airborne operations was one in which the Allies had a real opportunity and the capacity to get ahead of the enemy. Now in February 1944 Marshall was complaining that the Allies had not properly exploited air power in combination with ground forces. He believed that the reason was not lack of aircraft but a poverty of ideas. He said that if he were the Supreme Commander he would be looking for a single large airborne operation. In considering the possibilities he rejected the idea of three landings to block the movement of enemy reserves, and also of a single landing 30 miles inland, in the region of Argentan, for the same purpose. But he did ask Eisenhower to consider a landing south of Evreux, where there were four large airfields. Such a landing would be within reach of the crossings over the Seine, would threaten Paris, and would completely upset the German defensive plans. Eisenhower confessed that he spent much time in contemplation of plans for airborne operations but he did not agree with Marshall's idea as part of the initial invasion. He believed that such a landing would be immobile on the ground at a time when the airborne troops were out of reach of supporting action by other forces. The moment for such an operation was after the beachhead had been built up and the invading army was in a position to strike. Eisenhower saw the initial crisis of the campaign as the breaking of the beach defences and rapid exploitation to seize a port and to establish a firm base for future operations. To this end he would devote everything that could be profitably used, including airborne forces.[3] In the light of these ideas a British airborne division was allotted to cover the left flank of the British landing and to facilitate the attack on Caen. At the same time two United States airborne divisions were to land at the base of the Cherbourg peninsula and facilitate the attack on Cherbourg (see map p. 134). In approving the landing inside the Cherbourg peninsula Eisenhower had to come down on the side of Montgomery against the advice of Leigh-Mallory, who warned him that a landing in that area would mean that 'at most 30 per cent of the glider loads will become effective for use against the enemy'. Eisenhower accepted Leigh-Mallory's estimate of the casualties but said '. . . a strong airborne attack [in that area] is essential to the whole operation and it must go on. Consequently, there is nothing for it but for you, the Army

[3] Papers III, No. 1557

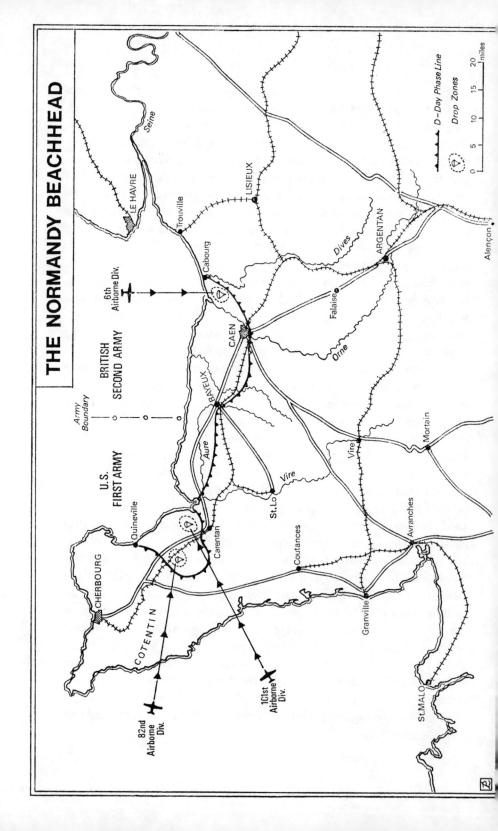

THE NORMANDY BEACHHEAD

BRITISH SECOND ARMY

U.S. FIRST ARMY

Army Boundary

6th Airborne Div.

82nd Airborne Div.

101st Airborne Div.

CHERBOURG

COTENTIN

Quineville

Carentan

Coutances

St.Lo

Granville

Avranches

St.MALO

Vire

Mortain

BAYEUX

CAEN

Cabourg

Trouville

LE HAVRE

Seine

Dives

LISIEUX

Falaise

ARGENTAN

Alençon

Orne

Aure

Vire

D – Day Phase Line

Drop Zones

0   5   10   15   20
miles

Commander and the Troop Carrier Commander to work out to the last detail every single thing that may diminish these hazards.'[4]

Eisenhower found the establishment of a truly allied team spirit in his headquarters staff easier than he had in the pioneer days in North Africa. On the other hand it was more difficult at first find to get the complete devotion to the idea of unity of command that he had had from Cunningham, Alexander and Tedder. No doubt there will be those who jump to the conclusion that it was Montgomery that was difficult. That is not so. At this stage the two men were in complete accord and saw the problem in the same light, but Eisenhower found both Ramsay and Leigh-Mallory what he called 'somewhat ritualistic in outlook'.[5] Nevertheless he realised their great ability and absolute integrity and soon, with the broader aspect of command of the strategic air forces settled, Eisenhower, Tedder and the three commanders-in-chief were working in complete unity. It must already be clear that Eisenhower was a master of decentralization. This mastery must not be imagined as in any way a willingness to forego responsibility nor as a relegation of his proper function as commander. As is clear in a note in his diary soon after he came to Overlord, he knew what some people said of him. In February 1944 he wrote: 'Generally speaking the British Press tries to show that my contributions in the Mediterranean were administrative accomplishments and friendliness in welding an Allied team. They dislike to believe that I had anything particularly to do with campaigns. They don't use the words initiative and boldness in talking of me—but often do in speaking of Alex and Monty.' He goes on to say that the bold British commanders were Cunningham and Tedder and to show how often it was his own orders that had demanded the holding of forward airfields in North Africa and—against more cautious advice—for the landing at Salerno rather than crawling up the leg of Italy.[6]

Nothing better illustrates the proper working of command than the way in which the threads of the Overlord planning were drawn together, the detailed plans made and the operation launched. Eisenhower saw himself responsible for the outline plan, for ensuring that the resources necessary for that plan were provided by the Combined Chiefs of Staff and for a workable command system. He also made it his business to see that all the

[4] Papers III, No. 1720
[5] Papers III, No. 1701
[6] Papers III, No. 1536

American commanders down to divisional commanders were men up to their task. Within the approved outline plan the three commanders-in-chief made a joint plan, very detailed in certain aspects but broad in others. That joint plan was the executive instrument which allowed the army commanders (Bradley and Dempsey) and their associated naval and air force commanders to make the plan for the assault and the follow up. From here comprehensive plans for the administration and maintenance of the force were made, comprising as they did the myriad loading tables for men and material, for ships and for landing craft. Right down the chain of command such details and all the tactical details had to be worked out before the Allied forces could be finally committed to this mighty venture.

Eisenhower knew that however well the plans might be worked out and tied together there would be little chance of success if the enemy realised exactly when and where the landings would come. The scope for surprise was very small because the Germans would now be certain that the invasion must come in 1944 and that the landings must come between the Belgian coast and the mouth of the Loire. They knew as well as the Allies the conditions of weather and moon and tide which would be most favourable. The most direct threat to the Ruhr was through the Pas de Calais and it was by playing on the German fears of this approach that an effective deception plan was made. Everything that was done—the concentration areas of troops, the location of craft, the pattern of air reconnaissance and bombing on the Continent, the wireless deception and the release of false information—was designed to persuade the Germans that any landing in Normandy would be a feint or a preparatory operation and that the real threat would come between Dunkirk and Boulogne. It is not pretended that this was Eisenhower's own idea; he inherited it from Morgan's original COSSAC plan. But he embraced it wholeheartedly and worked on it. He also saw that it was maintained throughout the critical days of the Normandy fighting. The result was that almost all the German military commanders predicted an invasion via the Pas de Calais and for two months after 'D' Day they believed that Normandy was a subsidiary operation and kept formidable reserves in the Calais area. In March 1944 Hitler had one of his flashes of intuition and saw that the landing would be in the Cotentin Peninsula. Happily he did not press his views. This is all the more surprising because the German Navy had the same idea and noted that Cherbourg and Le Havre were the only major French ports that were spared heavy air bombardment.

During the busy weeks of preparation Eisenhower determined to give his time to the men whose fighting power would determine the outcome of the hazardous operations which were being planned. Notwithstanding the weight of his headquarters duties and the demands on his time for the endless exchanges with political heads and with the Combined Chiefs of Staff, he made it his business to visit every division under his command, whether British, Canadian or American. Gault accompanied him on all his visits. He had been appointed his British Military Assistant after the landings in Sicily and he tells how Eisenhower was always able to inspire confidence in British, Canadian and American and in officer and man alike. There were no special tricks of showmanship but an easy and natural manner which exposed the warmth of the man and the spirit of the commander to those he was about to commit to battle. The ordinary soldiers reacted instantaneously to him and to his qualities.

Eisenhower had problems of a very different nature in dealing with the French. French naval, air, and airborne forces were taking part in Overlord but there were no other French formations available in Britain—the main French effort was to be part of Anvil. But Eisenhower knew how much he stood to gain from the work of the French Resistance both active and passive, and how much he would depend, after the landing, on French co-operation in guarding communications, police action and currency arrangements. De Gaulle's military respresentative in London was General Koenig and Eisenhower was ready to take him into his confidence. But British and American distrust of French security arrangements and de Gaulle's insistence that communications between himself and Koenig should go by French cypher made such a course dangerous. The situation was made more difficult by Roosevelt's distrust of de Gaulle. Roosevelt was determined that there should be no recognition of de Gaulle and his Committee of National Liberation as the future government of France. He went further and said that nothing should be done which might be thought to impose any government upon the French or even to colour their views in making their choice of government after their liberation. Roosevelt sent a number of personal signals to Eisenhower on his relations with the French and Eisenhower was not afraid to make quite clear to him the realities of the situation and the necessity for an Allied rather than a personal directive. On 16 May Eisenhower asked Marshall to pass the following message to Roosevelt:

You may be quite certain that my dealings with the French Committee will be confined to military matters and related civil administration and will be conducted on a military level. I understand your anxiety in the matter and I assure you that I will carefully avoid anything that can be interpreted as an effort to influence the character of the future government of France. However, I think I should tell you that so far as I am able to determine from information given to me through agents and through escaped prisoners of war, there exists in France today only two major groups, of which one is the Vichy gang, and the other characterised by unreasoning admiration for de Gaulle. This may merely be an indication of the shell shock to which you refer, but its effect will be a practical one when we once shall have succeeded in liberating areas that will fall outside the strictly military zone and should therefore be turned over to local self government. . . .

Because this is an Allied Command, I hope that your desires on this subject of which I am already aware, can eventually come to me as a joint directive of the two governments. This would help me.[7]

On 11 May Eisenhower suggested to the Combined Chiefs of Staff that de Gaulle should be brought to London and told about the Overlord plans. Roosevelt would agree only if de Gaulle would undertake not to leave London until after 'D' Day. Churchill considered it would be unwise to invite de Gaulle in terms that he would be bound to regard as insulting. The matter was not brought to a head until the end of May when Eisenhower insisted that de Gaulle ought to be asked to make an appeal to the French people to support the Allied Forces. It was proposed that de Gaulle should speak immediately after Eisenhower's 'D' Day broadcast and a text for de Gaulle's speech was prepared by Supreme Allied Headquarters. Eventually, in response to Churchill's invitation de Gaulle arrived in London on 4 June, just as it was known that bad weather necessitated the postponement of the landing from 5 June. As might be expected de Gaulle refused to use the text provided for him but he satisfied Eisenhower that he was anxious to help in every possible way and would speak on the lines suggested.[8] The difficulties were, however, not so easily removed and, in a series of political discussions in which Churchill participated, de Gaulle alternated between a refusal and a desire to broadcast. He did speak, immediately after Eisenhower's broadcast, but his speech was an exhortation to follow the government—the French Committee of National Liberation—and there was no attempt to emphasise the authority of the Allied Supreme Command.

[7] Papers III, No. 1681
[8] Papers III, No. 1733

De Gaulle's attitude did not have the serious results that it might have had because of all the preliminary work that had been done on a non-political level. Many of de Gaulle's officers and officials selected as liaison officers for the civilian organizations in the liberated areas were already working closely with Eisenhower's Civil Affairs representatives. There was also the French Resistance, and Eisenhower was careful to profit from all the preliminary work that had been done by the British Special Operations Executive. He regarded the Resistance as a strategic weapon and gathered together the threads in his Special Force Headquarters, a combination of representatives of Special Operation Executive and the American Special Operations, both of which had responsibilities outside those of Overlord. The contacts with the five movements of the French Resistance were well established and there were working arrangements for general direction, special instructions, and supply. Before 'D' Day a series of plans had been drawn up for specific operations to destroy certain railway and communication centres, electricity systems and headquarters. The signal to go would be sent out over the British Broadcasting Corporation network. All was as ready as could be, whatever the political controversies.

All preparations for Overlord were to be completed by 1 June and the invasion was to be launched on the first suitable day thereafter. The fixing of the day and the hour depended on an intricate combination of meteorological factors: moonlight for the airborne landings, darkness for the naval approach, sufficient light for supporting fire from aircraft, naval and support craft, and a rising tide to allow the landing of sufficient craft in the first flight. In early June only the 5th, the 6th and the 7th gave the required combination. But all depended on weather which would enable air forces, navies and merchant marine to carry out their appointed tasks. Eisenhower provisionally decided that 5 June would be 'D' Day but that he would meet his commanders and his meteorological experts at 4 a.m. on 4 June to confirm his decision.

Eisenhower knew how much would depend on his decision. All the Allied forces were keyed up to go; postponement even for a day would cause complications in the carefully worked out time-tables of loading, shipping and aircraft. The waiting would add to the burden on nerves and morale. The missing of the early June opportunity would be a heavy blow and there was no guarantee that a fortnight later conditions would be any better. Most serious effect of all was the possibility of discovery by the enemy of final preparations (loading of ships had to begin on 1 June) and the use of pilotless aircraft to destroy the assembled shipping. In order to be the better able to judge the meaning of weather forecasts and the basis on which they were made Eisenhower began towards the end of May to discuss them daily with his Chief Meteorological Officer. From 1 June he also brought in the Allied Commanders-in-Chief to consider the prospects with them. At the end of May the forecast was favourable but the weather worsened from 2 June and on the 3rd it looked as if the landing would not be possible on the 5th. Nevertheless Eisenhower allowed the preliminary moves that were necessary to go ahead.

At the decisive meeting in the small hours of the 4th it was clear that conditions on the 5th would not allow the air forces to carry out their programme. Montgomery was ready to go but neither Tedder, Ramsay, nor Leigh-Mallory thought the landing should be carried out in such circumstances. Eisenhower, conscious of how much depended on air superiority, decided on postponement for one day and said that a decision on the 6th would be taken that same evening at 9.30 p.m. That evening the weather men gave some hope of temporary improvement. Clearing skies would allow the air forces to operate during the night of the 5th and morning of the 6th. Ramsay said that the decision must be taken within the next half-hour if the navies were to be ready for the 6th and added that if it was not the 6th the necessity for shipping to refuel would require the postponement to be longer than one day, thus bringing the operation outside the suitable period. The airmen, Tedder and Leigh-Mallory, were still doubtful and Montgomery still anxious to go. The decision was for Eisenhower himself and those that were with him were struck by the calmness with which he faced a decision on which so much depended.[9] After weighing the alternatives Eisenhower said that the real risk lay in the decision not to go. How right he was to approach the decision in that way is now clear to us in the light of our subsequent knowledge of events. The decision to go having been made, it so happened that the next suitable period (19 June and successive days) saw the worst June storms in living memory.

Eisenhower had the remarkable habit in all his great military ventures of disarming fate by preparing a draft communiqué to hold in readiness to announce a failure, and to accept the full responsibility for such a result. These he would write out with his own hand. That prepared for Overlord

[9] Pogue, *op. cit.*, p. 170 and numerous personal accounts

came into the hands of Butcher and was preserved in the diary. It read:

Our landings in the Cherbourg Havre area have failed to gain a satisfactory foothold and I have withdrawn the troops. My decision to attack at this time and place was based upon the best information available. The troops, the air and the Navy did all that Bravery and devotion to duty could do. If any blame or fault attaches to the attempt it is mine alone.[10]

Happily this draft, like all the others, proved to be a work of supererogation, and did not have to be used.

[10] Papers III, No. 1734; Butcher, *op. cit.*, p. 525

11

The Battle of Normandy

Having launched the operation on the approved plan there was nothing else for the moment that Eisenhower could do. Montgomery had the responsibility for the land battle and Eisenhower had no intention of standing over him. Eisenhower was in his advanced headquarters near Portsmouth where he was in constant touch with Ramsay and Leigh-Mallory. One of the first messages Eisenhower got was from Leigh-Mallory telling of the success of the air operations and particularly of the airborne landings. In both there were less casualties than had been expected. Leigh-Mallory followed this up with a letter to Eisenhower confessing that he had been wrong in trying to dissuade him from the Cotentin landings and saying that never in his life had he been more thankful to be wrong. On the day after the landing Ramsay took Eisenhower on a tour of the beaches. He saw Montgomery as he was going ashore to set up his tactical headquarters and he also saw Bradley and a number of the principal commanders. He had meant to set foot on French soil himself but the fast mine sweeper in which he was travelling hit a sand bank.

The great success of the planning and concentration was that surprise was achieved in all the landings. Strategically too the Germans were kept guessing and they feared that a major effort was still to come through the Pas de Calais. The weather which had faced Eisenhower with such a crucial decision had helped in the tactical surprise. In his diary on 3 June Rommel had discounted the likelihood of an invasion during the period up to the 8th and had noted that the tides thereafter were most unfavourable. The very factors which set Rommel's mind at rest were those which made Eisenhower see that the risks of postponement were greater than facing the hazards of weather. Thus great men rise to the occasion and seize the opportunities which lie hidden behind the difficulties which fate deals out to them. Although the Allies got their first critical foothold ashore with fewer casualties than had been expected (only at Omaha Beach was there real anxiety) the Germans reacted quickly and fighting for an adequate beachhead was fierce and prolonged. So effective was Allied air action that the German Air Force could hardly intervene against the landings or shipping. Rommel wanted to get his armour quickly on the scene and now he and Rundstedt were of one mind, but the organization was against them. Rundstedt had eight panzer divisions of which two were in the south of France. The other six were in Rommel's area but only three were under his immediate command. Three were retained under O.K.W. (High Command of the Armed Forces) and could only be moved with Hitler's permission. Early on 'D' Day Rundstedt had asked for two of these divisions to move forward. He had first been refused, then the move of one permitted but orders given that neither was to be committed without orders from O.K.W. Even when the orders for release had been given air attack was so effective that the moves were largely balked. The commander of one division described the roads along which he had to move as a fighter-bomber race track. On 7 June Rundstedt ordered one of the panzer divisions up from the south and on 21st Hitler ordered two from the east. One panzer division was however left in the Pas de Calais area, so in mid-June there were eight in Normandy.

By the end of the first week the Allied beachhead was smaller than had been planned and, in particular, Caen, which it was hoped to take on the first day, was still in enemy hands. Nevertheless Eisenhower was not worried. Montgomery was well pleased, the casualties were still comparatively light and, owing to the success of the air operations and German fears for the Pas de Calais, the enemy had not been able to mount a major counter-attack. The beachhead was a continuous defended line some ten to 12 miles in depth. Montgomery's confidence was based on the knowledge that his master plan, which was well understood by Eisenhower, was working out. Montgomery's intention was to play upon the German fears for Caen and the eastward communications from there direct to Paris. The British Second Army would, he hoped, quickly capture Caen and would bring down upon themselves the main weight of the enemy, especially the panzer forces. The American First Army would be free first to capture Cherbourg and then to strike towards St Lo. With the possession of a major port and room in the beachhead the British and American armies would expand into army groups and the American Twelfth Army Group would carry out the exploitation to capture the Brittany ports and sweep round the enemy flank towards the upper Seine and Paris. After the formation of the two army groups Eisenhower intended to take control of the land battle.

On 18 June Montgomery issued his orders for the capture of Caen and Cherbourg. He hoped to get both by the 24th. Cherbourg was captured on 27 June and the whole peninsula cleared by the end of the month. On the other hand the attack on Caen met with little success, and both the town and the crossings over the Orne remained in enemy hands. Montgomery had failed in his aim of getting his armour out on to the high ground south-east of Caen but he had succeeded in his purpose of holding the greater part of the enemy strength. Of the eight panzer divisions on the Normandy front all, except part of one, were facing the British Second Army on the 20 mile front from Caen to Caumont. That the weight of armour lay in this direction must not be attributed solely to the way Montgomery was fighting the battle; rather was it the other way round. The country west of Carentan was close and intersected by high hedges and deep ditches—the bocage country—while south and south-east of Caen was the rolling country suitable for tanks. It was here therefore that the Germans must seek decisive results from their panzer forces. Montgomery knew this and made his dispositions accordingly. British Second Army was considerably stronger in armour than was First United States Army and would fight the battle—defensive in concept—to break the German armour and the German ability to launch a major counter-attack. Further west the Americans fighting in difficult, but essentially infantry country, would force the gap through which the exploiting forces could be pushed into the open country beyond.

Although they had held Montgomery at Caen, the Germans were by no means happy about the situation. They had failed in their counter-attack there and it seemed certain that the Allies could not be ejected from the beachhead. Rundstedt and Rommel both visited Hitler on 29 June. Hitler was talking of sealing off the beachhead but Runstedt believed that if the only possible attitude were a defensive one then the Germans must lose the war. Unknown to the Allies, therefore, the German field commanders were thinking of withdrawal and even contemplating defeat. As a result of Rundstedt's belief that he could not fight a sustained defensive action, Hitler decided to replace him by Kluge, although Rommel was still left in his command. Broadly speaking it may be said therefore that by 1 July Montgomery had laid the foundations of success. There were however by this time reasons for grave disquiet at Supreme Allied Headquarters. There were administrative troubles because of the great storm that had broken in the Channel on 19 June and had damaged both the artificial harbours (Mulberries). And even for what could still be landed in the retarded programme there was too little room in the beachhead. Far more serious was the lack of room for airfields. During the planning stages the airmen had made it clear that the air battle depended on the early capture of fighter airfields south-east of Caen. The COSSAC plan had attached great importance to their capture within 14 days of landing. Montgomery was aware of the problem and indeed hoped that the progress of the battle would keep to something like that time-table. But he attached much more importance to establishing a firm bastion to bar the progress of enemy forces from the east and to making ground further west for the eventual break-out to the south. The staff did prepare a phase map showing estimated progress but this was a forecast for administrative planning and not a promise of how the battle would go. De Guingand, Montgomery's Chief of Staff, tells how it was made clear during the planning stages that the air forces could not rely upon the early establish-ment of airfields in the Caen area because of the importance which the Germans were bound to attach to Caen.[1] War is a two-sided game and exact forecasts are obviously impossible. The true value of phase lines can be judged by the comparison (see map p. 146) which shows how the lateness in the early phases was more than counterbalanced by the speed of the break-out.

And now to come to Eisenhower's part in the battle. He had rightly left the assault and the establishment of the beachhead to Montgomery. But he was the commander responsible to the two governments for the conduct of the invasion and he could not let things go wrong. The question was whether they were going wrong and whether the battle was being fought as he thought it ought to be. The failure to take Caen was a great dis-appointment to Eisenhower but there is no evidence to show that the situation was one in which he thought he ought to interfere. His advanced headquarters was still at Portsmouth but he went over on 24 June to see Bradley and again spent 1 to 5 July in Normandy, visiting Montgomery but spending most of the time with Bradley. On the first visit Eisenhower had seen the possibility that, after the capture of Cherbourg, Bradley would be able to attack south while Montgomery still 'had the enemy by the throat in the east'.[2] During the second visit, after the failure to get Caen, Montgomery's assessment of the situation was clear to Eisenhower

[1] De Guingand, *Operation Victory*, p. 551
[2] Papers III, No. 1774

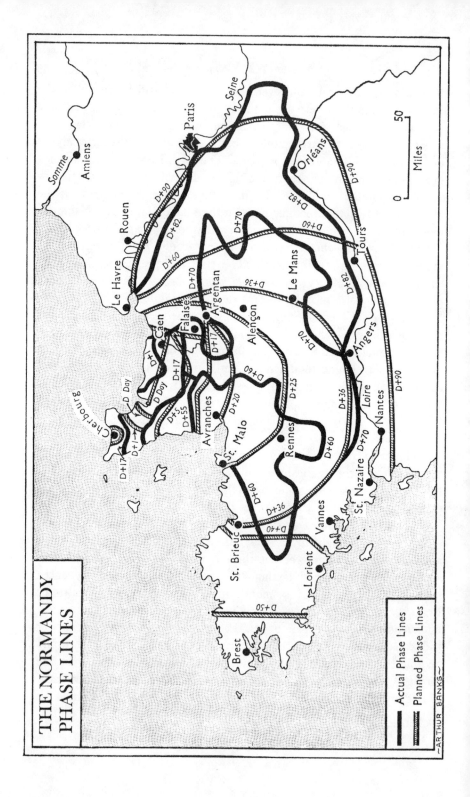

THE NORMANDY
PHASE LINES

Somme
Amiens
Seine
Paris
Orléans
D+90
D+82
D+60
D+90
Le Havre
Rouen
D+90
D+82
D+70
D+60
Tours
Falaise
Argentan
Le Mans
D+70
D+36
D+82
Caen
D+I
Alençon
D+I
D+17
Angers
D Day
D Day
D+60
D+36
Cherbourg
D+5
D+55
Avranches
D+20
St. Malo
D+25
Rennes
Loire
Nantes
D+17
D+I
D+60
St. Nazaire D+70
D+90
St. Brieuc
D+60
D+36
Vannes
D+40
Brest
D+50
Lorient

0   50
Miles

Actual Phase Lines
Planned Phase Lines

~ARTHUR BANKS~

and he agreed that if an early break-out were possible the Americans would have to make it.[3] But Eisenhower did not regard the British part as being defensive. His natural inclination was to hit everywhere and he saw that a successful thrust on to the high ground beyond Caen would considerably ease Bradley's task of fighting through the Bocage country.

On his return from Normandy Eisenhower reviewed the situation with Bedell Smith and Tedder. Tedder was sharply critical of Montgomery. He believed Montgomery was too cautious and attached too little import- ance to the capture of Caen and the airfields beyond. He was angry with Montgomery too because of critcism expressed that the air forces were not vigorous enough in support of the immediate land battle. Tedder had the impression that the army was not prepared to fight its own battle. He thought Eisenhower should 'tell Montgomery to get moving'.[4] Eisen- hower would not have been human if he had not been affected by the views of a trusted subordinate and a compatriot of Montgomery, especially when those views accorded with the way he himself would have fought the battle. Nor were there wanting senior British officers in the headquarters who thought in the same way, particularly Morgan, architect of the COSSAC plan. But Eisenhower was not the man to be shaken from his purpose or jockeyed into panic action. At this stage he confined himself to a letter to Montgomery which, while making clear the direction in which he wanted progress made, expressed his full confidence in Montgomery and promised him all the support he could give. In this letter he said:

> I am familiar with your plan for generally holding firm with your left, attract- ing thereto all of the enemy armor, while your right pushes down the Peninsula and threatens the rear and flank of the forces facing the Second British Army. However the advance on the right has been slow and laborious, due not only to the nature of the country and the impossibility of employing air and artillery with maximum effectiveness, but to the arrival on that front of [enemy] reinforcements. . . .
>
> It appears to me we must use all possible energy in a determined effort to prevent a stalemate or of facing the necessity of fighting a major defensive battle with the slight depth we now have in the bridgehead.
>
> We have not yet attempted a major fulldress attack on the left flank sup- ported by everything we could bring to bear. . . .[5]

In reply, on the next day, Montgomery outlined his thoughts and on

[3] Note by Bedell Smith reproduced in Papers III, No. 1982, no. 2
[4] Tedder, *op. cit.*, p. 537
[5] Papers III, No. 1807

the same day, 8 July, Second Army captured the main part of Caen but not the crossings over the river. In his letter[6] Montgomery dealt with the past and with his present intentions. He made it clear that he would take advantage of success at Caen but his real emphasis was on the opportunities which the British attack would make for the Americans, whose strength was now being increased by the arrival of the Third Army under Patton. He said he did not want the additional American armoured division which Eisenhower had offered him for the British attack and ended his letter: '... we really have all the armour we need. The great thing now is to get First and Third Army up to a good strength, and to get them cracking on the southward thrust on the western flank, and then to turn Patton westward into the Brittany peninsula.'

Two days later Montgomery gave Bradley and Dempsey their orders for the next phase. Second Army in an operation known as Goodwood was to cross the Orne and push out with a corps of three armoured divisions to the south-east, while First Army (operation Cobra) pushed south beyond St Lo. Bradley was to get a corps into Brittany but his main thrust was to be a wide wheel eastwards through Mayenne and Laval to a line from Alencon to Le Mans. Montgomery made it clear that his intention was unchanged: 'It is to draw the main enemy forces into the battle on our eastern flank, and to fight them there, so that our affairs on the western flank may proceed the easier.'[7] Bradley well understood Montgomery's intentions. Writing after the war of these phases of the Normandy fighting he said:

> While Collins was hoisting his VII Corps flag over Cherbourg, Montgomery was spending his reputation in a bitter siege against the old university city of Caen. For three weeks he had rammed his troops against those panzer divisions he had deliberately drawn towards that city as part of our Allied strategy of diversion in the Normandy campaign. Although Caen contained an important road junction that Montgomery would eventually need, for the moment the capture of that city was only incidental to his mission. For Monty's primary task was to attract German troops to the German front that we might more easily secure Cherbourg and get into position for the break-out. . . .
>
> For another four weeks it fell to the British to pin down superior enemy forces in that sector while we manoeuvred into position for the U.S. breakout.[8]

[6] Quoted in Pogue, *op. cit.*, p. 186
[7] *Ibid.*, p. 187
[8] Bradley, *A Soldier's Story*, p. 325-6

Despite Montgomery's clear statement of his intentions, his orders and his expressed hopes for the Goodwood operation led Eisenhower into expecting a considerable armoured breakout towards Falaise. The plan depended on overwhelming air support and in giving his approval Eisenhower wrote: 'We are enthusiastic about your plan. . . . I am confident it will reap a harvest from all the sowing you have been doing during the past weeks. With our whole front line acting aggressively against the enemy so that he is pinned to the ground, O'Connor's[9] plunge into his vitals will be decisive. I am not discounting the difficulties, nor the initial losses, but in this case I am viewing the prospects with the most tremendous optimism and enthusiasm. I would not be at all surprised to see you gaining a victory that will make some of the "old classics" look like a skirmish between patrols.'[10]

Montgomery had written to Eisenhower: 'My whole eastern flank will burst into flames'[11] and to Brooke he had written: 'And so I have decided that the time has come to have a real "show down" on the eastern flank and to loose a corps of three armoured divisions against the Caen-Falaise road.'[12] So hopes ran high when on the first day of the attack Montgomery expressed himself as well satisfied and thought that the effect of the air support had been 'decisive'. It is not surprising therefore that there was deep disappointment when, two days later, Montgomery instructed Dempsey to call off the armoured attack. VIII Corps had lost some 500 tanks and over 4,000 men but they had advanced six miles, taken 2,000 prisoners and exhausted the German armoured reserves, and Montgomery judged that the purpose of the attack had been accomplished.[13] But the success had been nothing like that which Eisenhower had expected. Apart from his own disappointment, Eisenhower was faced with a storm of criticism of Montgomery at his own headquarters. Tedder was outspoken in condemning Montgomery's conduct of the battle. Although he later discounted the gossip of the day that he advised Eisenhower to ask the Chiefs of Staff to sack Montgomery,[14] there is no doubt that, during this period, he was constantly trying to undermine Eisenhower's confidence in Montgomery. On 21 July, worried about the V1 (pilotless

[9] Commander VIII Corps
[10] Papers III, Nos. 1826-7
[11] Quoted Pogue, op. cit., p. 188
[12] Quoted in Ellis, Victory in the West, I, p. 329
[13] Blumenson, Breakout and Pursuit, p. 192
[14] Tedder, op. cit., p. 653

aircraft) attacks on Britain, Tedder said to Bedell Smith that if the Allies could not get to the Pas de Calais quickly 'then we must change our leaders for men who will get us there.'[15] On the same day news came in of the attempt on Hitler's life and Tedder told Eisenhower that Montgomery's failure to take action earlier had lost the Allies the opportunity which that attempt offered them. Tedder also frequently urged Eisenhower to set up a tactical headquarters in Normandy and end the situation by which Montgomery commanded both the British and American forces. Fortunately Eisenhower not only knew that Tedder was guided solely by the requirements of the air forces but also that he himself had a far better understanding than Tedder of the relationship of air action to the land battle.

On 20 July, the day before Tedder's latest outburst, Eisenhower had been to see Montgomery and after his talk with Tedder he wrote to Montgomery to assure himself that they saw eye to eye on the immediate problem. In this letter Eisenhower quoted an earlier statement of Montgomery's as expressing his own view: 'We are now so strong and are so well situated that we can attack the Germans hard and continuously in the relentless pursuit of our objectives. This will be done by First and Second Armies.' Eisenhower went on to say that the Allies were now relatively stronger than the Germans than they could hope to be at any time in the near future. 'Time is vital', he said 'We must not only have the Brittany Peninsula—we must have it quickly. So we must hit with everything.' Eisenhower then expressed some doubts whether, in view of the difficulty of the country and of the enemy strength, Bradley would be able to make such progress unless there was a simultaneous offensive on Dempsey's front. He said that he realised the difficulties of the British reinforcement problem and that eventually American ground strength would be much greater than the British. 'But,' he said, 'while we have equality in size we must go forward shoulder to shoulder with honours and sacrifices equally shared.'[16] Montgomery did not reply, as he might have, that Dempsey's army was successfully holding the greater part of the German army in Normandy. Montgomery did point out that he had no intention of halting offensive operations on his eastern flank and that Dempsey was continuing infantry attacks. Eisenhower expressed himself as completely satisfied.

---

[15] Tedder, *op. cit.*, p. 566
[16] Papers III, No. 1844

The Press, particularly in America, had now begun to take a hand. After the optimism with which the successful landings were hailed, there had been disappointment at the slow progress, and the memory of the stalemate of the 1914-18 War had begun to assert itself. Before Goodwood was launched there had been no reports of an impending offensive but the Press had been led to believe that Caen was the critical area and, from the point of view of deception of the enemy, it was no bad thing that this idea should be prevalent. But on the evening of the first day of Goodwood a most optimistic communiqué was issued and when territorially so little was seen to have been achieved there was much disappointment. The feeling of discontent at Supreme Headquarters, where the principal correspondents were located obviously became known and there was criticism both of Montgomery and of Eisenhower. In America there was a tendency also to point to the fact that most of the ground gained in the beachhead had been in the American sector and that First Army had suffered more casualties and taken more prisoners than Second Army. Eisenhower was determined that, whatever the Press said, there was not going to be an Anglo-American squabble—the severest critics of Montgomery were British, Tedder and Morgan. He was also determined that any criticism of the conduct of the battle should be centred on him and not on his subordinates. He wrote to the Director of Public Relations in the War Department pointing this out, saying: 'I realise that every writer is entitled to express his own opinions but the articles in question apparently ignore the fact that I am not only inescapably responsible for strategy and general missions in this operation but they seemingly ignore the fact it is my responsibility to determine the efficiency of my various subordinates and make appropriate report to the Combined Chiefs of Staff if I become dissatisfied. My only concern ... is that criticism directed against anyone of my principal subordinates and therefore by inference approving of my own actions and efforts is certain to disturb the spirit of teamwork that I have so laboriously worked for during the past two years.'[17]

It is, however, no good pretending that Eisenhower was satisfied with the position. His headquarters was still in England and he often lunched with the Prime Minister. On more than one occasion he expressed the opinion to Churchill that Montgomery was too cautious. He knew that the British could not afford heavy casualties—every division except one that

[17] Papers IV, No. 1870

could be provided for the European front was already there and replacement of casualties would be a problem. But he still felt that this factor weighed too heavily with Montgomery and he hankered after an all-out offensive along the whole front. Churchill had the same desire for action all the time and he passed on Eisenhower's fears to Brooke. On 27 July the two met Eisenhower and Bedell Smith at dinner. Brooke's diary note for the same day[18] shows Eisenhower's concern which persuaded Brooke, rightly or wrongly, that Eisenhower did not understand Montgomery's conception of the way the battle should be fought and the way it was going. Brooke told Eisenhower that if he was not satisfied he should tell Montgomery exactly what he thought but that he, himself, would be happy to help in any way to explain these views. The gist of the conversation is shown by the letter Brooke sent to Montgomery next day. He wrote: 'It is quite clear that Ike considers that Dempsey should be doing more than he does: ... I drew his attention to what your basic strategy has been, ... I explained how in my mind this conception was being carried out, that the bulk of the armour had continuously been kept against the British. He could not refute these arguments, and then asked whether I did not consider that we were in a position to launch major offensives on each front simultaneously.'[19]

While these discussions were going on the battle was developing in a way that was to set Eisenhower's fears at rest. Operation Cobra had been intended for 21 July but had been put off day by day until 25th because of bad weather. Bradley's plan of a quick break-through after an intense air bombardment had been admirably executed by Collins's VII Corps. Indeed, the first results seemed disappointing because, as with the British at Caen, the soldiers expected more from the air bombardment and were displeased that they still had hard fighting to do. But despite the fact that the first infantry attacks had not secured all their objectives, Collins saw the opportunity to get his armour through into the more open country and, by the evening of 27 July one of his divisional commanders was able to say: 'This thing has busted wide open.'[20] The battle of the beachhead was over and the breakout could begin.

During the days of hard fighting in the beachhead Eisenhower had again been much concerned with an old controversy—Anvil. In March the

[18] Bryant, *op. cit.*, II, p. 243
[19] *Ibid.*, p. 244
[20] Blumenson, *op. cit.*, p. 251

operation had been left in abeyance with a target date of 10 July. Preparations and execution were the responsibility of Wilson, Supreme Allied
Commander in the Mediterranean. Eisenhower was still intimately
concerned because the date of Anvil depended on the release of assault
shipping and airborne forces after the Normandy landing, and because the
Anvil forces would eventually link up with his. Matters became more
complicated when Churchill suggested that instead of Anvil an amphibious
operation should be mounted to capture Bordeaux. On 16 June, ten days
after the Normandy landings and the almost simultaneous capture of
Rome, Eisenhower agreed that, if it were possible, a successful operation at
Bordeaux would be more profitable than a similar success in southern
France. He thought however that naval and air factors militated against a
quick success and therefore he did not favour the Bordeaux operation.[21]
Wilson agreed with Eisenhower and at the same time pointed out that
Anvil could not take place until 15 August. He sent Gammel, his Chief of
Staff, to see Eisenhower on 22 June. The storm in the Channel was then
at its height and there was great consternation about the consequent delays
in the Allied build-up. Eisenhower told Gammel he wanted Anvil 'and he
wanted it quick'. He had already told Marshall that he could not understand how an operation that had been under consideration for a year could
take so long but he now accepted 15 August as the date. Eisenhower and
Marshall were of one mind that only by the use of Marseilles or some such
great port could the full flow of American forces necessary for carrying
the war into Germany be ensured. But Churchill and the Chiefs of Staff
looked at Anvil not from the point of view of the battle for France,
which they did not think it could affect, but for its effect on the exploitation of the victory at Rome. Churchill made one last effort to persuade
Roosevelt to agree to cancel Anvil but Roosevelt would not yield. Wilson
was instructed to carry out Anvil on 15 August. On 6 July, after hearing of
Wilson's arrangements, Eisenhower expressed himself as completely
satisfied. Such are the vagaries of war and the demands of time that an
operation for which Eisenhower looked in mid-June to help him out of a
tactical and administrative impasse, was launched in mid-August when it
could have no immediate effect on the battle for France. It did however
provide the opportunity for de Gaulle's regular forces to join in the
liberation of their country and later for the build-up of American forces
along the Rhine. It might be thought that the Battle of Normandy would

[21] Papers III, No. 1755

have ensured the departure of the Germans from Marseilles, but judging by the tenacity with which German garrisons hung on to Brest and the Loire ports this is not certain. The effect of Anvil on the Italian campaign hardly concerns us here. Alexander thought to the end that it deprived him of the full fruits of his victory; Brooke was not so sure that this was so.

To return to the Battle of Normandy. On 27 July Montgomery met his army commanders and issued instructions to take advantage of Bradley's success. At that time all six German panzer divisions facing the British were on the east of their front, about Caen. Dempsey was therefore to further Bradley's advance by an attack from Caumont towards Vire, an area in which the enemy had few tanks. The attack was to be carried out with at least six divisions not later than 2 August. On 28 July Eisenhower, having received a copy of Montgomery's written instructions, cabled to Montgomery begging him to insist on a vigorous and determined blow by the British and Canadian Armies (Crerar's First Canadian Army had become operational on 23 July). He said that on ten miles of Second Army front the enemy only had four regiments and an occasional dug-in tank, and added: 'I feel very strongly that a three-division attack now on Second Army's right flank will be worth more than a six-division attack in five days' time. Follow-up units, if needed, can reach the scene while the initial breakthrough progresses. Now, as never before opportunity is staring us in the face. Let us go all out on the lines you have laid down in your instruction and let us not waste an hour in getting the whole thing started. I am counting on you and as always I will back you to the uttermost limit.'[22] Montgomery had already told Dempsey to accelerate his attack to 30 July and that, if the weather was bad, it should go in without air support,[23] and when Eisenhower visited Montgomery and Bradley on the afternoon of 29 July he was well satisfied.

By 1 August the Americans had taken Avranches, the British were within two miles of Vire and the Canadians were fighting grimly east of Caen to prevent the enemy moving his armour away. On that day a change in the command structure took place. There were now four armies in action. 21st Army Group under Montgomery consisted of First Canadian (Crerar)[24] and Second British (Dempsey) Armies; 12th Army Group under Bradley of the First (Hodges), and Third (Patton) U.S.

[22] Papers IV, No. 1866
[23] Ibid., note 5, Ellis, op. cit., p. 386
[24] About one third of this Army was British

Armies. Patton's arrival in Normandy was not announced in the press. The location of Patton's headquarters (disguised as an army group headquarters) near Dover had been an essential part of the deception plan and Eisenhower wanted to keep alive for as long as possible the German fears of a landing in the Pas de Calais. Eisenhower decided that for the time being Montgomery would retain general direction of the two army groups and that he would take over operational control on 1 September. This decision was obviously right. Supreme Headquarters was still in England (advanced headquarters was set up in Normandy on 7 August) and it would have been madness to change operational control at this vital stage of the battle. Nevertheless the general command situation could not be the same as when Bradley had been one of two direct subordinates of Montgomery. Now Montgomery and Bradley each had two armies and Bradley was on the flank where the situation was changing quickly and immediate opportunity offered. Eisenhower had always been as close to Bradley as he had been to Montgomery. The position was now one in which a joint effort was being co-ordinated by Montgomery and in which there was great temptation for Eisenhower to intervene direct with Bradley—a course he had been careful to avoid in the bridgehead battle.

In planning the breakthrough it had been envisaged Patton would drive west to overrun Brittany while First Army wheeled on the right of 21st Army Group to take part in a concerted advance to the Seine. As the battle developed this no longer appeared to be the most profitable action. Montgomery saw that the only hope the enemy had of saving their armies was a staged withdrawal to the Seine, but that after the losses they had suffered their chances of achieving this were small. The Germans were extremely vulnerable to a thrust round their southern flank to Paris and any attempt they made to buttress that flank would render them open to a thrust from east of Caen. Montgomery decided therefore to use a single corps to clear Brittany and seize the ports there while the whole of the rest of the Allied force would be used to encircle the German Army. Montgomery's directive of 6 August gave the main role to Bradley. He was to thrust east and then north-east to the Seine near Paris. At the same time Crerar was to push to Falaise and Dempsey to Argentan. At this stage, on 7 August, the Germans altered the whole picture by launching a counterattack to recover Avranches, the scene of Bradley's breakthrough. Some progress was made and Mortain was captured, but Bradley handled the situation calmly and skilfully. He did not allow the counter-attack to interfere with Patton's move south, although its success would have cut off Patton. First Army fought tenaciously to hold Avranches and the Germans were pounded unmercifully from the air. On the next day Eisenhower visited Bradley. By this time XV Corps of Patton's army was well on the way to Le Mans and Bradley saw that a wheel north-east would close the mouth of the sack into which the Germans had thrust themselves. After Eisenhower and Bradley had talked over the situation Bradley talked to Montgomery on the telephone. Thus was born the plan in which Montgomery now directed that the Americans would secure Alencon while the Canadians captured Falaise and that they would then meet at Argentan to close the gap. If that were achieved, as Montgomery said in his directive of 11 August 'We shall have put the enemy in a most awkward predicament.' The gap was not completely closed but a major defeat was inflicted on the enemy. Patton was at Alençon by 12 August and on the next day he was on the outskirts of Argentan. The Canadians had been within eight miles of Falaise on 9 August but had made no more progress. Patton wanted to fight on to Falaise but Bradley, with no reference either to Montgomery or Eisenhower, halted him. Instead he ordered Patton to hold Argentan, which he did with two divisions, and sweep with the rest of his army to the Seine. When the Canadians reached Falaise on 16 August there was still a 15-mile gap between the two armies.

Simonds, who was commanding II Canadian Corps, was undoubtedly the most able and thrustful commander produced by Canada during the war. He considered that from 18 to 21 August the gap was as effectively closed as was possible in such country and in conditions of day and night. The enemy that did get through the so-called gap were only able to do so because the German II Panzer Corps, which was already east of Falaise, turned about for a determined counter-attack. 1st Polish Armoured Division, which was part of II Canadian Corps, made them pay heavily for this attack but the remnants did get away and lived to fight effectively again in the Arnhem battle. During this phase the air took tremendous toll from the retreating Germans, but Simonds is sure from his own observation and from the reports of operational research teams that most of the destruction in the Falaise pocket was caused by Allied tank and artillery fire.[25]

Whether anything more should or could have been done to cut off the

[25] Letter from Lt.-Gen. Guy Simonds to the author 25 November 1971 supported by reports of immediate interrogation of German generals

retreating Germans will always be a subject for controversy. Patton was prepared, as he always was, to stick his neck out but Bradley 'preferred a solid shoulder at Argentan to the possibility of a broken neck at Falaise'.[26] It is probable that a hurried change in the boundaries and meeting point of two armies of different nations might have led to chaos, and certain that it would have much complicated the task of the air forces which at that moment were playing such havoc with the retreating enemy. On these grounds Eisenhower seemed satisfied with Bradley's decision both at the time[27] and in retrospect.[28]

At this time Eisenhower suffered much criticism in the press and some misunderstanding in the War Department because of his command reorganization. First there was an unjust suggestion that Eisenhower had withheld an announcement of Patton's arrival in Normandy because of jealousy of his reputation. Then there was a premature announcement that Bradley had become the equal of Montgomery. British papers deplored Montgomery's apparent demotion and when the report was officially denied the American papers wondered why, since the number of United States divisions exceeded those of 21st Army Group, Bradley was not put on an equal footing with Montgomery and why Eisenhower did not himself command the battle. And so on to inferences that Eisenhower was a figurehead. On 18 August Marshall told Eisenhower that Stimson and he 'and apparently all Americans' believed that the time had come for Eisenhower to take direct command, adding ominously 'at least of the U.S. forces'. Eisenhower sent back a strong answer pointing out the failure of the critics to understand the communications or air command problems. He said that he did not care what the *New York Times* or any other newspaper said, but it deeply concerned him that Stimson and Marshall should so misunderstand the situation. He said: 'No major effort takes place in this theatre by ground, sea, or air except with my approval and that no one in this Allied command presumes to question my supreme authority and responsibility for the whole campaign.'[29]

In reviewing Eisenhower's performance in the Battle of Normandy we must ask whether his direction showed a genius for command and whether Brooke was justified in his criticism that Eisenhower did not understand Montgomery's strategy. In the forefront of our answer we must say that,

[26] Bradley, *op. cit.*, p. 377
[27] Butcher, *op. cit.*, p. 550
[28] *Crusade in Europe*, p. 505
[29] Papers IV, No. 1900; Pogue, *op. cit.*, pp. 203–4

whatever his fears and doubts, they did not prevent Eisenhower from giving Montgomery his fullest support. At Supreme Headquarters there were all the makings of a major inter-service row, due to the genuine beliefs of a number of senior air force officers and others, and to the hard facts of ground actually gained in comparison with planning forecasts. There were seeds for an inter-Allied dispute too, but Bradley's understanding made this less likely. But Eisenhower would have none of this. He gave Montgomery the support he needed; he ensured that he was insulated from all except the battle, and he saw that he had all the resources that could be given to him. It is more difficult to judge whether Eisenhower fully understood Montgomery's handling of the battle. He certainly understood the plan to hold the enemy in the east and unhinge him from the west. Theoretically too he understood the need for a flexible rather than a rigid plan. But he did not have Montgomery's feel of the battle as a two-sided encounter in which he kept the initiative by actions which put the enemy at a disadvantage and kept him at a disadvantage. Eisenhower did not see that by the fighting round Caen the enemy was placing himself in a position from which he would not be able to recover, that what mattered was not the number of yards gained but that the enemy was wasting himself and was dancing to Montgomery's tune.

It is unprofitable to reconstruct the might-have-been of battle with a series of ifs. There is no doubt that if Eisenhower had been in direct command of the land battle it would have been handled differently, but it would be a bold man who would say that the outcome would have been better. From 6 June to 25 July German and Allied army casualties were about equal—notable because the Allies were always in the offensive or more expensive role. By the end of the battle the Germans had lost more than 300,000 and the Allies less than 210,000. The German Seventh Army had lost most of its equipment and had been virtually destroyed. Eisenhower had rightly delegated command of the land battle to Montgomery: he himself had wider tasks. All credit therefore to Eisenhower that throughout the hazards and strains and doubts the whole resources of the Allied force, land, sea and air, were directed from beginning to end to a common pattern and to victory.

12

The Pursuit to the Rhine

From the moment when Avranches was captured, Eisenhower had begun to see the possibility of the destruction of a substantial portion of the enemy. He knew Patton and he knew that he was just the man for the task of a wide enveloping sweep. While the fighting at the Falaise gap was still going on the Third Army was advancing to cut off the enemy a second time at the Seine. Five days after reaching Argentan Patton's divisions covered an average of 80 miles. By 16 August Orléans and Dreux were captured, on the 18th Chartres, and by the 20th Patton had secured a crossing over the Seine at Mantes. It was not considered desirable at that time to capture Paris; it was hoped rather to pinch it out and avoid fighting for the city. Moreover it was necessary to get on with the immediate task of destruction of the enemy rather than at that moment to assume the responsibilities of the liberation and supply of the French capital. The immediate task was complicated by the fact that at Mantes the Americans were well across the dividing line between the two army groups. All was happening much more quickly than orders in advance had foreseen. Quick conversations on the telephone between Patton and Bradley and between Bradley, Dempsey and Montgomery showed that troops of 21st Army Group were not in a position to take over at Mantes or to continue the sweep up the Seine. Montgomery would have preferred Patton's thrust to have come in much nearer to Falaise, but he took advantage of the existing situation and authorised Patton to continue down the south bank of the Seine to Elbeuf about 10 miles from Rouen, where the river widens into its estuary. Montgomery authorised direct contact between all commanders down to division in order to settle local differences until the normal boundaries were restored. Patton took Elbeuf on 25 August and the Canadians took over from him on the next day.

While these operations were taking place Eisenhower was rightly giving his mind to operations much further ahead. On 19 August he went to see Bradley, who had already been visited by Montgomery on the 17th. Then on the 23rd Eisenhower visited Montgomery; he took Bedell Smith with him but Montgomery insisted on talking to Eisenhower alone. Eisenhower, Montgomery and Bradley thus each knew what was in the others' mind. Eisenhower's idea was to get three army groups all thrusting for the Rhine. Montgomery's Army Group of the North would make first for the Pas de Calais and then for Antwerp and north of the Ardennes to encircle the Ruhr from the north. For the first essential step of the Pas de Calais, where the V1 sites were a real and increasing threat to Britain, Montgomery was to be given the whole of the Airborne Army (two British and two American divisions, and a third American in course of arriving in England). Bradley with Army Group of the Centre was to assemble east of Paris with a view either to striking north-east to ensure that the Calais area was captured quickly, or if, as Eisenhower hoped, enemy strength did not demand this, then to push south of the Ardennes to Metz and the Saar. The landing in the south of France had already taken place and was going well and Eisenhower looked forward to the Army Group of the South coming under his command on Bradley's right. Montgomery had very different views: he believed that he should retain the direction of Bradley's army group and that as many divisions as could be maintained by the combined Allied resources should thrust north of the Ardennes, clearing the coast up to Antwerp, establishing a powerful air force in Belgium and advancing into the Ruhr. Montgomery thought that Bradley agreed with this concept but Bradley wanted the main thrust through the middle of France to the Saar and over the Rhine to Frankfurt. This would be an American effort with Patton in the van.

Eisenhower was convinced that in one thing Montgomery was right: the overriding priority was to clear the Channel ports, capture the V1 sites and press on to secure a base at Antwerp. As he wrote to Marshall: 'For a very considerable time I was of the belief that we could carry out the operation in the northeast simultaneously with a thrust eastward, but later have concluded that due to the tremendous importance of the objectives in the northeast we must concentrate on that movement.'[1] He issued a directive accordingly to Montgomery and gave Bradley the principal task, for the moment, of supporting Montgomery in the attainment of his objectives. Eisenhower emphasised the importance of a secure base at Antwerp for the advance into Germany. He insisted too on the importance of using the whole strength of the airborne army so that the

[1] Papers IV, No. 1910

tasks in the north-east could be quickly accomplished. He thought there could be no reason for Montgomery requiring Bradley's support if the airborne forces were left idle.[2] During their meeting Montgomery had strongly pressed Eisenhower to leave the command arrangements as they were for the period of the pursuit. He believed that with the whole resources of the two army groups he could finish off the Germans in 1944. In the letter to Marshall already referred to, one in which he lays bare his thoughts at the time, Eisenhower said he was going to adhere to the date of 1 September for taking over operational control. His signal communications would not be anything like ready by that time but he saw that the moment had come to recognise a change that had already come about. As he said, Bradley had been operating with a considerable degree of freedom for some time. Montgomery could still have the task of co-ordination between his own forces and Bradley's left wing, but the large and steadily increasing body of American troops could not be left to the direction of Montgomery.[3]

Eisenhower's desire to leave the liberation of Paris for the time being was thwarted by a rising of the Free French Forces of the Interior within the city. Eisenhower had under his command one veteran Free French division, Leclerc's 2nd Armoured Division, which had fought with Eighth Army in the Desert and had landed in Normandy early in August as part of Third Army. To this division was given the honour of being the first of the Allied troops to enter the city. Eisenhower immediately asked de Gaulle to precede him into Paris but de Gaulle had already established himself there. Eisenhower wanted to make a formal Allied call on de Gaulle, accompanied by Montgomery, but Montgomery was too much concerned with the battle to spare the time. Eisenhower, accompanied by Bradley and Gault, made the call. De Gaulle asked Eisenhower for help by sending in supplies, uniforms and equipment for additional French divisions. According to Eisenhower he also asked for two American divisions to help keep order in the city. De Gaulle denies this. Certainly by 2 September de Gaulle was in full control and screaming for Leclerc's division to be sent eastwards to take part in the battle.[4]

On 2 September Eisenhower visited Bradley at his headquarters at Chartres. Patton and Hodges were also there and all three used every effort

[2] Papers IV, No. 1909
[3] Ibid.; Pogue, op. cit., pp. 249–52; Montgomery, op. cit., pp. 266–9
[4] Pogue, op. cit., pp. 241–3; Crusade in Europe, pp. 326–7; De Gaulle, op. cit., p. 319

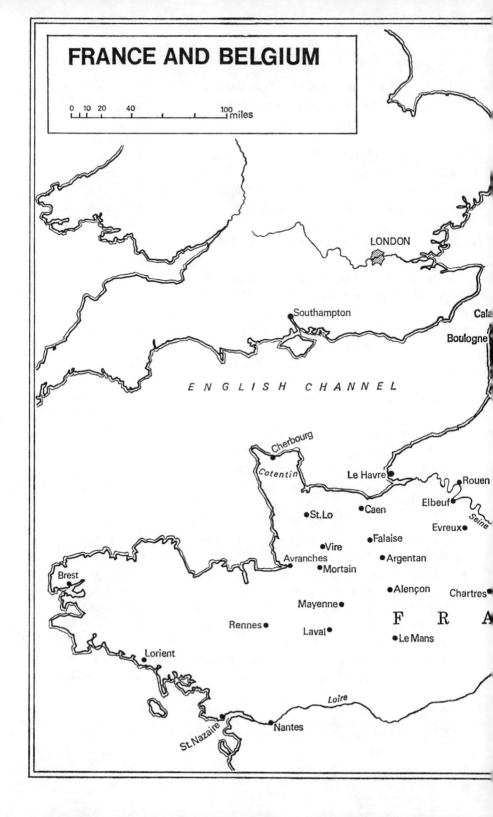

FRANCE AND BELGIUM

0 10 20   40   100 miles

LONDON

Southampton

Cala

Boulogne

E N G L I S H   C H A N N E L

Cherbourg

Cotentin

Le Havre

Rouen

Elbeuf

Caen

St.Lo

Evreux

Seine

Falaise

Vire

Argentan

Avranches

Mortain

Brest

Alençon

Chartres

Mayenne

F R A

Rennes

Laval

Le Mans

Lorient

Loire

St.Nazaire

Nantes

to persuade Eisenhower to authorise a drive by Third Army through Mannheim, Frankfurt and Coblenz. Their views tallied with Allied Intelligence opinion which declared: 'The August battles have done it and the enemy in the west has had it. . . . [The German Army is] no longer a cohesive 'force but a number of fugitive battle groups, disorganized and even demoralized, short of equipment and arms.'[5] Things had been going equally badly for the Germans on the eastern front. The Russian offensive had begun within a week of the Normandy landing and by 5 September attacks stretching from Finland to the Black Sea had succeeded in forcing the capitulation of Finland and Rumania and the turning to the Allies of Bulgaria. In the centre East Prussia had been overrun and the Russian advance continued to the gates of Warsaw where inexplicably, and unhappily for the Polish Resistance, it had halted. In the light of the general belief that the war was near its end, Eisenhower gave qualified approval for Bradley's advance. However, he made it clear that the supply and transport position was such that even against weak opposition widespread movement would be difficult and that at present Montgomery's operation must have priority.

This is a suitable moment to interrupt the account of the pursuit and to discuss Eisenhower's handling of the immediate situation which arose from the near destruction of the German Seventh Army in Normandy. It must be remembered that only one of the two armies which comprised Army Group 'B' had been defeated. Fifteenth Army, which had been retained for the defence of the Pas de Calais and the coast north of the Seine, was still largely intact. The resulting situation poses two questions: was there an opportunity to complete the destruction of Army Group 'B' west of the Rhine and if so, what was Eisenhower's part in the failure to seize it?

In the planning for Overlord it had never been expected that the battles for the beachhead and in Normandy would do more than drive the Germans back to the Seine. The Allies intended to get possession of Brittany for the sake of its ports and to launch a second great battle for the heart of France. The situation had been completely changed by the way Hitler demanded that the battle should be fought. Rundstedt was not allowed to make the withdrawals that he and Rommel saw were necessary and then, after Rundstedt had been dismissed, Kluge was ordered to carry out the Mortain counter-attack. Thus he thrust the whole of his

[5] SHAEF Intelligence summaries quoted in Pogue, *op. cit.*, p. 244

panzer forces into the net which Montgomery, by his handling of the Normandy battle, was setting. The question whether the mouth of the net could have been better closed has already been discussed but one thing is certain, the Germans suffered a major disaster. The scale of the disaster can be measured from the German Army Group 'B' strength statements of 23 August. These show a total of between 70 and 80 tanks and about 7,000 men for the whole ten panzer divisions. On 'D' Day a single S.S. panzer division mustered 20,000 men and 150 tanks.

There has been endless discussion of the pursuit from Normandy to the Rhine in the form of controversy over the broad or narrow front. Such discussion has usually centred on the direction of the advance into Germany and the question where the final battle for Germany should be fought. It is often forgotten that the magnitude of the defeat suffered by the Germans offered two opportunities. The first was the immediate exploitation of the victory in Normandy by destroying all the German forces west of the Rhine, the second, the possibility of an advance into Germany to overcome such forces as had got away and those which Hitler had been able to gather from elsewhere to hold the West Wall. By giving attention too soon to the requirements of the second task it may be that the opportunity to accomplish the first was missed.

Eisenhower was always thinking ahead and he was well able to see what was necessary for the advance into Germany. But he was not equipped to deal with the immediate crisis of an exploitation battle for the destruction of a retreating enemy. As has been shown his command post had only arrived in France on 7 August and the advanced element of Supreme Headquarters itself did not arrive in France until 31 August, the day before Eisenhower took over command of the battle. Neither of these headquarters had the communications or facilities for direct control of a fluid battle. In exploitation of success much must be left to the initiative of the lower echelons of command, but the direction of the battle must be in the hands of one man with the whole picture in his mind and nothing outside the battle to distract him. A moment's reflection will tell the reader that Eisenhower, as Supreme Commander, could never have the same close control over operations which Montgomery had had throughout the Normandy battle. Montgomery had his finger on the pulse of the battle, he knew what every division was doing—possibly even brigade actions came within his scan. His highly trained personal liaison officers brought him the latest information. He was in immediate touch with the commanders concerned and knew from them what the enemy was doing. Simonds, commanding II Canadian Corps in the thick of the battle wrote about the passage of intelligence in this situation:

> Normally the best strategic intelligence comes from the top down, because the top headquarters has at its disposal all the means of collating and collecting intelligence. In a confused broken battle the leading formations really have the best picture. From the quick tactical squeeze of captured senior commanders and staff officers there was a very clear picture of the temporary collapse of the German command structure.[6]

It was with such considerations in mind that Montgomery protested when Eisenhower told him on 23 August that he would take over direction of the battle on 1 September. Unfortunately Montgomery did not limit himself to the immediate situation. He asked not only to be allowed to finish the battle then going on but went further and said that Eisenhower should never take over direct command. Montgomery thus weakened his case and pushed the argument into a sphere in which Eisenhower knew he could never give way.

Eisenhower was undoubtedly right in thinking that the close single control under which the Normandy battle had been fought would not be possible for an advance into Germany against organized resistance. He saw that in order to deploy all the Allied forces now coming forward a much looser direction would be necessary. But he was wrong to fix an arbitrary date for the change over of command. He should have made it clear that until every effort had been made to destroy all the German forces west of the Rhine, Bradley would remain under Montgomery's command and, in addition, all the air and administrative resources available to Eisenhower would be used for the furtherance of Montgomery's operations. At the same time it should have been made clear to Montgomery that this state of affairs would probably only continue for the fighting west of the Rhine and that in the event of the enemy being able to organize resistance along their West Wall, Eisenhower would take over command in the field.

It is easy to be wise after the event and in imagination to recreate the battle as it might have gone. The phases of an operation can be seen—or even invented—more easily by a historian than by the actual commanders. It is certainly not claimed here that if Eisenhower had handled the command problem in the way suggested, complete German defeat west of

---

[6] Letter from Lt.-Gen. Guy Simonds to the author November 1971

the Rhine would have been assured. It might have been achieved, but despite their disorganization the Germans did nothing that played into Allied hands. There was no attempt to fight on any intermediate position but all units made hot foot for the West Wall. Behind it there were time and facilities for reorganization. Moreover, by the time it came to a battle for the West Wall the Allied supply problem would be formidable indeed Much has been made of the fact that de Guingand disagreed with his own chief and supported Eisenhower in his broad front strategy. De Guingand tells us that this was the only major point during the war in which he disagreed with Montgomery. But de Guingand bases all his arguments on the difficulties that would be incurred beyond the Rhine and by inference suggests that more could have been achieved west of the Rhine.[7]

Probably the factor that weighed most heavily with Eisenhower in his decision to take over direction of the battle on 1 September was the pressure being put on him by Marshall, Bradley, and American opinion generally to do so at once and to give the United States forces the independent role that their strength and performance justified. There is no doubt that if Eisenhower had seen the tactical opportunity he would have resisted all such national feelings and interests. If Eisenhower had made his intentions clear, Bradley would have loyally accepted Montgomery's command as he had throughout the Normandy battle. Montgomery would have been happy, at least for the moment, to concentrate on his immediate task and much fruitless argument about the future would have been avoided.

In weighing up all the factors there are good grounds for thinking that, although Eisenhower's policy of the broad front was right in the long run, he put it into effect too early. By doing so he may have missed an opportunity for an even greater victory west of the Rhine than was achieved.

On 1 September, the day that Eisenhower took operational control of the two army groups, Montgomery was made a Field Marshal. Three days later he again urged Eisenhower to concentrate his resources in the northern thrust. He did not believe that the supply situation allowed a double thrust but he thought the Allies had 'now reached a stage where one really powerful and full-blooded thrust towards Berlin is likely to get there and thus end the German war.'[8] Eisenhower did not believe that any juggling with the administrative resources could sustain an advance to

---

[7] De Guingand, 'Operation Victory', pp. 411–13
[8] Montgomery to Eisenhower September 4 1944; Montgomery, op. cit., p. 272

Berlin. No thrust deep into Germany seemed possible until Le Havre and Antwerp were open. Antwerp had already been captured on 4 September with the port almost undamaged, but the Germans still held Walcheren and South Beveland and the south side of the Scheldt estuary with the result that shipping could not approach. What Eisenhower did believe was that the near destruction of the German Army in the west had made possible an advance on a wide front to breach the West Wall, sometimes wrongly called the Siegfried Line. The Allies would then be in a position to cross the Rhine and encircle the Ruhr and the Saar. The loss of her great industrial areas would largely destroy Germany's ability to wage war. Montgomery did not relent in his own views and Eisenhower gave way so far as to get his staff to review the possibilities. Montgomery sent de Guingand to talk to Eisenhower's staff. As a result of this visit it was found that 80% of Montgomery's demands for rail transport could be met. Northern Army Group would also have priority for air transport and the airborne army would be available to clear Walcheren and the south of the Scheldt estuary. The necessary motor transport could be made available only by immobilising a number of United States divisions and other fighting units. This Eisenhower said he was prepared to do as an emergency measure for a limited period in order to get Montgomery across the Rhine and to enable him to capture the approaches to Antwerp.

In returning from a visit to the forward areas on 2 September Eisenhower had wrenched his knee in a forced landing. He had been laid up for several days, but despite this he went to see Montgomery on 10 September. He also sent Bedell Smith to see him on the 12th and on the 13th issued a new written directive. He did not alter his previous instructions to Montgomery and Bradley but he emphasised even more strongly than before the importance of securing the approaches to Antwerp, or as an alternative Rotterdam, and also the Channel ports and Brest. Despite the priority given to the clearing of the Scheldt, the role given to First Airborne Army was to assist Northern Group of Armies in seizing a crossing over the Rhine.[9]

It may be helpful to reiterate the thoughts of Eisenhower and his principal commanders at this time and to consider the state of the troops both allied and enemy. Eisenhower was confident that he could get quickly to the Rhine and while he was doing so Antwerp and Le Havre could be opened up. Montgomery thought he could finally defeat the German army

[9] The two directives are given in Papers IV, Nos. 1933 & 1946

provided the whole effort was directed by him. He would need at least one American army as well as First Airborne Army and all the transport facilities of both army groups. Bradley believed that the Ruhr should be approached from both north and south before attempting one main drive on Berlin. Patton went further than his chief and was determined to get so deeply involved that he could not be held back. Ramsay was most disturbed that nothing seemed to be being done about Antwerp. He gave a severe warning that if the Allies did not act quickly the Germans would mine the Scheldt.[10] Tedder now had all the room for airfields he wanted and was not much concerned in present controversies; he did however support Eisenhower's views. Northern Army Group having overrun the whole of France and Belgium was triumphant but exhausted. The British, Canadian and First United States Army had borne the heat of the Normandy battle and the pursuit across France and Belgium. Vehicles were breaking down and petrol was scarce. Horrocks's XXX Corps had captured Brussels and Antwerp. They had exhausted themselves in the great pursuit and thoughts of Walcheren and Beveland did not enter their minds. Horrocks had quite rightly ensured first the capture of the port intact but he admits that he did not think of turning west to cut the retreating Germans off from the Scheldt. His mind was on the Rhine.[11] Horrocks does not attempt to excuse himself, but he might well do so. The decision required was at a much higher level than that of corps commander. First Canadian Army was following along the coast behind the British but was making slow headway in dealing with the determined but local German resistance at the whole chain of ports from Le Havre to Dunkirk. The German Seventh Army defeated in Normandy was streaming back, largely without equipment and with less than 100 tanks. Its commanders saw little hope of anything but sporadic resistance short of the West Wall. The Fifteenth Army, which had been kept North of the Seine by Eisenhower's deception plan, was in better shape and was now south of the Scheldt and crossing to Walcheren and South Beveland, at all of which places they were destined to offer fierce resistance. Isolated garrisons were still holding out at the ports. Brest was held until 20 September and was then so badly damaged that it was never used by the Allies. St Nazaire and the Loire ports held out so long that the Allies abandoned all hope of using them. Le Havre held out until 12 September and was not in working order until

[10] Ellis, *op. cit.*, II, p. 5
[11] Horrocks, *A Full Life*, pp. 203-4, and correspondence with the author

9 October; Boulogne was held until 22 September, and Calais until 1 October. Hitler had reinstated Rundstedt as Commander-in-Chief West and Model remained as Commander of Army Group 'B'. Model asked for at least 25 fresh divisions and in addition 6 panzer divisions to enable him to hold from the West Wall to the Meuse. Hitler also took the action which Ramsay so greatly feared; he ordered that the approaches to Antwerp should be held at all costs, and that the Scheldt should be heavily mined.

In this phase First Canadian Army had been given a task of which the difficulty was not fully appreciated. It had to take the Channel ports from Le Havre to Ostend and to clear the Scheldt west of Antwerp. This involved crossing a series of rivers where they were widest and operating through country where there were no Maquis to help in preventing the Germans from blowing the bridges, as they did for Second British Army advance to Brussels and Antwerp. The absence of Maquis was due to the fact that this area of the VI sites had been subject to the most stringent German security precautions. Simonds, commanding II Canadian Corps, saw the problem in its proper light. He believed it was a waste of time to do more than mask the Channel ports, whose garrisons offered no offensive threat but would take time to overcome. He saw that his opportunity was to race along the coast to Breskens and then turn east to cut off the Fifteenth Army from the Scheldt. For his advance bridging material, ammunition and petrol would have to be supplied by landing craft, thus easing 21st Army Group administrative problem. Simonds could not succeed in making his army commander see the problem in the same way. Crerar would not question the orders he had received from Montgomery to take the Channel ports. Simonds says that he would have given anything for ten minutes with Montgomery, who would have seen the possibilities in a flash.[12] Antwerp could have been opened quickly and the delay in opening the Channel ports, even if it had been more than a few days, would not have affected the supply situation.

By mid-September Eisenhower's armies had reached the frontiers of Holland and thence along the borders of Germany through Trier to Metz. There they linked up with the forces which had landed in the south of France and were in process of extending the front through Epinal and Belfort to the Swiss frontier. These forces now came under Eisenhower as the Southern Group of Armies. As they were maintained through Mar-

[12] Letter from Lt.-Gen. Guy Simonds to the author 25 November 1971

seilles their activities put no burden on the stretched lines of communication in the north. Although Cherbourg and Dieppe were the only ports available to supplement supply over the beaches and by the one Mulberry in working order, Eisenhower was nevertheless prepared to let operations for the clearance of the Scheldt estuary take lower priority than the effort to force a crossing over the Rhine at Arnhem. Commenting on the Arnhem operation in retrospect he said he not only approved it, he demanded it.

The Arnhem operation has gone into history as a glorious failure. It is not the tactical conduct of the battle that concerns us here, but its place in the strategic picture. First Allied Airborne Army was Eisenhower's only reserve and the only force that could intervene without the restraint of the supply and transport situation. Eisenhower had been looking for an opportunity to use it ever since the victory in Normandy, but Montgomery and Bradley's rapid advance across France and Belgium had outrun the opportunity to use it. Both commanders had always preferred to use the aircraft involved in its lift for augmenting their overworked road transport. Now that the forces had outrun their communications the time had come. Eisenhower had already allotted the airborne army to Montgomery in furtherance of the priority he had given to the northern advance. The alternatives were clear; either a landing north of the Scheldt estuary or the forcing of a crossing over the Rhine. Two factors made both Eisenhower and Montgomery prefer the second: the thought that the enemy was finished, and a false optimism about the time First Canadian Army would be able to clear the coast and deal with the Scheldt.

There were two possibilities for airborne operations to cross the Rhine. One, favoured by Dempsey, to cross close to the Ruhr at Wesel; the other, that actually attempted, further downstream where the Rhine had divided into three main rivers. The decision for Arnhem was Montgomery's, one in which he was strongly supported by the air force, who considered that a landing at Wesel would come too close to the strong anti-aircraft defences of the Ruhr. But Montgomery's real reasons were that the Arnhem crossing would give the opportunity to outflank the West Wall; that it gave the greatest opportunity for surprise, and that it was closest to the base of the airborne troops. Eisenhower did not participate in this debate. It is possible that he should have. Wesel would have brought the attack within easy reach of support from Bradley. One of the causes of failure at Arnhem was that the land advance, restricted to one narrow corridor

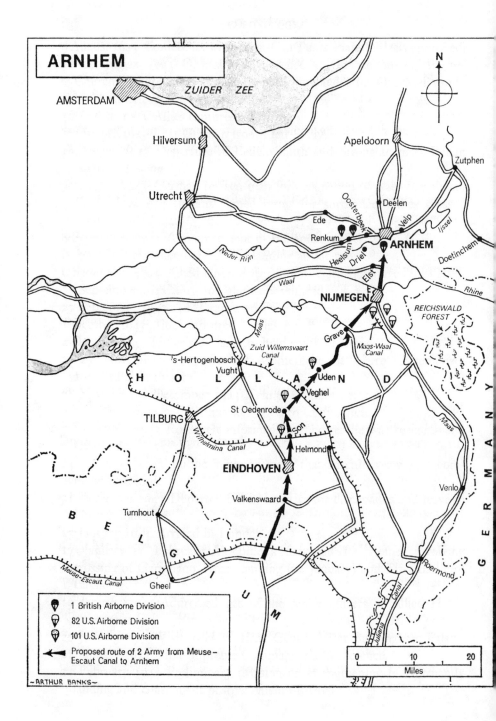

ARNHEM

N

AMSTERDAM

ZUIDER ZEE

Hilversum

Apeldoorn

Zutphen

Utrecht

Oosterbeek

Deelen

Ede

Velp

Ijssel

Renkum

Heelsum

Driel

ARNHEM

Neder Rijn

Doetinchem

Waal

Elst

Rhine

NIJMEGEN

REICHSWALD
FOREST

Maas

Grave

Maas-Waal
Canal

Zuid Willemsvaart
Canal

's-Hertogenbosch

Vught

Uden

H   O   L   L   A   N   D

Veghel

TILBURG

St Oedenrode

Son

Wilhelmina Canal

Helmond

EINDHOVEN

Venlo

Valkenswaard

B

Turnhout

E

Maas

L

G

Roermond

Meuse-Escaut Canal

Gheel

I

U

M

G   E   R   M   A   N   Y

Juliana Canal

1 British Airborne Division

82 U.S. Airborne Division

101 U.S. Airborne Division

Proposed route of 2 Army from Meuse–
Escaut Canal to Arnhem

0	10	20
Miles		

~ARTHUR BANKS~

overlooked by the enemy, had no real effect on the battle fought by the airborne troops.

The airborne attack involved one corps of three divisions which was to land along a narrow carpet across the water obstacles from Eindhoven to Arnhem (see map p. 172). 101st (U.S.) Airborne Division had the task of capturing Eindhoven and the crossings over the Wilhelmina Canal. 82nd (U.S.) Airborne Division was to capture the bridges over the Maas and the Vaal at Grave and Nijmegen. 1st (Br) Airborne Division was to capture the bridge over the Neder Rijn at Arnhem. There was a most ambitious plan for XXX Corps, the leading corps of Second British Army. It was to use the corridor made by the airborne troops to advance north to Apeldorn and the Zuyder Zee. VIII Corps on its right and XII Corps on its left were to expand the corridor. The whole army was then to face east on the line Zuyder Zee—Arnhem for the advance to the north face of the Ruhr. This bold plan was made on the assumption that the Germans were incapable of offering effective resistance. None of the airborne divisions was expected to meet opposition from more than one brigade. This was a major misappreciation because the Germans had got their defeated armies helter-skelter across France and Belgium without further engagement and were at last in a position to offer resistance along the line of the Meuse and the Rhine. Their section along the Meuse-Escaut Canal, opposite XXX Corps was held by First Parachute Army under command of Student, one of the most capable German generals. Moreover, at the moment of the Arnhem attack Model, an even more formidable character, was having lunch within a mile of the dropping zone of 1st (Br) Airborne Division. Apart from Student's army Model had in the vicinity two panzer divisions, resting and refitting and in good order. The Germans not only held the Arnhem bridge but managed to seal off the corridor along which XXX Corps was striving to reach the isolated 1st Airborne Division.

The failure at Arnhem may be attributed to the skill with which the Germans countered the Allied moves. But undoubtedly there were faults in the planning of the operation which were an important contributory factor. The airborne operation seems to have been planned in isolation and the supporting land operations tacked on. It should have been one comprehensive operation under a single commander, with the airborne forces playing an essential but subsidiary part. That was the way airborne forces had been used in the Normandy landing and were subsequently to be used in the crossing of the Rhine. It was Eisenhower's idea of the way they should be used (see p. 133), but there is no doubt that he gave his full support to the plan of operations as it was actually carried out.

While the Arnhem battle was still going on, Eisenhower was discussing future operations with his army group commander. They went over much of the ground already covered. Eisenhower thought there was not much difference between Montgomery's views and his own but Montgomery was sure that there was a fundamental difference. Eisenhower was prepared to give priority to the northern advance but also wanted Central Army Group to take every opportunity of advancing to Frankfurt so that he could move on the Ruhr from the south. Montgomery felt that if Bradley's army group were given this latitude, Patton would get himself involved in offensive operations which would absorb transport resources and would negative the priority given to the north. This indeed is what Patton said he intended to do, and he said it both at the time and again subsequently.[13] Another difference was that Montgomery was looking for a final thrust north of the Ruhr and on to Berlin; Eisenhower was looking at two very definite stages, first the capture of the Ruhr and the opening of Antwerp and then, as a subsequent stage depending on the success of those operations, a drive to Berlin. There was yet one more difference which neither of them recognized at the time: their respective attitudes to the opening of Antwerp. Eisenhower had consistently and continually demanded the clearance of Antwerp at the earliest possible moment and had emphasised that its use was a prerequisite of any advance beyond the Rhine. The only occasion on which Eisenhower in any way departed from this demand was when he allowed—and indeed encouraged—Montgomery to use the airborne army for Arnhem rather than for the clearance of the Scheldt. Montgomery seems to have accepted Eisenhower's directions in this matter without giving his mind to their true import. He made First Canadian Army responsible for clearing the Channel ports and Antwerp, but when progress was slow and it was obvious he was not within reach of clearing the Scheldt, he did nothing about it. His mind was on Dempsey's army and its dash for the Rhine. The result was that it was only after the failure at Arnhem, with its portent of the German recovery, that serious efforts were made to clear the Scheldt estuary. Antwerp had been captured almost undamaged on 4 September, but it was not in action as a port until the end of November.

<hr>

[13] Pogue, *op. cit.*, p. 293; Patton, *War as I Knew It*, pp. 125, 133, 265

After the failure of the Arnhem operation neither Eisenhower nor Montgomery had given up hope of continuing operations to secure the Ruhr, but subsequent delays in clearing the Scheldt virtually removed the possibility of ending the war in 1944. On 2 October First Canadian Army failed both to destroy the enemy south of the Scheldt and to cut their way through the isthmus leading to South Beveland. In order to comply with Eisenhower's insistent demands that Antwerp should be opened, Montgomery was forced to use a considerable part of Second British Army and to call on Eisenhower to increase the support given to him by Bradley. There was no longer any question of Montgomery being able to carry the Ruhr by a single thrust from the north, still less of a deep advance towards Hamm and Cologne. Even an attack much closer in against the western Ruhr would have to await the opening of Antwerp. Nevertheless Montgomery believed that some changes in the command arrangements would be necessary for operations against the Ruhr. He believed that future operations could not be efficiently conducted except under one single field commander. Eisenhower was at last stung into using his full authority as Supreme Commander. He replied on 13 October:

... If you could have a similarly clear picture of [the state of the supply situation in the Allied armies as a whole] you would understand why I keep reverting again and again to the matter of getting Antwerp into a workable condition. . . .

With one of your statements, I am in emphatic agreement. This is that for one major task on the battlefield there must be *a single battlefield commander* ; a man who can devote his entire attention to that particular operation. That is the reason we have Armies and Army Groups. When however we have a battlefront extending from Switzerland to the North Sea, I do not agree that one man can stay so close that he can keep a 'battle grip' upon the *overall* situation and direct it intelligently. This is no longer a Normandy Beachhead! Operations along such a *wide* front break themselves into more or less clearly defined areas of operation. . . . The overall commander, in this case myself, has the function of adjusting . . . the tasks . . , assigning support by air or rein- forcements . . . and shifting the emphasis in maintenance arrangements.[14]

Eisenhower said he would like to meet Montgomery with Bradley to discuss the future attacks to cross the Rhine. He suggested that both should spend the night with him at Reims. In fact the meeting took place at Montgomery's headquarters in Brussels on 18 October. Bradley is almost certainly right in suggesting that this was the only way of ensuring that Montgomery would be present in person.

[14] Papers IV, No. 2038

Before the meeting of commanders Montgomery had replied to Eisenhower's letter, saying that he had got his answer and that Eisenhower would hear no more from him on the question of command. He promised Eisenhower that he could rely on him to do what he (Eisenhower) wanted.[15] At the meeting Eisenhower, for the first time since the Normandy break-out, gave Bradley the principal role. Montgomery was left to give his undivided attention to the clearance of Antwerp. Bradley was to use his three armies to clear west of the Rhine and attempt to force a bridgehead south of Cologne. Further south Devers's army group of one French and one United States army was also directed to cross the Rhine. At this conference concern was expressed at the growing shortage of artillery ammunition, due not to transport difficulty but to premature reduction in output in America. Eisenhower not only pressed the matter through normal supply channels but telegraphed specially to Marshall on the subject.

The results of Eisenhower's October directive were disappointing. Mud, rain, fog and even snow hampered operations, but it was stiffened enemy resistance which held the Allies. By the end of November Antwerp was working and Metz captured, but the enemy was still firm along most of the West Wall. One cheering result of the battles was the success of de Lattre's First French Army in the southern sector where Belfort and its industrial area was captured, much of Alsace overrun and the Rhine reached near Colmar.

When Eisenhower visited him on 28 November and later in writing, Montgomery took the opportunity of pointing out to Eisenhower what he described as 'a strategic reverse'. He said that a new plan was required and added: 'In the new plan we must get away from the doctrine of attacking in so many places that we are not strong enough to get decisive results. We must concentrate such strength on the main selected thrust that success will be certain. It is in this respect that we failed badly in the present operations.' Despite his earlier promise Montgomery also raised once more the command question. He wanted a single operational commander north of the Ardennes, even if he could not have it for the whole front. He pointed out that he and Bradley were a good team who worked together well in Normandy to win a great victory. One or other should now have full operational control north of the Ardennes.[16] Eisenhower sent a long

[15] Ellis, *op. cit.*, II, p. 71
[16] Montgomery to Eisenhower 30 November 1944; Bryant, *op. cit.*, II, pp. 342–4

reply questioning Montgomery's diagnosis of a strategic reverse. He obviously took the criticism as referring to strategy since Normandy rather than, as expressed, since the end of October. He did not agree that things had gone badly since Normandy simply because the Allies had not done all that they had hoped. He said: 'Had we not advanced on a relatively broad front, we would now have the spectacle of a long narrow line of communication, constantly threatened on the right flank and weakened by detachments of large fighting formations. . . . As it is we now have a rear that is cleared of the enemy. We can look to the front. . . . I have no intention of stopping Devers's and Patton's operations . . . but I do not intend to push these attacks senselessly. It is going to be very important to us later on to have two strings to our bow.'[17]

Churchill was as worried about the situation as Montgomery, but Roosevelt refused to be moved by his fears. Brooke dissuaded Churchill from approaching Eisenhower direct. Although Brooke at this time had a low opinion of Eisenhower's ability to conduct a battle, he saw the realities of the situation; he knew that the relative size of the British and American forces must prevent Eisenhower from giving Montgomery control over the whole of Bradley's army group. At the same time Brooke doubted whether Bradley was suitable as Land Forces Commander, and knew that Eisenhower shared his doubts. Brooke believed that the only solution of the problem was for Montgomery to handle Eisenhower properly. Nevertheless, Brooke himself decided to take a hand and Eisenhower was invited to come over with Tedder to discuss the strategic situation with Churchill and the Chiefs of Staff. Eisenhower explained his intention of making a double advance, north of the Rhine and by Frankfurt. Brooke was brutally critical and made it clear that such dispersal of effort could only lead to failure. Later at dinner, the argument continued and Brooke found Churchill talking Eisenhower's side against him. Later Churchill told Brooke that Eisenhower was his guest, that Brooke had been very rough with him, and that he was bound to support one American faced with five British.[18]

In his diary Brooke makes one criticism of Eisenhower that ought not to go unchallenged. In the entry for 24 November he wrote that he was most concerned about the command of the land battle. He went on: 'Eisenhower though supposed to be [controlling the campaign] is on the golf links at

[17] Papers IV, No. 2145
[18] Bryant, *op. cit.*, II, pp. 343 & 350–2

Reims—entirely detached and taking no part in the running of the war.'[19] Such an entry might be taken, and has indeed been taken, to mean that Eisenhower was playing golf instead of giving his whole attention to command. To think so shows a complete misunderstanding of the man and of the way Eisenhower worked at his advanced headquarters. The site of the headquarters was the golf course at Reims and the very position of the tents would prevent the course being used for the game of golf. In fact the golf course as such did not exist and Gault affirms that Eisenhower never had a golf club in his hand during the whole period of their association. Gault explains Eisenhower's use of his forward headquarters. He was accompanied only by a small number of officers, and Gault was the senior. There was a British signals officer and American pilots for the two L5 light aircraft. The two requirements for the headquarters were good communications and that it would give Eisenhower the ability to get quickly to see Montgomery and Bradley. The senior officers from the main headquarters had to come forward to him frequently. The most regularly called forward were Bedell Smith, Strong and Whiteley.

Eisenhower gave his whole time to the prosecution of the war, but he did not think out the tactical operations in the way that Montgomery and Bradley had to; his was a much wider task. He visited Bradley more often than he visited Montgomery, because he felt himself responsible much deeper down the chain of command for the American forces. He felt it his business to know the qualities of every divisional commander. For the British that was Montgomery's business.

Besides constant thought about the campaign—always trying to be one step ahead of events—Eisenhower gave much time to visits to the forward divisions. As has been stated, he felt he must know at first hand how his commanders, at any rate down to divisions, were meeting the strain and problems of battle. He understood too the problems of morale and his papers are full of examples of how he looked to the well-being of the fighting soldier. He came down heavily on any base commander who appropriated the best facilities for administrative echelons or neglected those for the rest and recreation of the fighting man.

Responsibility for signals at the advanced headquarters was British. British equipment was of a more rugged field type than that used by the Americans in large headquarters. Smijth-Windham, the senior signals officer, tells how when he showed Eisenhower his field telephone complete

---

[19] Bryant, *op. cit.*, II, p. 338

30 *With Brooke and Churchill near the Rhine, March 1945*

31 *Montgomery, Zhukov, Eisenhower and Koenig at a flag-raising ceremony at the Allied Control Council, Berlin, September 1945*

with winding handle, he was invited to 'take away that Goddam meat-grinder and get me a telephone'.

Whatever other men's doubts Eisenhower could be sure of Marshall's full support and he continued his habit of unburdening himself regularly to his chief. In one of these letters in November he commented on how well the army group, army and corps commanders were standing up to the strain, adding somewhat whimsically that they were spared the burden of politics, priorities, shipping and maquis and were also spared the direct battle strain borne by the divisional commanders.

As a result of the second Quebec Conference (Octagon) the arrangements for the command of the air forces had undergone a change as early as mid-September. The command of the strategic air forces was taken away from Eisenhower and vested jointly in the British Chief of Air Staff and the Commanding General United States Army Air Forces. Eisenhower protested at the time but he later admitted that it made no difference. He continued to make his requests for strategic air action through Tedder and the confidence and good relations he had built up with Harris and Spaatz during Overlord ensured the smooth working of the new arrangement.

Eisenhower's handling of the immediate situation after the victory in Normandy has already been discussed. Accepting his decision to take over command on 1 September and considering the broader aspects of the phase from the Seine to the Rhine there are two questions. Was Eisenhower right in his broad front strategy? If he was right, or at any rate justified, did he make his intentions clear and bend his subordinate commanders to his will? Nobody will ever know for certain the answer to the first question. It is possible that Montgomery, given all the forces and all the administrative support that could be mustered, might have finished off the German armies. The German commanders, after the war, were almost unanimous in thinking that he could have. It is even possible that Bradley given the same priority for an advance further south might have enabled the dashing Patton to do the same. That would however have been an unsound decision because of the danger to England from the V1 sites in the Pas de Calais. Looking at his decision in the light of what happened later it is probable that Eisenhower adopted the soundest plan. The success of the Germans in dealing with Arnhem shows that by the time they got back to the Rhine they would have been in a position to deal with any single thrust. Once there was no longer an opportunity for the immediate destruction of the enemy, the advance to the Rhine on as broad a front as possible, with priority first for the V1 sites in the Pas de Calais and second for the opening of Antwerp, was almost certainly the wisest course.

On the second point it is not so easy to defend Eisenhower. Certainly he made it clear from the beginning that he wanted Antwerp. As certainly he gave the north priority, but he was not firm enough with Bradley in ensuring that this priority worked even at the cost of stopping Patton. Even more important he was too inclined to let Montgomery think that he could get his own way. If in the endless discussions with Montgomery he had not only held to his plan, as he did, but made it abundantly clear that his priority lasted only up to the Rhine, then Montgomery might have realised that the opening of Antwerp really did matter.

In saying that Eisenhower ought to have been firmer with Montgomery and with Bradley it is easy to gloss over the realities of the situation. There is no doubt that the speed of advance after the break-out took everyone, including Eisenhower, by surprise. All the commanders saw opportunities ahead if only they could be supplied with petrol and ammunition. Montgomery was the senior British commander. He was in constant touch with the Chiefs of Staff through Brooke, and they were wholeheartedly behind him in wanting the northern advance, first for the V1 sites, then the Rocket (V2) sites, and then for the victorious dash for Berlin. This was a national pull right up to government level. On the other hand by this time the great preponderance of forces was American and they could hardly be held back just to make a British victory. Thus, despite the true unity of the western Allies, there were those national pulls which are unavoidable even in the closest alliance. Although Eisenhower can be criticised for controlling with a light rein on both sides, there was no giving way through weakness. His was a technique which was alive to the problem of command of Allied forces.

13

The Ardennes Counter-Offensive

While Eisenhower was thinking of the battle to destroy the German forces in the Rhineland, Hitler was insisting on a blow that would finally disrupt the Allied offensive in the west. He aimed to cut the Allied army in two by a thrust to Brussels and Antwerp and then to turn to destroy the northern portion. He had begun to think of such an offensive in September and had got Jodl at OKW[1] to prepare plans which were then presented to Rundstedt to carry out. Neither Rundstedt nor Model was as hopeful as Hitler of the far-reaching consequence of such a counter-offensive. They would have preferred a less ambitious movement to encircle a substantial part of the Allied forces between the Meuse and the Moselle. Hitler, with some support from Keitel and Jodl, insisted and Rundstedt and his subordinates prepared the offensive with customary German efficiency. Two Panzer Armies were to form the principal striking force; Sixth Panzer Army to strike north-west to make for Antwerp and the Albert Canal, and Fifth Panzer Army to make for Antwerp from the south through Brussels to Givet. The Fifteenth Army in the north and the Seventh in the south were to hold the shoulders of the salient and to engage the Allies on each flank of the main attack. There was an elaborate deception plan to hide German intentions and all preliminary moves were made by night into hidden concentration areas. Knowledge of intention was confined to a very few senior officers and Sixth Panzer Army was only brought into the area at the last possible moment.

Despite the German precautions almost all the moves were known to the Allied Intelligence and the shift in strength to the Ardennes was clearly identified. Yet neither Eisenhower nor any of his senior commanders suspected that they were about to be subjected to a major attack. This state of affairs brings out the crux of the Intelligence problem, which is the difference between the gathering of information and the interpretation that is put upon it. It also brings out the danger of a preconceived idea. The real reason why the available information was not properly

[1] Supreme War Headquarters

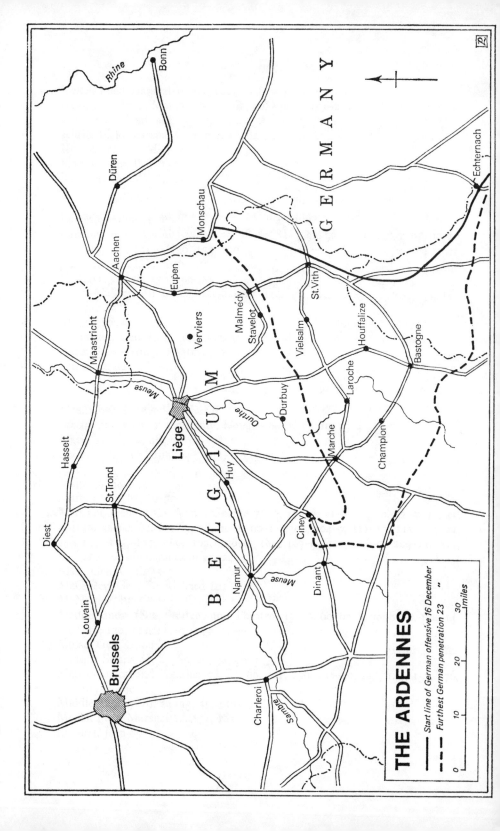

THE ARDENNES

— Start line of German offensive 16 December
--- Furthest German penetration 23 "

0 10 20 30 miles

interpreted was that Eisenhower and all the commanders were convinced that the German Army was no longer capable of offensive action, and that all efforts were directed to holding the Allied attacks towards Cologne and the Ruhr.

Broadly speaking it is the business of the Intelligence staff to say what the enemy could do, whereas it is the business of the commander himself to deduce what they are most likely to do. Strong, Eisenhower's head of Intelligence, and his staff had much the same idea as the commanders of the German inability to launch a major attack. But he had a deep knowledge of the German army and he was always conscious of what they could do. At several of Bedell Smith's staff meetings in the first week of December, about a fortnight before the attack, Strong drew attention to the existence of a major German panzer force. He thought it might be being prepared to go to the eastern front or that it was being held to deal with any major Allied penetration. But he warned Bedell Smith that it might be used for a major attack in the Ardennes which could be launched any time that there was a prospect of six days bad weather to offset the Allied air superiority. Bedell Smith was anxious that Bradley should be warned of the danger. Although the possibility had already been reported to Bradley, Strong went to see him. Bradley said he was aware of the danger and had prepared to move certain divisions into the Ardennes should an attack come there. But Bradley's attitude is best indicated by his remark to Strong: 'Let them come!'[2] It is not unjust to suggest that Eisenhower consented to that view. He had commented to Bradley on the fact that in the Ardennes four divisions were holding some 75 miles of front, but neither of them thought the danger sufficient to draw in divisions from elsewhere. Eisenhower wanted as few troops as possible in defensive areas so that his offensive in the Rhineland could be delivered in sufficient strength.

The German attack came in the early hours of 16 December. The whole weight of the attack, some 24 divisions with a preponderance of panzers, came against VIII Corps of three divisions. As might be expected the early reports which came into 12th Army Group gave an imcomplete picture, and Bradley, who had just arrived at Eisenhower's headquarters, was inclined to discount the seriousness of the attack. However, Eisenhower urged on him the necessity of moving an armoured division both from north and south on to the flanks of the attack. Bradley gave the necessary

[2] Pogue, *op. cit.*, p. 365; Strong, *op. cit.*, pp. 154–5

orders and the next morning returned to his own headquarters. During that day the strength of the enemy effort and the extent of his penetration became apparent. Eisenhower saw that the first necessities were to hold the shoulders at Monschau in the north and Bastogne in the south, and to prevent the enemy crossing the Meuse to the west. At the same time reserves had to be gathered to counter-attack from north and south to cut the enemy salient. The immediate problem was command. The attack had split Bradley's army group. Patton's army and a small part of Hodges's army were to the south of the salient while the greater part of Hodges's army and all Simpson's were to the north. Bradley at Luxembourg was badly placed to command his two northern armies. Eisenhower left Bradley in command in the south but decided that both Hodges and Simpson must be taken from his command and put under Montgomery. In the cold light of military necessity this may seem a very obvious decision but nothing shows more clearly that Eisenhower was able to put Allied considerations before national, and probably personal, feelings. The national implications were very real. It might well appear to the world that Eisenhower regarded this crisis as an American failure from which they had to be rescued by the British. Even more obviously it might be regarded as Bradley's failure. Bradley was left with only one subordinate, and that Patton, who always got the publicity whoever else was involved. Most of Bradley's command was put under Montgomery who, in the eyes of the British press was the only general, and who in the American press was always portrayed as being in rivalry with Bradley. At this moment Eisenhower was much encouraged by getting letters expressing complete confidence in him from both Churchill and Marshall. Eisenhower showed his own confidence in Bradley by suggesting to Marshall that this was the time to promote him to four star general's rank. The promotion could not be made because Congress was not then sitting. Curiously enough, despite this, Eisenhower heard on 20 December that he himself had been promoted to the newly created rank of General of the Army.

In a special order of the day Eisenhower pointed out to the Allied armies that by rushing out from his fixed defences the enemy had given them the opportunity to turn his greatest gamble into his worst defeat.[3] The difficulty of achieving this admirable aim was that Eisenhower had no substantial reserves immediately available and that air action was impossible because of fog which persisted from the beginning of the attack and

[3] Papers IV, No. 2195

did not lift until 23 December. As a result of the broad front strategy, his only reserve was an airborne corps of two divisions, 82nd and 101st, which were refitting near Reims. Both were ordered to Bastogne, although by the time they arrived Bradley had ordered 82nd to the northern sector. Montgomery had already moved his reserve corps to ensure that the Meuse could be held. Patton's army was engaged in offensive operations in the Saar and their employment against the southern flank of the salient required withdrawal, regrouping and a complete change in direction, a task to which Patton set himself with his customary energy and which he speedily accomplished. Montgomery went about his task more methodically. It was first necessary to get the feel of the American commanders that had been put under him. Both Hodges and Simpson had co-operated with him on his flank but neither of them had previously been under his command. Eisenhower made it clear to Montgomery that he had confidence in both of them and that if because of 'physical exhaustion' it became necessary to make any change in command, Eisenhower himself would make the decision. In the event, despite some prejudice against Montgomery in both the army headquarters, the new command worked smoothly.

It had been one of Montgomery's tenets of command since well before the war that when an enemy attack had got beyond the immediate stage no counter-attack could be launched until a new defence line was established and the enemy dispositions identified. He believed that a counter-attack required just as careful preparation as any other form of attack. The application of this doctrine to the present situation caused some impatience at American headquarters, Bradley's and Patton's as well as those under Montgomery. However, Eisenhower was of the same mind as Montgomery and indicated that, provided every effort was made to safeguard the line of the Meuse from Namur to Liège, he was prepared to give ground in order to adopt good defensive positions and to establish a strategic reserve for eventual counter-attack.[4] Eisenhower was anxious that such reserves as could be collected should not be squandered piecemeal and he feared especially that Patton might persuade Bradley to let the Third Army attack without waiting for a full counter-offensive. Eisenhower therefore directed that Patton should not be allowed to go beyond the relief of Bastogne, which was at that time surrounded by the enemy.

By 23 December the defensive stage of the battle was virtually over and

[4] Pogue, *op. cit.*, p. 377; Papers IV, No. 2184

to add to the German difficulties the sun came out and the Allied air forces could again go into action. On Christmas Day First Army re-established communication with all its units. Montgomery was confident that with some minor withdrawals the line could be held but he was worried about the American replacement situation. He did not know that as a result of Eisenhower's immediate reaction 17,000 reinforcements for First and Third Armies were promised by the end of December. Apart from what had come over from American camps in Britain every effort had been made to scrape together all infantrymen from administrative and base units. In addition the flow from the United States had been accelerated and administrative units everywhere made responsible for their own protection.

On Christmas Day Montgomery and Bradley met. Bradley thought that Montgomery showed too defensive an attitude and he did not agree with the further shortening of the line that he had ordered. As a consequence he asked Eisenhower to let him have his two armies back under his command, and to facilitate this he proposed to move his headquarters from Luxembourg to Namur. Eisenhower did not agree; he insisted that the command should remain unchanged for the time being. He also ordered Devers to make some limited withdrawals on the Vosges front so as to free two or three divisions for the reserve.

Unknown to the Allies Rundstedt realised that he could do no more and that he ought to pull back from the salient to a line through St Vith. Hitler did not agree; he wanted the Allies pushed to the Meuse and he wanted a further effort to capture Bastogne. He also pressed for a new attack in the Vosges to take advantage of the thinning out that had taken place there.

On 28 December Eisenhower went forward to see Montgomery. He made full notes of their conversation at the time. Montgomery thought that Rundstedt would make one more effort in the north. Eisenhower was prepared to wait for this attack but believed that if it did not come by 1 January Montgomery ought to begin his attack. Eisenhower emphasised that the Germans must not be allowed to push in infantry to take over from his armour and so provide for a reserve to regain the initiative. He believed that the enemy must be broken while he was still out in the open.[5] Eisenhower thought that Montgomery agreed and that on 1 January he would drive south to cut the base of the salient including in his attacking

5 Papers IV, No. 2206

force XXX British Corps, so far not committed, while Bradley came in from the south. However, on 30 December de Guingand arrived at Eisenhower's headquarters to say that Montgomery would attack on 3 January. He believed that the Germans were exhausting themselves in the salient and that nothing would be worse than an ill-prepared offensive. Eisenhower was furious at the postponement. Hodges and Collins, commander of VII U.S. Corps, had been trying for some days to convince Montgomery that the moment for attack had come. Eisenhower was very sore with Montgomery on another point, a letter on command that he had just received which will be discussed below. Eisenhower said subsequently that he was so angry that he sat down and prepared a note asking Marshall to request Churchill or Brooke to relieve Montgomery.[6] De Guingand was, as usual, a most effective peacemaker but he warned Eisenhower that on the timing of the attack it was most unlikely that Montgomery would change his mind. He returned next day to confirm that this was so.

Montgomery had chosen the very moment when Eisenhower was impatient with him about the attack from the north to raise again the question of command of future operations. On the day after Eisenhower had visited him to urge an attack not later than 1 January Montgomery wrote to him saying that previous command arrangements had not worked and that for the coming operations to capture the Ruhr it would not be enough merely to have co-ordination. He went on: 'The person designated by you must have powers of operational direction and control of the operations that will follow your directive. . . . After the battle is joined one commander must have powers to direct and control the operations; you cannot possibly do it yourself. . . . I suggest that your directive should finish with this sentence "From now onwards full operational direction, control, and co-ordination of these operations is vested in the C-in-C, 21 Army Group, subject to such instructions as may be issued by the Supreme Commander from time to time".'[7] Montgomery no doubt believed, surely wrongly, that the placing of two American armies under his command in an operational emergency was a confession of Eisenhower's own and Bradley's failure in command.

There was no lack of firmness in Eisenhower's reaction but he did not let his anger affect his judgment. He did not disturb the existing command

[6] Ambrose, *The Supreme Command*, p. 573; John S. Eisenhower, *The Bitter Woods*, p. 383
[7] Montgomery, *op. cit.*, p. 318

arrangements and he undertook to leave with Montgomery one American Army, the Ninth, after the closing of the Ardennes battle. But he made it clear that he wanted the Ardennes salient reduced by immediate attacks from north and south. He told Montgomery: 'Enemy action within the salient indicates his determination to make this battle an all-out effort with his mobile forces. *Therefore we must be prepared to use everything consistent with minimum security requirements to accomplish their destruction.*'[8] In the same message he said that as soon as the armies linked up again Bradley would resume command of First Army. Then the two army groups were to revert to the original plans for the destruction of the enemy forces west of the Rhine with a view to forcing a crossing over the river. The main effort would be made north of the Ruhr by 21st Army Group with Ninth U.S. Army under command. This formal instruction was accomplished by a personal letter to Montgomery explaining that these were the same instructions as Eisenhower had given on 28 December and adding: 'You know how greatly I've appreciated and depended upon your frank and friendly counsel, but in your latest letter you disturb me by predictions of "failure" unless your exact opinions in the matter of giving you command over Bradley are met in detail. I assure you that in this matter I can go no further. . . . I know your loyalty as a soldier and your readiness to devote yourself to assigned tasks. For my part I would deplore the development of such an unbridgeable gulf of convictions between us that we should have to present our differences to the CC/S. The confusion and debate that would follow would certainly damage the good will and devotion to a common cause that have made the Allied Force unique in history.'[9] In addition to this letter de Guingand was able to convey to Montgomery something of Eisenhower's anger both at the reopening of the command question and the delay in the counter-attack. De Guingand also said that both Eisenhower and Bedell Smith were more worried than he had ever seen them. Montgomery saw that he had gone too far and he immediately signalled to Eisenhower telling him that whatever his decisions he would do everything to make them work.[10]

At this time Eisenhower was subject to a good deal of criticism in the British press but he got the strongest support from where it was most welcome. Both Churchill and Marshall again sent special messages of

[8] Papers IV, No. 2211
[9] Papers IV, No. 2210
[10] Montgomery, *op. cit.*, p. 322; De Guingand, *op. cit.*, pp. 434-5; and *Generals at War*, pp. 107-12

confidence in him. Marshall had been disturbed by predictions that Eisenhower would have to leave all United States forces north of the Ardennes under Montgomery. In expressing complete confidence in Eisenhower's command he told him that his own feeling was that no concession of any kind should be made and that there would be strong national reactions to leaving American forces under Montgomery. Montgomery too realised that the British press was being unjust to Eisenhower and Bradley and he decided to do what he described as 'put the record straight'. But unhappily, in talking to the press, Montgomery did not always show the same caution and skill as he did in battle, and the result of what he said was to make matters far worse. Eisenhower subsequently said that that press conference caused him more distress than any similar event in the war.[11] Montgomery has published the text of the notes on which he based his talk and has admitted that it was a mistake to hold the conference.[12] He meant to, and did, give full credit to the part the American soldier had played in the battle. The *New York Times* giving a dispassionate account of the conference said: 'No more handsome tribute was ever paid to the American soldier than that of Field Marshal Montgomery in the midst of battle.'[13] But the battle was painted entirely as Montgomery's own and the impression given that he had saved the Americans. The fact that few British troops had actually been committed was obscured, as was the fact that the situation on both flanks had been restored by American troops fighting under their own army commanders. Patton's feelings can be imagined and the more modest and phlegmatic Bradley was so angry that he went to Eisenhower to ask what he intended to do and to make clear that he would never again be willing to serve under Montgomery. Deeply as Eisenhower felt in the matter his judgment was not affected. He was still the Allied commander; he chided Bradley for his attitude[14] and he still left both American armies under Montgomery's command while operations so demanded.

In an attempt to regain the initiative in the Ardennes battle, Patton had begun his attack on 22 December and on 3 January Montgomery had set First Army in action. Both made the preliminary progress necessary for the full-scale co-ordinated attack and for this Montgomery and Bradley issued orders on 10 January. The attack was launched on the 13th, first to join

[11] *Crusade in Europe*, p. 389
[12] Montgomery, *op. cit.*, pp. 311–14
[13] *New York Times*, 9 January 1945
[14] Bradley, *op. cit.*, p. 487

up the divided portions of First Army and then to cut the enemy's lateral communications running south from St Vith. The Germans fought stubbornly but Rundstedt had already warned Hitler that there was no further prospect of success and on 8 January Hitler had authorised limited withdrawal. On 12 January the Russian offensive in the east had begun and a week later Hitler ordered the transfer of Sixth Panzer Army to the east. By the 17th the link up of the First Army had been achieved and its command was restored to Bradley. By the 28th all the ground lost in the Ardennes had been regained.

The importance of the Russian offensive and its effect on his offensive in the Rhineland were prominent in Eisenhower's mind at this time. In early January he had received a most secret personal message from Churchill which told him of the Prime Minister's exchanges with Stalin. Eisenhower had had permission from the Combined Chiefs of Staff to send Tedder to Moscow because no information of any importance was coming through normal liaison channels. Tedder's departure was held up by bad weather and Churchill, after consultation with Eisenhower, had decided to see what information he could get by personal approach to Stalin. Stalin responded generously. He said that the weather was at that time unfavourable for the Russian offensive but in view of the position on the western front large-scale operations along the whole central front would begin irrespective of weather conditions not later than the second half of January.[15] On the strength of that statement the Russians later claimed that their offensive had enabled the western Allies to defeat the Ardennes offensive. Tedder was dealing with matters further ahead and informed Stalin that Eisenhower's interest was in the Russian ability to engage the Germans from mid-March until late May when his own offensive would be at its height. Stalin was not sure that a full-scale offensive could be maintained for so long, but he believed that he could prevent the enemy from moving troops from the east to the west. Stalin thought the Germans showed more determination than intelligence and that their Ardennes offensive had been a mistake. Nevertheless he did not foresee the end of the war until the summer. Tedder's meeting with Stalin was acknowledged to be one of the most fruitful exchanges between the west and Russia of the whole war. The direct military approach had been more effective with Stalin than any number of diplomatic niceties.[16]

[15] Churchill, op. cit., VI, pp. 242–4
[16] Pogue, op. cit., pp. 406–7; Tedder, op. cit., pp. 646–51

Perhaps this was to have an effect on Eisenhower's subsequent dealings with the Soviet Union.

Eisenhower's efforts during the Ardennes battle to thin out on all other parts of the front in order to strengthen forces for his own counter-attacks led to some difficulties in Alsace. He ordered Devers to provide a corps of two divisions for this purpose even if it meant he had to draw back to a suitable defensive line along the Vosges. At the same time as these orders were given it became apparent that the Germans were preparing for a second offensive this time to regain Alsace and part of Lorraine. Eisenhower had hoped that the First French Army, part of Dever's group, would have been able to eliminate the pocket of enemy resistance at Colmar and then take over the whole defence of Alsace-Lorraine. But the Colmar pocket held out and the American Seventh Army was still engaged in Lorraine and north Alsace, including support for the French garrison of Strasbourg. Devers could only carry out Eisenhower's orders by withdrawing from Strasbourg and taking up a defensive line in the Vosges further back. The French commanders on the spot protested about the withdrawal and de Gaulle felt so strongly on the subject that he threatened to withdraw the French forces from Eisenhower's command. Eisenhower looked at the question from a purely military pont of view. He had to be prepared to give up ground to take up a firm position if he were to create an effective reserve. But he sensed that de Gaulle was not being unreasonable and that the loss of Strasbourg might undermine de Gaulle's hold over France and so lead to insecurity in the whole country. He therefore gave in and cancelled his orders to Devers.

It might be supposed that having brought the Ardennes battle to a close, having made peace with Montgomery and de Gaulle and having succeeded in overtures to Stalin, Eisenhower would be left in peace to carry on the war. It was not to be. The British Chiefs of Staff chose this moment to take up the debate on command which Eisenhower had effectively closed with Montgomery. Both in an exchange with the Joint Chiefs and by personal approach from Churchill to Roosevelt, the British made it clear that they were not happy about the command situation. The Americans were furious at the reopening of a question which they thought had been properly settled by the commanders concerned.[17] Eisenhower was quite certain that the Ruhr would be a natural dividing line between army groups and that there was no way in which a land forces commander

[17] Ehrman, *op. cit.*, VI, pp. 89–90

could better co-ordinate army groups than could the Supreme Commander himself. A moment's consideration of the military problem will show that Eisenhower was right. It could hardly be supposed that a new command, with all the enormities of staff and communications involved, could be interposed between army groups and Supreme Headquarters. If Montgomery or Bradley were to take over the control of land operations were they to do so as well as command their own army group? The analogy of Montgomery in the Beachhead and Alexander in Italy was absurd. Each of them had been in effect an army group commander with two armies under command. The solution that a deputy at Eisenhower's own headquarters, and using his own staff, might command is equally absurd. He would either be a deputy and work in Eisenhower's name and on his commands or he would make Eisenhower a cipher.

In order to ease the situation with the British, Eisenhower did suggest that it would be a suitable moment to substitute Alexander for Tedder as his deputy. Such a change would be in keeping with the changed emphasis of land and air operations in Eisenhower's command. It also coincided with Churchill's own idea. But Eisenhower made it clear that if Alexander did come to him it must be as Deputy and not as Land Forces Commander, or even as 'Deputy for Land Operations'.[18] The Chiefs of Staff did take up the idea of substituting Alexander for Tedder and in fact decided on this change. By this time Montgomery had agreed with Eisenhower that the existing command structure was right and had asserted to him 'that any thought of an intermediate ground commander, or of any interference with the clear line of authority extending from [Eisenhower] to him, should be carefully avoided.'[19] Eisenhower made the situation clear to Brooke when he explained that he would certainly have no objection to Alexander's appointment but that the appointment must be made in the knowledge that there would be no fundamental change in the command structure or the role of the Deputy.[20] Churchill wrongly took this to be an indication that Alexander would be excluded from the intimate family relationship that had always been a feature of Eisenhower's headquarters. Eisenhower thereupon wrote to Churchill to explain that no one would be more welcome at his headquarters than Alexander, but that he did not want him to be appointed with any misunderstanding of the role of the Deputy

[18] Papers IV, Nos. 2233 & 2235
[19] Papers IV, No. 2284
[20] Papers IV, No. 2284

Commander. Such a course might 'compel public announcements that would injure Alexander's feelings'.[21] The Chiefs of Staff, faced with the knowledge that Alexander would in no sense become the executive land force commander, decided to leave matters as they were.

[21] Papers IV, No. 2294

14

The End of the Battle for Germany

Before the German attack in the Ardennes had begun the Allies had been posed for their Rhineland attacks, and by the end of December Eisenhower was able to turn his mind once more to this operation. He was not prepared to put his whole weight into the advance north of the Ruhr although he fully realised the importance of this thrust and intended to leave Ninth U.S. Army under Montgomery for it. He also wanted Bradley with First and Third Armies to strike south of the Ruhr from Bonn. Brooke was not inclined to accept Eisenhower's view but wanted to continue the argument which Eisenhower had already had with Montgomery. Accordingly the Chiefs of Staff asked that Eisenhower should submit his proposals for a review by the Combined Chiefs of Staff at the end of January.

One of Brooke's fears was that Eisenhower's broad front strategy would prolong the war unnecessarily: every day the war went on increased the almost unbearable strain on the British economy. There was something of a suggestion that Eisenhower showed a lack of urgency and that his inexperience had already thrown away an opportunity to finish the war in 1944.[1] Such an attitude is difficult to understand if the Allied expectations before Overlord are remembered. There can have been few in high positions—certainly not Churchill or Brooke—who believed that the defeat of the Germans could be achieved in 1944.

The real difference between the British and Eisenhower's view was that Brooke was looking for a quick advance across the Rhine and foresaw the major battle the other side because the Germans were bound to fight to prevent the heart of Germany being separated from the Ruhr. Eisenhower believed that Hitler would never allow his commanders to fight a fluid battle of that nature. The Allies would have to contest every yard up to the Rhine and in the destruction of the German Army in the Rhineland lay the key to Allied success. Out of this difference came Brooke's belief that the priority which Eisenhower accorded to the northern thrust was an empty

[1] Bryant, *op. cit.*, II, pp. 378-9

32 *De Gaulle expounds*

33 *De Gaulle presenting Eisenhower with one of Napoleon's swords—a gift which Eisenhower later presented to France*

34 *With Churchill, May 1945*

35 *Eisenhower, having been given the Freedom of the City of London, is greeted by Churchill*

pronouncement and that his orders for Bradley's advance did not accord with that priority. Eisenhower's answer to that criticism was that Montgomery had told him that only 25 divisions could be maintained north of the Ruhr. Eisenhower had insisted that at least 35 would be required and told his staff that means to support that number must be devised.[2] This decision meant that Eisenhower was prepared to support Montgomery with more American divisions than the total of British and Canadian divisions in 21st Army Group.

One of the reasons why Eisenhower attached great importance to closing up to the Rhine along the whole front was the desire to get to a firm defensive line. Unless he did that, he would not be able to thin out in some areas to provide the preponderant forces for the advance deep into Germany and he would be subject to the dangers of counter-action such as he had already met in the Ardennes and Alsace. Notwithstanding this factor Eisenhower was not only aware but constantly affirmed that the nature of the ground, the communications and the important objectives all pointed to the fact that the main attack must be made in the north.[3] But looking ahead he saw the situation that would face him when the armies got across the Rhine. The Ruhr was an effective barrier through which no attempt to advance would be made. By closing up to the Rhine along almost the whole front he would have a choice of the most suitable area in which to develop his supporting attacks. It seemed to him that the country opposite Cologne and Bonn would be difficult and that a more effective line to join up with the northern advance would be through Frankfurt to Kassel.

Eisenhower welcomed the review by the Combined Chiefs of Staff of his projected operations and he put forward his ideas in two very full telegrams to Marshall.[4] The discussion took place on 30 January at Malta, where the Combined Chiefs met before going on to join their political heads and the Russians at Yalta. Eisenhower's views were presented by Bedell Smith. The Chiefs of Staff were not satisfied. They feared Eisenhower would not cross the Rhine in the north until the enemy was completely cleared from the west bank of the Rhine. On Marshall's instructions Bedell Smith wired to Eisenhower for his remarks. Eisenhower replied: 'You may assure the Combined Chiefs of Staff in my name that I will seize the Rhine crossings in the north just as soon as this is a feasible

[2] Papers IV, No. 2232
[3] Papers IV, No. 2233
[4] Papers IV, Nos. 2232–3

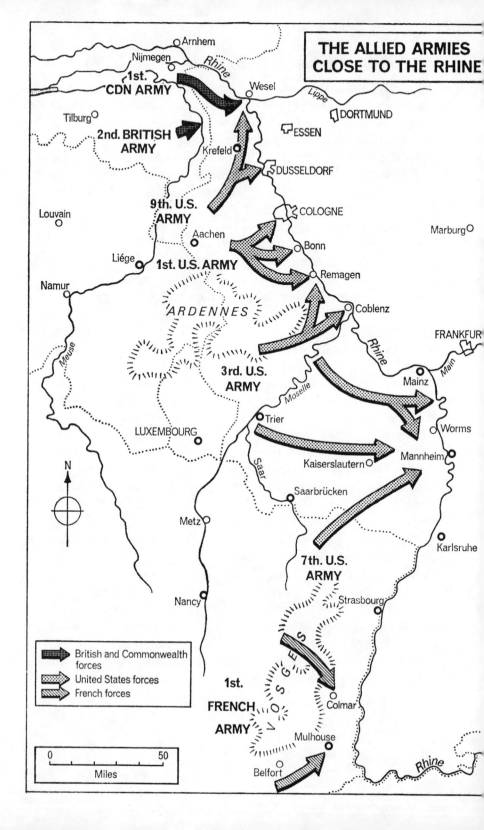

THE ALLIED ARMIES
CLOSE TO THE RHINE

Arnhem

Nijmegen

Rhine

1st.
CDN ARMY

Wesel

Lippe

DORTMUND

Tilburg

2nd. BRITISH
ARMY

ESSEN

Krefeld

DUSSELDORF

Louvain

9th. U.S.
ARMY

COLOGNE

Marburg

Aachen

Bonn

Liége

1st. U.S. ARMY

Remagen

Namur

Coblenz

ARDENNES

FRANKFUR

Rhine

Meuse

3rd. U.S.
ARMY

Main

Mainz

Moselle

LUXEMBOURG

Trier

Worms

Saar

Kaiserslautern

Mannheim

Saarbrücken

Metz

Karlsruhe

N

7th. U.S.
ARMY

Nancy

Strasbourg

V O S G E S

1st.

FRENCH

Colmar

British and Commonwealth
forces

United States forces

French forces

ARMY

Mulhouse

0   50

Miles

Belfort

Rhine

operation and without waiting to close the Rhine throughout its length. Further, I will advance across the Rhine in the north with maximum strength and complete determination immediately the situation in the south allows me to collect necessary forces and do this without incurring unreasonable risks.'[5]

The reference in Eisenhower's signal to the south and to collecting forces makes it worth while examining what he did to make the priority to the north effective. He demanded that 35 divisions should be maintained in the northern front. In Montgomery's British and Canadian armies there were 15 divisions plus two airborne divisions. Montgomery asked that Simpson's Ninth Army, which by the end of the Ardennes campaign had only five divisions, should be brought up to a strength of 16 divisions. Eisenhower was willing to bring it up only to 12 and the additional seven divisions were not forthcoming until Bradley had completed his operations to clear the enemy up to the West Wall beyond Roermond. It was not until 1 February that Bradley gave the orders for these divisions to join Ninth Army, which was due to begin its attack on the 10th. Bradley did not then go on to the defensive but, without specifically letting Eisenhower know, although as he says within the spirit of his instructions, permitted Patton to go on with limited attacks north of the Moselle.[6]

Bradley's action is important because, as can be seen above, the divisions under Montgomery's direct control numbered only 29. The remaining strength of the northern thrust was to be made up by operations under Bradley to protect the right flank of Ninth Army. A preliminary attack entrusted to Bradley was to capture the Roer dams and so remove the possibility of the Germans flooding the Roer valley. Bradley's attack went in as arranged but before the capture of the dams the Germans had released the waters. In consequence flooding delayed the Ninth Army attack for about a fortnight.

Despite the postponements of Simpson's attack, Montgomery's main attack by Crerar's First Canadian Army (ten British and three Canadian divisions) went in as planned on 8 February. The ensuing battle was one of the hardest fought of the war. Over difficult country and in terrible weather Crerar's army battered its way between the Meuse and the Rhine towards Wesel. It was an August 1918 type of battle; an infantry battle with overwhelming artillery support, modern air support and

[5] Papers IV, No. 2268
[6] Pogue, *op. cit.*, pp. 417–18; Bradley, *op. cit.*, p. 501

every type of armoured fighting vehicle added, even amphibians to cross the floods. The Allies were to get some advantage from the delay in Simpson's attack. The Germans were deeply engaged with the relentless blows of 21st Army Group just at the moment when Ninth Army thrust right through them to the Rhine opposite Wesel. This battle cost the Germans some 90,000 men[7] and considerably affected the German ability to offer effective resistance on the far side of the Rhine. It was one of Montgomery's greatest battles, and by brilliant manipulation of his army and corps headquarters and by sound administrative foresight and effort he was ready almost immediately to stage a major crossing of the Rhine. This phase of the battle was to be commanded by Dempsey and was planned to begin two weeks after reaching the Rhine.

While the Rhineland battle was going on Bradley's armies had to take second place. First Army was fully engaged in securing the right flank of Ninth Army but Patton was screaming to be let loose for a break-out such as he had achieved in Normandy. As required by Eisenhower, Bradley restrained him for the moment. In early March when Crerar and Simpson had linked up and had a secure footing on the west bank of the Rhine, Bradley began to clear Cologne. From there he began to sweep the whole area up to the junction of the Moselle with the Rhine. It hardly seemed possible that a crossing could be bounced over the Rhine but that is what happened. By a stroke of good fortune armoured elements of First (U.S.) Army arrived at the railway bridge at Remagen while the German destruction parties were still waiting for the last German parties to cross. The opportunity was not allowed to slip and, although some charges were blown and the bridge partially destroyed, a bridgehead was secured. When he heard the news Bradley ordered that everything possible should be got across to exploit this unexpected success. Bradley reported his action to Eisenhower who enthusiastically endorsed it. In reporting the crossing to the Combined Chiefs of Staff, Eisenhower said Bradley's action would be a most effective supporting effort for the main attack in the north. South of Remagen, Patton was in action up to the Moselle, while Devers, with his Army Group of American and French troops, cleared the Saar triangle.

By 21 March Eisenhower had not only achieved his aim of clearing up to the Rhine but he had taken advantage of Hitler's refusal to give ground and had dealt a blow from which the German Army could not recover. In the

[7] Ellis, *op. cit.*, II, p. 277

series of Rhineland battles the Germans lost some 250,000 prisoners and altogether their losses amounted to the equivalent of 20 full divisions.[8] In a last attempt to retrieve his fortunes in the west Hitler dismissed Rundstedt and brought Kesselring from Italy to take his place.

When Patton had reached the Rhine he had not stopped but in the early hours of 23 March made a successful assault crossing of the river just south of Mainz. He was, as always, ready to steal a march on Montgomery and had six battalions across just one day ahead of Montgomery's massive operation in the north. For that Eisenhower was present and he watched the British and American airborne assault on 21st Army Group front.

The Germans had been too heavily defeated to be able to offer effective resistance on the line of the river and Montgomery's two armies, Second British and Ninth (U.S.), achieved overwhelming success. First Canadian Army was soon set free for the much needed relief of the Northern Netherlands. On the second day of the battle Eisenhower, Churchill and Brooke met together on the far side of the Rhine. Brooke congratulated Eisenhower on his success. There is some difference in the memory of the two men about what was said. Eisenhower believed that Brooke confessed that Eisenhower's policy for the Rhineland battles had been right and thanked God that Eisenhower had stuck to his guns. This is confirmed by Gault who was with Eisenhower and had it from him immediately and also by what Eisenhower wrote on the next day to Marshall. On the other hand Brooke, writing in the 1950s, said that he still believed that Eisenhower's strategy was wrong and that his congratulations, hearty and sincere though they were, expressed the thought that 'with the Germans in their defeated condition, no dangers now existed in a dispersal o effort'.[9] There are certainly differences in emphasis in these accounts but it is clear that Brooke saw that the severity of the German defeat west of the Rhine had put final victory beyond doubt. That defeat was what Eisenhower had set out to achieve.

All the Allied armies were quick to exploit the crossings of the Rhine. North of the Ruhr, Second British and Ninth U.S. Armies pressed rapidly eastwards while First Canadian Army went into North Holland. South of the Ruhr First U.S. Army from Remagen and Third U.S. Army from south of Mainz made converging attacks against crumbling resistance. On

[8] Pogue, *op. cit.*, p. 427
[9] Bryant, *op. cit.*, II, pp. 436–7; *Crusade in Europe*, p. 407; Papers II, No. 2355; Letter Sir James Gault to author November 1971

GERMANY

BALTIC
SEA

NORTH SEA

Lübeck • • Wismar
Stade • • Hamburg
Stettin

• Bremen   Elbe   Oder

Amsterdam •   • Celle   • BERLIN
Rotterdam •   Minden •   Hanover
    Arnhem   Magdeburg •
    Nijmegen   Wittenberg
        Wesel
Antwerp •   RUHR   Paderborn •   Weser
    Roermond   Ruhr
• Ghent   Düsseldorf   Kassel •   Leipzig   Dresden
Brussels   Cologne   Erfurt •   Elster
Liège • • Aachen   Bonn
    Meuse   Remagen •   Meiningen   Karlsbad
ARDENNES   Frankfurt •   Prague •
        Moselle   Main   Bayreuth   Pilsen •
LUXEM-   Mainz Main
BOURG   Mannheim   • Nuremberg   BÖHMER WALD
    SAAR
Metz •   Saarbrücken •   Regensburg
        Karlsruhe   Danube   Linz
Strasbourg •   • Stuttgart
    Rhine   Neckar
    WURTTEMBERG   Augsburg   • Munich

FRANCE   Basel   Berchtesgaden

• Dijon   AUSTRIA

SWITZERLAND   TYROL

NETHERLANDS

BELGIUM

Maas

Ems

Aller

Leine

Weser

Saale

CZECHOSLOVAKIA

Vltava

Meuse

Rhine

Rhine

ITALY

West Wall

0 10   50   100
                miles

1 April the two army groups, Montgomery's and Bradley's, made contact with each other east of the Ruhr. The Germans were also assailed on other fronts. Since early February the Russians had had a bridgehead across the Oder, only 30 miles from Berlin, although they had made little progress since. In Italy Alexander was in process of dealing the final blow which resulted in the destruction of Vietinghoff's army group in the Po valley. Clearly the Germans were defeated and it was only a question of the final rounding up of their forces and the imposition of surrender on their government. In this situation political considerations became more important than military. But effective as the politico-military machinery of the western Allies normally was, it was quite incapable of dealing with events at the pace at which they now unfolded. Telegraphic exchanges were necessary between the British and American Chiefs of Staff to resolve differences before they could speak with one voice at the Combined Chiefs of Staff. The close rapport which existed between Churchill and Roosevelt could no longer serve because Roosevelt was on the point of death. The time was at hand when Eisenhower would have to take decisions which would have far reaching political results. If there was time to consult anyone it would be Marshall to whom he would first turn, as was his wont.

There was one political factor which made for stability in this otherwise fluid phase: the agreement which had already been reached on eventual Allied zones of occupation of Germany. Churchill, Roosevelt and Stalin had formally accepted the delineation of these zones at Yalta in February 1945. There had been no wrangling over the zones and this was certainly not an occasion on which Stalin had wrung the last pound of flesh from his allies. The zones agreed were those which had been suggested by British political representatives in January 1944 and discussed from time to time by British, American and Soviet political committees. The only difference in boundaries suggested by the British and those used after the war was that France was given a zone carved from the British and American zones.[10] Eisenhower had had an opportunity to discuss the zones before 'D' Day. He was of the opinion that the British and American zones should be left as one and their occupying forces left under a supreme Allied commander, but his advice was not taken.[11] There is no evidence that Eisenhower expressed any view on the possible dividing line with the Soviet forces up to the time his forces crossed the Rhine.

[10] Pogue, *op. cit.*, pp. 463–4
[11] *Ibid.*, pp. 349–50

Churchill, Brooke and Montgomery had all presumed that Montgomery, with the Ninth U.S. Army still under his command, would be left to race along the north German plain for Berlin, but other ideas were gradually developing in Eisenhower's mind. In the days of the Rhineland battles he had been working out with his staff how he might direct operations after the crossing had been achieved. He had in mind the possibility of a large-scale airborne operation deep in Germany at the beginning of May, using seven to ten divisions. Looking closer in he thought it might be necessary to alter the grouping of his armies. 21st Army Group might have to have the primary task of clearing the Netherlands, while Bradley with Ninth and First U.S. Armies advanced north of the Ruhr. Then Devers would take over Third Army and his army group would thrust north-east from Mainz and Frankfurt.[12] As the extent of the success of the Rhineland battles became apparent Eisenhower changed his mind. It would not be necessary to use the whole of 21st Army Group in Holland and he believed that he had put as much into his northern thrust as could be maintained east of the Rhine. He was much impressed by the dash displayed by First and Third U.S. Armies, each of which had secured a bridgehead over the Rhine very cheaply, and he saw the opportunity of widening the base of operations. On 24 March, the day of Montgomery's Rhine crossing and after he had seen Montgomery, he told the Combined Chiefs of Staff that the situation offered opportunities that must be seized boldly and that he had in mind a major thrust from the south that would assist the northern operations.[13] As often before he was attracted by the idea of an advance from the Saar towards Kassel and he was now thinking beyond Kassel to Leipzig and Dresden.

On 28 March Eisenhower told Montgomery that Ninth Army would revert to Bradley's command as soon as he had gained contact with Bradley east of the Ruhr. For the first time he disclosed his thoughts about Leipzig and Dresden and he gave Montgomery the role of protecting Bradley's northern flank. He said that after reaching the Elbe it might be necessary to put Ninth Army back under Montgomery's control but for the present there was no doubt that the priority between Montgomery and Bradley had been reversed. Montgomery's advance was now subsidiary to Bradley's.[14]

[12] Papers IV, Nos. 2332, 2347–8
[13] Papers IV, No. 2351
[14] Papers IV, No. 2364

In his message to Montgomery Eisenhower said that he was co-ordinating his plans with Stalin and on the same day he sent a message through the Military Mission in Moscow to Stalin himself. It may be wondered how Eisenhower had come to make this direct approach without consulting the Combined Chiefs of Staff. The fluid situation has already been mentioned as has the success of Eisenhower's previous direct contact with Stalin, although that was with permission of the Combined Chiefs of Staff and after political consultation. On this occasion the nearest approach to political consultation occurred when Churchill and Roosevelt met on the Rhine and Churchill told Eisenhower of Russia's suspicion that the British and Americans were negotiating behind Russia's back for German surrender. Churchill said that Eisenhower was angry at this unjust accusation and had confessed that if there were any opportunity he would accept the unconditional surrender of any body of troops in the field. He thought that political consultation on such a matter would prolong for three or four weeks what he could do in an hour. Churchill agreed that such matters should be left to Eisenhower's discretion but there was no suggestion of a direct approach from Eisenhower to Stalin.

In his message Eisenhower told Stalin his future intentions. He said that his immediate aim was to encircle the German forces in the Ruhr and to cut off the Ruhr from the rest of Germany. He hoped to do this by 1 April and his object would then be to divide the enemy forces by joining hands with the Russians. For this purpose the axis of his main effort would be through Leipzig and Dresden, and a subsidiary advance would also be made to effect a junction in the Regensburg-Linz area. Eisenhower's last two paragraphs read:

> Before deciding firmly on my future plans, I think it most important that they should be co-ordinated with yours both as to direction and timing. Could you, therefore, tell me your intentions, and let me know how far the proposed operations outlined in this message conform to your probable action.
> If we are to complete the destruction of the German armies without delay, I regard it as essential that we co-ordinate our action and make every effort to perfect the liaison between our advancing forces. I am prepared to send officers to you for this purpose.[15]

A copy of this message was sent to the Combined Chiefs of Staff.

It will be noted that Eisenhower said nothing about Berlin, nor about halting on the Elbe, which broadly speaking served as the dividing line

[15] Papers IV, No. 2363

between the agreed zones of eventual Soviet and Western occupation. Stalin very soon replied to Eisenhower. He agreed with the proposed plan and the areas for linking up. He did mention Berlin. He said that Berlin had lost its former strategic importance and that the Soviet High Command had decided to send only secondary forces in that direction.

Churchill and the Chiefs of Staff were not as pleased as Stalin was at Eisenhower's message. It seemed to them that Eisenhower had gone far outside his proper sphere by sending a personal message to Stalin. It was, to them, the same as if some Russian commander had sent a personal message to Roosevelt or Churchill asking about Alexander's intentions in the Italian campaign. Moreover, whatever the means of communication, they disagreed with Eisenhower's expressed intentions. The Chiefs of Staff believed that northern Germany was not getting the attention it required. To them it seemed imperative to prevent a renewal of the submarine threat. Accordingly they were anxious that the ports of northern Germany should be captured quickly, that forces be got into Denmark to control the Baltic and the possibility of liberating Norway opened up. They said to Washington: 'The emphasis placed by General Eisenhower on the main thrust on an axis Kassel—Leipzig—Dresden causes us much concern. We are forced to doubt whether there has been sufficient appreciation of issues which have a wider import than the destruction of the main enemy forces in Germany.'[16]

Churchill was quick to see that in the light of the severe defeat inflicted on the German Army, the Chiefs of Staff exaggerated the importance of these wider matters. He himself took a more realistic view of Eisenhower's decision. He reminded the Chiefs of Staff that the British had only a quarter of the troops employed in the fighting in Germany and that they could not regard the situation as in any way the same as it had been in June. He pointed out how high Eisenhower's credit now stood with the Joint Chiefs of Staff because he had proved his strategy by deeds in closing up to the Rhine along its whole length and by his ability to make the double advance instead of staking all on the northern advance. He went on: 'These events, combined with the continued arrival of American reinforcements, have greatly enhanced Eisenhower's power and prestige, and the Americans will feel that, as the victorious Supreme Commander, he has a right, and indeed a vital need, to try to elicit from the Russians their views as to the best points for making contact by the armies of the

[16] Ehrman, op. cit., VI, p. 135

West and of the East.'[17] He also thought that the use of the phrase about issues with a wider import than the destruction of the main enemy forces laid the Chiefs of Staff 'open to a charge of extreme unorthodoxy'.

However, Churchill was strongly critical of Eisenhower, but for another reason. He thought Eisenhower was wrong to shift the main axis of advance from Berlin to Leipzig and Dresden, and in supposing Berlin to have lost its military and political importance. He said: 'The idea of neglecting Berlin and leaving it to the Russians to take at a later stage does not appear to me to be correct. As long as Berlin holds out and withstands a siege in the ruins, as it may easily do, German resistance will be stimulated. The fall of Berlin might cause nearly all Germans to despair.'[18]

At the same time as they got the views of the Prime Minister, the Chiefs of Staff received the reply from Washington. The Joint Chiefs of Staff disagreed completely with their British counterpart. They believed that Eisenhower's consultation with the Soviet was an operational necessity in view of the rapidity of his advance into Germany, and they considered that he should remain free 'to communicate with the Commander-in-Chief of the Soviet Army'. The Joint Chiefs did not argue about the merits of Eisenhower's strategy except to take up the point which Churchill had described as 'extreme unorthodoxy'. They believed that if Eisenhower achieved his primary aim of destroying the German Army everything desired by the Chiefs of Staff would be accomplished far more quickly than by direct pursuit of dispersed aims. It is ironic that the British, who had so often blamed Eisenhower for a failure to concentrate on a single aim, were now being soundly beaten by the Americans with the same stick. The point, however, on which the Joint Chiefs of Staff felt most strongly was that Eisenhower must be left free to make his own operational decisions. 'The battle of Germany', they said, 'is now at the point where the Commander in the Field is the best judge of the measures which offer the earliest prospect of destroying the German Armies or their power to resist.'[19]

Eisenhower himself elaborated his view in two signals to Churchill and another to the Chiefs of Staff. In each of them he emphasised that his aim must be 'to divide and destroy the main German force, as when that is achieved the rest will follow'. By using his main weight in the Leipzig

Churchill, *op. cit.*, VI, pp. 403-4; Ehrman, *op. cit.*, VI, p. 135
[18] *Ibid.*, p. 403; *Ibid.*, pp. 135-7
[19] Quoted in Ehrman, *op. cit.*, VI, pp. 139-40

area he would retain the flexibility which would enable him then to turn to the north or south as the situation developed. It looked to him as if Montgomery would be able to get to the Elbe with his own resources and later, for the crossing of the Elbe and an advance at least to Lubeck, he would be reinforced as necessary by American troops. He thought that the principal importance of the southern area lay in the fact that a junction with the Russians there would prevent the establishment of a Nazi fortress in southern Germany.[20] Eisenhower also signalled Montgomery to the same effect in reply to Montgomery's plea that he might be allowed to keep Ninth Army until he had reached the Elbe. Eisenhower also said: 'You will note that in none of this do I mention Berlin. That place has become, so far as I am concerned, nothing but a geographical location, and I have never been interested in these. My purpose is to destroy the enemy's forces and his power to resist.'[21]

Eisenhower's correspondence with Marshall at this time discloses how he had come to his decision. Just before Eisenhower sent his signals of 28 March to Stalin and to the Combined Chiefs of Staff he had received a signal from Marshall suggesting that, in view of the apparent break in German resistance, he might want to push eastward on a broad front towards Nuremburg—Linz or Munich. Marshall asked Eisenhower what his ideas were about control and co-ordination as his own and the Russian forces approached each other through disintegrating German forces. Marshall said: 'The arrangements we now have with the Russians appear quite inadequate for the situation you may face and it seems that steps ought to be initiated without delay for the communication and liaison you will need with them. . . .' In his reply on that same 28 March Eisenhower said that he put Leipzig—Dresden first but that he agreed on all other points. In telling of his signal to Stalin he said that he did not feel he could tie himself down to a demarcation line but that he would suggest that when the forces met, either side would withdraw to its own occupational zone at the request of the other.[22]

Bradley also had considerable influence on Eisenhower. When the two met after the main Rhine crossing they discussed the future advance. Bradley was anxious as soon as he had mopped up the Ruhr, to speed to the Elbe and then to fan out with two of his armies and send the third

[20] Papers IV, Nos. 2374, 2379, 2381
[21] Papers IV, No. 2778
[22] Papers IV, No. 2365

down the Danube to link up with the Red Army in Austria. Bradley knew that an advance on Berlin would mean leaving Ninth Army with Montgomery and he thought he might have to give more of his divisions to Montgomery. This can hardly have left him unprejudiced. Eisenhower himself described his relations with his senior commanders as dealing with several prima donnas in the same bed. Bradley was conscious that Allied bridgeheads were almost 200 miles from Berlin while Zhukov with more than a million men on the banks of the Oder was only 30 miles from the capital. Even when the Allies reached the Elbe they would still have 50 miles to go, and Bradley reckoned it would cost 100,000 casualties to reach Berlin. In giving this estimate to Eisenhower Bradley said: 'A pretty stiff price to pay for a prestige objective, especially when we've got to fall back and let the other fellow take over.'[23] It must be remembered that this estimate was made, not when the Allies had reached the Elbe, but when they had only just crossed the Rhine.

On 30 March Eisenhower opened his heart to Marshall about the objections which Churchill and the Chiefs of Staff were making. He confessed himself in the dark over the protest on procedure since he had been instructed to deal direct with the Russians on military co-ordination. He said that there had been no change in his basic strategy. He had kept his undertaking to give priority to the northern attack for the isolation of the Ruhr and now it looked as if this were about to be achieved successfully. Even before 'D' Day he had explained to his staff and senior officers that his plan was to link up his various advances in the Kassel area and then make a great thrust eastwards. He thought that even a cursory examination of the problem would show that Leipzig was the best direction for the main thrust. He understood the naval aspects and once the primary thrust had put him into a decisive position he would make the clearance of the northern coast his next aim. Then he would be in a position to thrust south-east to prevent a Nazi occupation of a mountain citadel. He said that he thought Berlin was no longer a particularly important objective because even the government was preparing to move to another area.[24]

Eisenhower never lost sight of the fact that as organized German resistance became impossible, Hitler and the other principal Nazis might gather for a final stand in a national redoubt constructed in a mountain fastness near Berchtesgaden. The fact that the Nazis intended to do so and to

[23] Bradley, *op. cit.*, pp. 531–5; Papers IV, No. 2330
[24] Papers IV, No. 2373

leave their people in the lurch was a constant subject of Allied propaganda. Whether or not Eisenhower was misled by his own propaganda is not certain, but he did allow the possibility to affect his strategy. Strong told him that he was by no means certain that such a redoubt had been constructed but that it was 'possible that some such scheme might be regarded seriously by fanatical Nazis who could not bring themselves to accept the reality of the liquidation of the Third Reich.'[25] British Intelligence discounted the idea and in the outcome Hitler chose to meet his end in Berlin.

On 1 April Churchill sent one of his last messages to Roosevelt. He began with a special expression of his confidence in Eisenhower and 'admiration of the great and shining qualities of character and personality which he has proved himself to possess in all the difficulties of handling an Allied Command.' Churchill also paid tribute to the glorious victories of the American armies in the centre. But he thought that the question of the importance of Berlin was one in which he and Roosevelt should have some say. He repeated his belief that the loss of Berlin would be the supreme signal of defeat to the German people. He said: 'On the other hand if left to itself to maintain a siege by the Russians among its ruins, and as long as the German flag flies there, it will animate the resistance of all Germans under arms.' He also put before the President the thought that the Russians seemed certain to overrun Austria and take Vienna. 'If they also take Berlin will not their impression that they have been the overwhelming contributor to our common victory be unduly imprinted in their minds, and may this not lead them into a mood which will raise grave and formidable difficulties in the future?'[26] But it was too late to appeal to Roosevelt. He had already left Washington never again to return. He died on 12 April. He might have acted on Churchill's pungent appreciation of the political factors. Without him it is certain that the Joint Chiefs of Staff would not be moved from the view they expressed on 6 April: 'Such psychological and political advantages as would result from the possible capture of Berlin ahead of the Russians should not override the imperative military consideration, which in our opinion is the destruction and dismemberment of the German armed forces.'[27] There is no doubt that at this time the Americans were very conscious that Germany

---

[25] Strong, *op. cit.*, p. 188
[26] Churchill, *op. cit.*, VI, pp. 406–7
[27] Quoted in Pogue, *op. cit.*, p. 445

was only one of her enemies and that it then appeared that a large part of the forces in Germany would be required in the Far East before Japan could be defeated. This was not at the moment Eisenhower's concern but, as he himself said in a cable to Marshall: 'I am the first to admit that a war is waged in pursuance of political aims, and if the Combined Chiefs of Staff should decide that the Allied effort to take Berlin outweighs purely military considerations in this theatre, I should cheerfully readjust my plans and my thinking so as to carry out such an operation.'[28] The Combined Chiefs of Staff made no such decision. In fact there is no evidence that the Combined Chiefs ever considered the question, despite Eisenhower's message and Churchill's to Roosevelt, sent on the same day.[29]

The Allied advance went even more quickly than Eisenhower had expected. 21st Army Group crossed the Weser on 9 April and by 16 April were within striking distance of the Elbe. On their right Bradley's armies had reached the Elbe. Simpson, now under his command, had suggested that Ninth Army should be allowed to dash for Berlin but he was told he must hold on the Elbe. Eisenhower, who went to London on 17 April, felt that a continuation of his advance across the Elbe would, for supply reasons alone, prevent the necessary progress on his two flanks. He thought that the Germans might possibly prolong resistance by holding out in Norway and in Bavaria and Austria, where the bogey of the 'National Redoubt' still worried him. If they succeeded the war might not be over before winter made operations in these mountainous areas even more difficult. In the north therefore he wished to secure the Baltic coast as far as Lübeck and in the south to join up with the Russians in the Danube valley. Berlin must take a lower priority than both. In discussion Churchill and the Chiefs of Staff were more inclined to agree with Eisenhower than formerly. With the reduced strength of the northern thrust the competition of Berlin for priority was with Bremen, Hamburg and Lübeck. The importance of these was just as apparent to the Chiefs of Staff as to Eisenhower. Churchill tried again to get Eisenhower to make one decisive effort to capture Berlin but eventually he too agreed with Eisenhower. On 21 April, this time with the agreement of the British Government and the Combined Chiefs of Staff, Eisenhower sent another message to the Soviet High Command, but Stalin was not mentioned by name as in the previous

[28] Papers IV, No. 2401
[29] Pogue, *op. cit.*, p. 446

message. He said that he had decided to halt on the Elbe and explained his plans for the flanks.

From this time forward Eisenhower had the explicit authority of the Combined Chiefs of Staff to work with Moscow on plans for linking up the Allied and Soviet forces. He had complained on 15 April to Marshall that: 'The intervention of the British Chiefs of Staff in my military dealings with the Soviet has thrown quite a monkey-wrench into our speed of communications.' In reply to a message sent after revision demanded by the Chiefs of Staff the Russians had asked whether the message implied an attempt, under the guise of military necessity, to change occupational boundaries already agreed. Eisenhower had gone on: 'Frankly, if I should have forces *in the Russian occupational zone* and be faced with an order or "request" to retire so that they may advance to the points they choose, I see no recourse except to comply.'[30]

Although Eisenhower showed no desire to anticipate the Russians in an area which they would eventually occupy, he was enough of a realist to want to make quite sure that the Russians did not anticipate the Allies in their own zones. The possibility that they might do so at Lübeck caused him some anxiety. He had already made it clear to Montgomery that after reaching the Elbe he would give him the American troops and administrative support necessary to enable him to carry out his role on the northern flank. Later he made sure that both Montgomery and Bradley understood this. Montgomery thought he had sufficient resources and all he wanted was a slight adjustment of his boundary with Bradley. This was made. On 27 April Eisenhower wrote to Brooke emphasising the importance he attached to Montgomery's advance to Lübeck and expressing some fears of the Russian activity on that front. He explained that he was not criticising Montgomery but he wanted to be sure that nothing was held back which Montgomery might require. On 30 April Eisenhower, at the request of the Combined Chiefs of Staff, again signalled the Soviet High Command to explain that the Elbe was the boundary only in the central sector and that he intended to cross the lower Elbe to secure Lübeck. Montgomery took Lübeck on 2 May.

In the meantime on 25 April the Soviet forces had surrounded Berlin and on the same day American and Russian forces had met on the upper Elbe east of Leipzig. Eisenhower had achieved his aim of cutting the German forces in two. Further south the situation was still fluid. The

[30] Papers IV, No. 2418

British, thwarted over Berlin, had suggested that at any rate there was great political advantage in liberating Prague and as much of Czecho-slovakia as possible. As Czecho-Slovakia was an area for liberation rather than occupation there was no political agreement which could invalidate such action. Marshall in putting these representations to Eisenhower had said that he 'would be loath to hazard American lives for purely political purposes'. Eisenhower replied that it looked as if the Russians could certainly reach Prague before his own forces, but he intended to act to destroy any remaining German forces and that a move into Czecho-Slovakia might be necessary. In his signal to the Soviet of 30 April Eisenhower said that he intended to hold the line of the 1937 Czecho-Slovakia frontier but that the situation might require him to advance to Karlsbad-Pilsen.

As it turned out Patton's Third Army made faster headway than the Russians. Further south the Russians had entered Vienna on 13 April but Devers's Army Group too was making rapid progress. It captured Munich on 30 April and went on into Austria to Innsbruck and to link up with the Allied forces coming up from Italy in the Brenner Pass. Patton's rapid advance to Linz and the Czecho-Slovakian border brought his forces nearer to Prague than were the Russians. On 4 May Eisenhower gave orders to Bradley that Patton was to occupy the line Karlsbad-Pilsen and to be ready to continue his advance. At the same time he informed the Soviet High Command that he was prepared to advance to the Elbe (on which Prague stands) and to clear the west bank while the Russians cleared the east. This brought an immediate response from the Russians asking Eisenhower not to advance beyond his originally suggested line lest such a move should lead to confusion of forces. They strengthened their request by reminding Eisenhower that they had complied with his request not to get involved in the Baltic area near Lübeck. Eisenhower complied with the request.[31]

The situation in Prague was complicated by a rising of the Czech partisans who on 5 May took independent action to liberate the city. The Germans reacted and on the 6th the Czechs called on Eisenhower for assistance, asking also that the Czech Brigade, which was part of Bradley's army group, should go into Prague. A direct call was also made to Patton. By the time the requests came into Supreme Headquarters on 7 May the German surrender had already been agreed and no action was taken.

[31] Papers IV, Nos. 2482 & 2496

Owing to the seizure of the Prague Radio station by the partisans the German commander got no official news of the surrender and refused to believe the partisans. Despite an approach from Churchill to President Truman no political guidance was given to Eisenhower, who confined his action to informing the Czechs that he had halted at the request of the Russians and that requests for assistance should be made to them. Confusion continued for some days after the agreed surrender date and it was not until 12 May that Soviet forces entered Prague, nor until the end of the month that the Czech Brigade from Bradley's forces was allowed into the capital.[32]

Apart from the tragic events in Czecho-Slovakia the German surrender came into force without a hitch although the Germans made every effort to surrender to the Western Allies alone. Eisenhower not only took a rigidly correct attitude, insisting that he could not receive their emissaries unless they surrendered to all the Allies, but he also demanded the inclusion in the surrender of all the forces in Norway and Denmark. On 7 May he was able to send to the Combined Chiefs of Staff the message drafted in his own hand: 'The mission of the Allied Force was fulfilled at 0241, local time, May 7th, 1945.'[33]

From a strictly military point of view little cause for criticism of Eisenhower will be found in this final phase of the war in Europe. The Rhineland battles, the several crossings of the Rhine, and the rapidity with which Germany was overrun as far as the Elbe may be seen as a justification of Eisenhower's strategy—at any rate in its later stages. Yet no part of his campaign has been subjected to so much bitter critcism after the event. Although there were already plenty of reasons to mistrust the Russians, there is no doubt that criticism of his decision not to take Berlin and his later decision not to enter Prague have their roots mainly in knowledge of what happened after the war. Such criticisms also suggest the idea that if the British or Americans had captured Berlin the later history of Europe would have been different. This idea is surely unproven. It is easy enough now to forget that the Russians were our Allies and that, at British initiative, an agreement had already been drawn up for the occupational zones after the war. The task given to Eisenhower was 'to . . . undertake operations aimed at the heart of Germany and the destruction of her armed forces.' As he said in his final message, that task he did fulfil.

[32] *Command Decisions*, pp. 385-6
[33] Papers IV, No. 2499

Strategy cannot be divorced from politics, but it was certainly no part of Eisenhower's task to put the Western Allies at an advantage over the Russians. Not even Churchill included that in his policy.[34] If it had been among the political aims it would have been for the governments to give the necessary directive to Eisenhower through the Combined Chiefs of Staff. Nevertheless the question remains whether Eisenhower saw his military task too narrowly and whether he was moved away from his normal Allied attitude to a desire to give the American forces, and particularly Bradley, pride of place. It has already been shown how Marshall as well as Bradley did influence him. Bradley's estimate of 100,000 casualties to take Berlin looked foolish by the time the Elbe was reached. But the thought that Eisenhower had any small-minded desire to deprive Montgomery and the British of the glory of capturing Berlin can be discounted by the fact that when Bradley's own army group was within reach of the capital the task was also refused to them. Undoubtedly Churchill was right to emphasise the strategic importance of Berlin, but it can hardly be claimed that the defeat of Germany was delayed by a single day as a result of Eisenhower's decision to halt at the Elbe.

The decision not to make the effort to liberate Prague is a different matter. It would have been hard to go on in the face of the definite Soviet request not to do so. But the operational situation required that Eisenhower should do so. There is little doubt that the Czech Brigade and such additional American troops as were necessary should have been in a position to take over from the partisans the liberation of their capital.

[34] Ehrman, *op. cit.*, VI, pp. 150–1

15

Appraisal

Although Eisenhower's military career did not end with his final victory over the Germans little more happened that could affect his standing and reputation as a Commander. In November 1945, after a few months as commander of the American occupational forces in Germany, he was appointed to the highest position in the United States army, Chief of Staff of the Army. In Washington his principal task was the demobilization of the army. It was necessary in discharging this duty to remind his political masters and his countrymen that the unwinding of the work of creating an army that had operated from the Arctic to Australia could not be done in a moment. It was even imperative to remind them also that the defeat of Germany and Japan had not necessarily ushered in an era of world peace. However, one more task of military organization remained to be performed, and that was the creation of an independent United States air force.

During the whole of the war the American air force had been the Army Air Force and Arnold had sat on the Joint Chiefs of Staff Committee as a subordinate to Marshall, his army chief. The most vehement opponents of an independent air force were in the navy but their objections were hardly relevant to the issue. The United States Navy had operated during the war largely as a floating air force, a character that it retains to this day. But Eisenhower knew that the air force must have a voice in military matters equal with that of each of the two older services. He very soon brought together the senior air force officers to discuss the question and immediately afterwards assembled a group of the principal senior army officers. Norstad, who it will be remembered was one of Eisenhower's air commanders in the North African campaign, was invited to attend both meetings. He tells[1] how 'Eisenhower stated categorically that the Air Force had come of age and should be given a position of parity with the two older services. He clearly stated, and more forcefully to the

[1] Letter to the author April 1971

Army than to the Air Force group, that he proposed to support such action.' With Eisenhower's strong support the measures necessary were taken and the National Security Act of 1947 created an independent air force within the structure of the United States Defence Department as it now exists.

Eisenhower's advocacy of an independent air force did not mean that he had moved in any way from his belief in a single commander over all three services and an integrated staff. Such commands were set up for all the United States forces overseas and an integrated staff system was also used in the Pentagon. Eisenhower was determined that in the Pentagon, in turbulent days when the future was even less easy to define than usual, day-to-day business should not obscure the task of deciding on future needs and new concepts of security. He was careful to use not only the experience of those who had held responsible appointments during the war but also the ability of those young officers who had seized the opportunities offered by war to show their capabilities. Norstad, Chief of Plans and Operations, was still under 40, and can therefore be said to belong to both categories. Another future Supreme Allied Commander in Europe, Goodpaster, was used to set up an 'Advanced Study Group'. He had under him a group of three relatively young officers of the highest intellect and capable of independent and creative thinking. The group was kept free of ordinary routine tasks and had direct access both to Norstad and to Eisenhower.[2]

Early in 1948 Eisenhower retired from the army but less than three years later he was recalled to service. A succession of events had convinced most of the nations of the free world that they must unite or risk the gradual submission of Western Europe to Soviet domination. On 4 April 1949 the North Atlantic Treaty was signed and on 19 December 1950 Eisenhower was appointed Supreme Allied Commander in Europe. In that position Eisenhower set up SHAPE, the first Allied military headquarters ever to have existed in peace. As can be imagined he was exactly the man for the task. Although the western European nations had already begun to organize themselves it must be confessed that little had been achieved that was effective. The military organization had suffered from the fundamentally different views of Montgomery and de Lattre. The latter expressed even at this early stage the French dislike of integration which was to reappear later. But the arrival of Eisenhower brought to the

[2] Letter from General Goodpaster to the author August 1970

scene the man who had already made an Allied headquarters function successfully.

The whole spirit of SHAPE was that it was an Allied and an integrated headquarters. Every officer who served there in those early days shared in that spirit and knew and acknowledged its source. But Eisenhower was not content just to infuse SHAPE with the spirit of an Allied headquarters that had stood the test of war. He was determined also to ensure that the international structure was right. In this Eisenhower worked closely with Ismay, the first Secretary General, and great advantage came from the friendship and confidence that had grown up between them while Ismay was Secretary to the Chiefs of Staff Committee and Principal Staff Officer to Churchill. Eisenhower insisted that he should have a clear statement of his responsibilities and authority from his political head, the NATO Council, and that he should have the right of direct access to the heads of government of each of the NATO nations. This last provision, which still exists today, is the corner-stone of the confidence between political and military authority which, through the years, has been an essential feature of the Alliance.

When Eisenhower came to SHAPE, NATO had at its disposal, in the face of the mobilised might of the Soviet army and air force, 12 divisions, many of them unfit for an active role, 400 aircraft and 400 ships. The member nations were thinking of peace and reconstruction. Eisenhower understood the need to reconcile the political, economic and military factors of this difficult time and yet create a convincing pattern of defence. His appointment signified the commitment of the United States with its overwhelming advantage at that time of the possession of atomic weapons, but the effort had to come from the other members of the Alliance too. Eisenhower's great contribution was in the building of the confidence of Europe in its ability to make and maintain an effective military structure.

We must return to the war years to find Eisenhower's place as Military Commander. Of his personal qualities there can be no doubt. His absolute integrity and the humanity that shone from him, his ability to get the best out of those who served him, his impartiality in international matters and his selfless devotion to the task entrusted to him were apparent to all who worked with him. Despite his charm of manner and his ability to reconcile conflicting opinions, he knew when to be firm and even severe. For example, his handling of Patton was masterly. Where a weaker or less patient man would have taken the easy way out and dismissed him for one or more of his indiscretions, Eisenhower was able to bring him under control and to use him for the great cavalry leader that he was. In Montgomery he had a difficult subordinate of a very different kind, but Eisenhower was always conscious that he was dealing with the commander of the army of his principal ally and with a man who had proved himself a master in battle. Yet Eisenhower was firm with him too and Montgomery learnt that there was a line beyond which he must not go.

There is not the same unanimity in assessing Eisenhower's strictly military ability. Marshall had absolute confidence in him, but Marshall had chosen him and some thought that he reflected too easily Marshall's views. Brooke, probably the man who had the clearest idea of all of the strategy necessary for the Allies to win the war, did not have a high opinion of Eisenhower except for his personal qualities and his ability to handle allies. Indeed it can hardly be doubted that Brooke underestimated Eisenhower. He never quite forgot Eisenhower's rather naive approach to the possibility of landing on the Continent in 1942, or the difficulties and disappointments of the North African campaign. What Brooke did not appreciate was the way in which Eisenhower developed as a commander and the skill with which the enormous Allied armies were directed to final victory. Brooke was a man of great magnanimity but it is possible that after his disappointment in not getting the Supreme Command, which had been promised to him by Churchill, he saw throughout the campaign what he himself would have done. No doubt his command would have been more incisive, but whether it would have been more successful with an Allied and a preponderantly American army will never be known.

Curiously enough Churchill had a higher opinion of Eisenhower than Brooke had. He liked him from the first and from the time of his appointment for the North African campaign had confidence in him and was proud to place the British forces under his command. Possibly the way Eisenhower liked to talk out a problem pleased Churchill; neither hid his thoughts from the other. Even at the time of his disagreement with Eisenhower over Berlin, Churchill was able to express to Roosevelt his confidence in Eisenhower and to describe the difference with a latin tag '*Amantium irae amoris integratio est*'.[3] Eisenhower also had the confidence of another great political figure. Occasionally de Gaulle felt that the

[3] Churchill, *op. cit.*, VI, p. 409, quoted from Terence 'Lovers quarrels are the essence of love'

honour of France demanded a political veto but he trusted Eisenhower's military judgment and political understanding.

Eisenhower's relationship with Marshall, his superior, and Bedell Smith, his trusted subordinate and Chief of Staff, shed an interesting light on his military character. After working directly under Marshall in the War Department, Eisenhower came to England with the impression that Marshall would eventually become Commander-in-Chief for the invasion of the Continent and that he would be his Chief of Staff or his Deputy. The relationship formed in those days never quite changed. When Eisenhower was Supreme Commander he acted under the direction of the Combined Chiefs of Staff. Marshall was much the most powerful American member of that committee and it was natural that Eisenhower should look to him for guidance and interpretation so long as they were not at variance with the directives of the Combined Chiefs of Staff. In the same way Montgomery always kept his link with London and continually consulted Brooke about his differences with Eisenhower. The British Chiefs of Staff were suspicious of the influence Marshall had with Eisenhower. Brooke and Marshall were men of a very different stamp and seldom saw eye to eye. Brooke feared that some of the impression that had been made by discussion in Committee might be lost in the exchanges which he knew went on between Marshall and Eisenhower. The fears were not so serious while Dill was in Washington, because Marshall and Dill were close friends and Dill had a great deal of influence. Dill and Marshall were on Christian-name terms, a rarity if not unique between the austere American Chief and his military associates. When Dill died in November 1944 that special link no longer existed and it was all the more unfortunate that this was the period in which the Americans attained a considerable preponderance of forces in Europe.

Although the 100 or more letters that Eisenhower sent to Marshall[4] reveal a similar strategic outlook and show that Eisenhower regarded Marshall as his mentor, there is no indication that Eisenhower looked to Marshall to tell him how to run his campaign. Eisenhower was certainly not a yes-man. The exchanges were rather the means by which the men kept in each other's mind and, occasionally, the means by which Eisenhower could blow off steam or unburden himself of his troubles. The majority of them dealt with questions of purely American concern like

---

[4] All published in the Eisenhower Papers, and the principal ones also published separately under the title *Dear General*

promotion, comments on the performance of senior officers, efficiency or shortcomings of American equipment and views on training. When Marshall expressed definite views on action which Eisenhower should take, Eisenhower weighed up the advice carefully but he was not afraid to modify or disregard it.

Just as Eisenhower was not a yes-man he did not choose to have yes-men about him. His chief of staff was a really tough man and a most capable soldier. Brooke thought he had 'far more flair for military matters' than Eisenhower. It is not easy to see deeply into the relations between a commander and his chief of staff, but those closest to Eisenhower are unanimous that the relationship was exactly what it should be. Eisenhower liked to talk over his problems with Bedell Smith, he listened to him seriously but it was he who made the decision. There was no question which was the commander. It must be remembered too that Eisenhower spent much of his time away from his main headquarters, where Bedell Smith normally was, either at his advanced headquarters or visiting commanders. Whiteley, the senior British operations officer on Eisenhower's staff, who worked closely with Bedell Smith and had a great regard for him, was in no doubt that Eisenhower used Bedell Smith in the same kind of way that the best British commander would use his chief of staff.[5]

Montgomery's opinion of Eisenhower quoted at second hand is apt to seem somewhat patronising. Anyone hearing it personally at first hand gains a quite different impression. Montgomery has said without equivocation that no one else could have carried out the task as Eisenhower did; no one else could have controlled the air force and naval commanders and satisfied the politicians. 'No one else could have done it', but he added, 'he knew nothing about how to fight a battle.'[6] Enough has been written here to support the first part of the opinion and it remains to consider Eisenhower's direction of his forces to battle.

In his first campaign in Tunisia it cannot be pretended that Eisenhower showed the boldness and skill with which the Germans deployed forces no larger than his own to forestall him. It is not a complete defence but it can be said that no Allied commander ever did beat the Germans at that particular game. Time and again small German forces were used to seize a fleeting opportunity or to stave off a threat. This was not only a

[5] Conversation with General Whiteley, June 1970
[6] Conversation with Field Marshal Montgomery, August 1970

question of the genius of command, it was a mark of the extent to which all ranks of the German Army were masters of their craft. Eisenhower came untried and with largely untried forces to his task at a time when the Germans had, in addition to their major operations, shown these special skills in Norway, in Belgium and Holland, in Greece and Crete and in the Desert.

In the campaigns in Sicily and in Italy, Eisenhower showed the same inability to take complete and immediate advantage of German forces outnumbered on land, at sea and in the air. The decision not to risk the airborne landing in Rome was probably the most serious failure. But here again there are circumstances not to be overlooked which may be quoted in extenuation, even though they may not completely exonerate him. The first is the way democracies, particularly when in alliance, must and do wage war, their refusal to take the big risks when the object can be achieved more slowly and at less apparent cost. The other is to ask which of the Allied commanders showed a better understanding of what should be done. Alexander, Montgomery, Cunningham and Tedder, all among the best British commanders, were there.

When Eisenhower became Supreme Commander for Overlord the scope of his command began to change. For the actual landing the command was as it had been in Sicily and Italy. Eisenhower had under him one army group commander responsible for fighting the battle. But he had already shown his understanding and genius for command by his grasping of the roles of navy and air forces and the technical services to make for a complete and overwhelming assault. After the battle of Normandy, Montgomery's battle, Eisenhower began to take command of the land campaign. Enough has been said about the possibility of destroying German resistance in the autumn of 1944 in a single battle, so much in fact that all that is certain is that no one will ever know whether the opportunity existed or not but that if it did it was certainly lost. It is far more likely that Eisenhower was right to look to the development of his whole strength along the Rhine. In this phase there was only one flaw, his underestimate of the German power to riposte which left him without a reserve to deal with the Ardennes offensive. That too was a failure shared by all the Allied commanders, but the chief responsibility must rest with Eisenhower. The ability to sense what is on 'the other side of the hill' is one of the essentials of the great commander in battle.

In his handling of the Allied forces from Normandy to the Elbe

Eisenhower showed his understanding of the problem of directing great forces to battle. He realised the necessity for a single commander to fight a particular battle and he realised that this was what an army group commander was for. The extent of the battlefield and the size of the forces were too great for all to participate in the same battle. But Eisenhower ensured that they were all participating to the same end and it was he who decided where and with what forces the main battle was to be fought. He never forgot that his was an Allied Army: that in Montgomery he had not just a subordinate commander but a commander who represented the views and handled the army of his most important ally. It was as the commander of allied forces that Eisenhower will be remembered. His work lay in fields hardly trodden by Foch and under complexities probably not seen since the less scientific days of Marlborough, days when you were at least safe from the air and from immediate communication with your political superiors. The technique which Eisenhower adopted from the start, and which evolved as his experience grew, remained firmly rooted in a full and lively consciousness of the problem inherent in commanding allied forces.

We are left with the picture of a commander of manifest integrity who warmed the heart and uplifted the spirit of everyone who worked with him. His special genius was his skill at management. He managed the generals, the admirals and the air marshals, and even the politicians, and he managed mighty armies. One special facet of this quality was his ability to draw the best from those under him, to draw from them and not to steal the praise. His own heart and mind were with the fighting man, and his preference would have been to be in command in the forefront of the battle. But that was not to be his destiny or his métier. His task was to weld together a force which was not only an Allied force but one drawn from all Services, and to direct it so that its whole weight was used most effectively to the single aim of the defeat of the common enemy. That he did superbly.

Glossary of Code Names

Anvil The attack against the south of France.

Arcadia The first Washington Conference December 1941.

Avalanche The landing at Salerno.

Baytown Eighth Army crossing of Straits of Messina.

Bolero The concentration of American forces and material in Britain for the assault on Europe.

Buttress Projected landing in the toe of Italy N.E. of Messina.

Cobra First U.S. Army attack at St Lo to achieve the break-out.

Cossac Planning Staff for Overlord before appointment of Eisenhower.

Crossbow Allied efforts to destroy German rocket sites.

Dragoon Final name for Anvil.

Goodwood Second (British) Army attack S.E. of Caen July 1944.

Gymnast First name for Torch.

Husky The landing in Sicily.

Mulberry Artificial harbours used off Normandy coast.

Neptune Assault phase of Overlord.

Octagon Second Quebec Conference September 1944.

Overlord The cross-Channel attack in 1944.

Pointblank The combined bomber offensive against Germany.

Quadrant First Quebec Conference August 1943.

Round-Up Cross-Channel attack contemplated for 1943.

Sextant Cairo Conference November 1943.

Sledgehammer Emergency landing on the Continent for 1942.

Torch Landings in North Africa with eventual objective Tunisia.

Trident Third Washington Conference May 1943.

V1 German pilotless aircraft for attacks against England 1944.

V2 German rockets for attacks against S.E. England 1944/45.

Bibliography

Official Histories and Reports

British. All published by H.M.S.O.
Grand Strategy, Vols 5 and 6 by John Ehrman, 1956
The Mediterranean and the Middle East, Vol. 4 by Major General I. S. O.
   Playfair and C. J. C. Molony, 1966
Victory in the West, two vols, by Major L. F. Ellis, 1962 and 1968
The Strategic Air Offensive against Germany, three vols, by Sir Charles
   Webster and Noble Frankland, 1961
The Despatches of Field Marshal The Earl Alexander of Tunis, 'The
   Conquest of Sicily'
The Despatches of Lieutenant-General K. A. N. Anderson, 'The Cam-
   paign' in North West Africa

American. All published by The Department of the Army
The Supreme Command by Dr Forrest Pogue, 1954
Strategic Planning 1941–1942 by Dr Maurice Matloff and Edwin Snell,
   1953
Strategic Planning 1943–1944 by Dr Maurice Matloff, 1959
The Mediterranean Command N.W. Africa by Dr George F. Howe, 1957
Cross Channel Attack by Gordon A. Harrison, 1951
Break-Out and Pursuit by Martin Blumenson, 1961
The Lorraine Campaign by Dr H. M. Cole, 1950
The Ardennes by Dr H. M. Cole, 1965
Global Logistics and Strategy by Dr Richard Leighton and Dr Robert
   Oakley, 1955

Biographies and Military Studies

Alexander of Tunis, Field Marshal The Earl, *Memoirs* (ed. John North),
   Cassell, 1962
Ambrose, Professor Stephen E., *The Supreme Commander*, Cassell, 1971
Belfield Eversley and Major-General H. Essame, *The Battle for Normandy*,
   Batsford, 1965
Bradley, General of the Army Omar N., *A Soldier's Story*, Eyre & Spottis-
   woode, 1951

Bryant, Sir Arthur, *The Alanbrooke Diaries*, two vols, Collins, 1957 & 1959
Butcher, Captain Harry C., *Three Years with Eisenhower*, Heinemann, 1946
Chandler, Professor Alfred and Ambrose Professor Stephen, (editors) *The Eisenhower Papers*, 5 vols, John Hopkins Press, 1970
Churchill, Rt Hon. Winston S., *History of the Second World War*, vols 4, 5 & 6, Cassell, 1951, 1952 & 1954
Clark, General Mark, *Calculated Risk*, Harrap, 1951
Cunningham of Hyndhope, Admiral of the Fleet Viscount, *A Sailor's Odyssey*, Hutchinson, 1951
de Gaulle, General Charles, *War Memoirs. Unity 1942–1944*, Weidenfeld and Nicholson, 1959
de Guingand, Major-General Sir Francis, *Operation Victory*, Hodder and Stoughton, 1947
de Guingand, Major-General Sir Francis, *Generals at War*, Hodder & Stoughton, 1964
Eisenhower Foundation. (Various authors), *'D' Day in Retrospect*, University Press of Kansas, 1971
Eisenhower, General of the Army Dwight D., *Crusade in Europe*, Heinemann, 1948; copyright 1948 by Doubleday & Co.
Eisenhower, General Dwight D., *At Ease*, Hale, 1968; used by permission of Doubleday
Eisenhower, Colonel John S., *The Bitter Woods*, Hale, 1969
Essame, Major-General H., *The Battle for Germany*, Batsford, 1968
Fergusson, Brigadier Sir Bernard, *The Watery Maze*, Collins, 1961
Greenfield, Kent Robert. 'American Strategy in World War II', John Hopkins Press, 1963
Greenfield, Kent Robert (ed.), *Command Decisions*, Methuen, 1960
Hobbs, J. B., *Dear General*, John Hopkins Press, 1971
Horrocks, Lieutenant-General Sir Brian, *A Full Life*, Collins, 1960
Jackson, Major-General W. G. F., *The Battle for Italy*, Batsford, 1967
Jackson, Lieutenant-General Sir William, *Alexander of Tunis as Military Commander*, Batsford, 1971
Lewin, Ronald, *Montgomery as Military Commander*, Batsford, 1971
Liddell Hart, Captain Sir Basil, *History of the Second World War*, Cassell, 1970
Macmillan Rt Hon. Harold, *The Blast of War*, Macmillan, 1967
Montgomery of Alamein, Field Marshal the Viscount, *Memoirs*, Collins, 1958

Murphy, Robert, *A Diplomat among Warriors*, Collins, 1964

Patton, General George S., *War as I Knew It*, Allen, 1948

Sixsmith, Major-General E. K. G., *British Generalship in the Twentieth Century*, Arms & Armour Press, 1970

Strong, Major-General Sir Kenneth, *Intelligence at the Top*, Cassell, 1968

Tedder, Marshal of the Royal Air Force Lord, *With Prejudice*, Cassell, 1966

Warner, Oliver, *Cunningham of Hyndhope*, Murray, 1967

Whiting, Charles, *Decision at St Vith*, Ballantine, 1969

Wilmot, Chester, *The Struggle for Europe*, Collins, 1952

Chronology

Notes

1. Except where otherwise stated the entries refer to Eisenhower.

2. Only the more important meetings between Eisenhower, the President, the Prime Minister, Brooke, Marshall and the principal subordinate commanders are detailed. In the period between the launching of Overlord and the establishment of an Advanced Command Post in Normandy, however, all visits to the beachhead are mentioned.

3. The principal authority for Eisenhower's personal movements and appointments is the diary in the Eisenhower Papers Vol. V, pp. 73–190.

Chronology

I. The Years of Preparation

14 October 1890 Birth of Dwight David Eisenhower.

14 June 1911 Joined U.S. Military Academy West Point and took the oath of allegiance.

July 1915 Graduated from West Point. Commissioned as 2nd Lieut. and joined 19th Infantry Regiment in San Antonio, Texas.

1 July 1916 Married Mamie Geneva Doud.

6 April 1917 U.S.A. entered war against Germany. Transferred from 19th Infantry as part of cadre to raise 57th Infantry Regiment.

July 1917 Became Instructor in Officer Training Unit at Fort Oglethorpe, Georgia, in rank of captain.

24 September 1917 Birth of son, Doud Dwight (died of scarlet fever December 1921).

November 1917 Posted to 65th Engineer Regiment at Camp Meade, Maryland, the parent unit organizing and training tank units for war service.

March 1918 65th Engineers reorganized as Tank Corps with headquarters in Washington. Eisenhower as Major commanded the tank training detachment at Camp Colt, Gettysburg.

14 October 1918 Promoted Lieut.-Col. (Rank relinquished after end of war and not regained until 1936 in Philippines).

11 November 1918 Armistice with Germany.

March 1919 Remaining nucleus of Tank Corps concentrated at Camp Meade.

7 July–6 September 1919 Duty with Trans-America convoy, Washington–San Francisco.

1919–1920 Commanding a heavy brigade of Mark VIII tanks as major and working with Patton on tank development and tactics.

1920 Abolition of Tank Corps, Eisenhower continued with his Infantry Tank Brigade at Fort Meade.

January 1922 Joined Brig.-Gen. Fox Conner as his Staff Officer in Panama Canal Zone.

3 August 1922 Birth of son, John Sheldon Doud.

August 1925–June 1926 Student at Command and General Staff School, Fort Leavenworth.

26 December 1926 Joined War Department on staff of Gen. Pershing, head of War Monuments Commission.

August 1927–June 1928 Student at War College, Washington.

June 1928–July 1929 Returned to War Monuments Commission and worked in Paris on revision of *War Monuments Guide Book.*

October 1929–December 1932 On staff of Maj.–Gen. Moseley, Deputy Secretary of War.

1 January 1933 Appointed Personal Military Assistant to Gen. MacArthur, Chief of Staff of the Army.

October 1935 Remained on MacArthur's staff on his appointment as Military Adviser to President Quezon of the Philippines.

December 1939 Departed from Philippines and took up appointment as Lieut.–Col. on staff of Army Commander San Francisco.

June 1940 Appointed Battalion Commander in 15th Infantry Regiment.

30 November 1940 Appointed Chief of Staff 3 Div.

1 March 1941 Appointed Chief of Staff IX Corps in rank of Colonel.

II. The United States Entry into the Second World War

10 June 1941 After British–American staff talks and consultation with Roosevelt the Secretary of War authorised the War Department to plan on the assumption that if war came Germany would be defeated first and then Japan.

1 July 1941 Became Deputy Chief of Staff and in August Chief of Staff to Third Army.

26 July 1941 MacArthur took command in Philippines.

9–19 August 1941 Churchill's meeting with Roosevelt and declaration of the *Atlantic Charter.*

7 December 1941 Japanese attack on Pearl Harbour.

8 December 1941 U.S.A. declared war on Japan.

11 December 1941 U.S.A. declared war on Germany and Italy.

14 December 1941 Appointed to War Plans Division as Deputy Chief in rank of Brig.–Gen.

17 December 1941 Appointed 'Action Officer' in War Plans Division for operations in S.W. Pacific.

22 December 1941–14 January 1942 First Washington Conference (Arcadia) between Churchill, Roosevelt and their Chiefs of Staff committees. Combined Chiefs of Staff Committee instituted.

15 February 1942 British surrender in Singapore.

16 February 1942 Appointed Chief of War Plans Division.

23 March 1942 War Plans Division reorganized as Operations Division. Eisenhower remained as Chief.

28 March 1942 Promoted Maj.–General.

8 April 1942 U.S. Surrender in Bataan.

26 May–3 June 1942 Visit to the United Kingdom to discuss Bolero.

11 June 1942 Appointed to command United States Forces European Theatre of Operations.

19–25 June 1942 Churchill's second visit to Washington.

19 June 1972 Attends informal meeting of Combined Chief of Staff.

21 June 1942 First meeting with Churchill.

21 June 1942 Germans capture Tobruk.

III. Eisenhower as Commander

24 June 1942 Arrived in London.

5 July 1942 First stay at Chequers with Churchill.

7 July 1942 Promoted Lieut.–General.

8 July 1942 Discussion with C.I.G.S. at which Eisenhower informed of British decision not to undertake Sledgehammer.

8 July 1942 Churchill's letter to Roosevelt suggesting that Allied landing in North Africa was true *Second Front* for 1942.

18–25 July 1942 Hopkins, accompanied by Marshall and King, in London to question abandonment of Sledgehammer and discuss alternatives.

23 July 1942 First meeting with de Gaulle.

23 July 1942 Germans captured Rostov.

30 July 1942 Roosevelt finally opts for Torch and requires landing not later than 30 October.

6 August 1942 Nominated as C–in–C Allied Expeditionary Force for Torch.

9 August 1942 Eisenhower's first plan for Torch completed. Landings to take place at Oran, Algiers and Bone, and later at Casablanca.

22 August 1942 Eisenhower's second plan. All landings within Mediterranean. Plan rejected by J.C.S.

25 August 1942 Dined with Churchill and worked late into the night on Torch.

28–30 August 1942 Working week-end with Churchill at Chequers.

31 August 1942 Roosevelt's counter-proposal to Churchill suggesting landings only at Casablanca and Oran.

1 September 1942 Churchill's message to Roosevelt that he would agree to Casablanca if Roosevelt would agree to Algiers.

3 September 1942 Roosevelt agreed Casablanca, Oran and Algiers. Churchill summoned Eisenhower to conference and plan finally approved on that basis.

3 September 1942 Cunningham nominated Naval C-in-C under Eisenhower.

21 September 1942 Final decision on 'D' Day for Torch 8 November.

22 October 1942 Clark's meeting with French collaborators on Algerian coast.

23 October–4 November 1942 Battle of El Alamein.

5 November 1942 Arrived in Gibraltar.

Night 7/8 November 1942 Allied landings at Casablanca, Oran and Algiers.

8 November 1942 Darlan agreed to cease-fire in Algiers.

8 November 1942 Giraud arrived in Gibraltar.

9 November 1942 Clark flew to Algiers to set up advance H.Q.

9 November 1942 Giraud arrived in Algiers.

9 November 1942 Germans began landing troops in Tunisia.

11 November 1942 Hitler ordered occupation of Vichy France. Darlan ordered cease-fire throughout French N. Africa, and ordered French troops in Tunisia to resist Germans. British detachments reached Bougie.

12 November 1942 British Commando landed at Bone.

13 November 1942 First visit to Algiers.

16 November 1942 First Army reached Tunisian border.

19 November 1942 First visit to Patton in Casablanca. Russian counter-offensive at Stalingrad began.

23 November 1942 First visit to Fredenhall in Oran.

27 November 1942 French fleet scuttled in Toulon.

28–29 November 1942 Visits to forward troops and first visit to Anderson's H.Q.

2 December 1942 First visit to Admiral Darlan.

23–24 December 1942 Visit to Tunisian front.

24 December 1942 Assassination of Darlan.

26 December 1942 Attended Darlan's funeral.

13-20 January 1943 Casablanca Conference. Eisenhower attended meeting of C.C.S. on 15 January.

23 January 1943 Eighth Army captured Tripoli.

31 January 1943 German surrender at Stalingrad.

11 February 1943 Promoted General.

14 February 1943 Rommel begins counter-stroke against flank of First Army.

16 February 1943 Eighth Army cross Tunisian border and in accordance with decision of Casablanca Conference. Eisenhower becomes Supreme Allied Commander Mediterranean.

20 February 1943 Rommel captured Kasserine Pass. Formation of 18th Army Group under Alexander.

23 February 1943 All Axis forces in N. Africa placed under Rommel.

5 March 1943 Patton took command II (U.S.) Corps.

6 March 1943 Battle of Medenine.

9 March 1943 Rommel left N. Africa to see Hitler and Mussolini and did not return.

13 March 1943 Met Cs-in-C and approved first plan for Sicily.

20–26 March 1943 Battle of Mareth Line.

14-15 April 1943 In Tunisia discussing with Alexander plan for final battle in North Africa.

2 May 1943 Meeting with Montgomery to discuss Sicily.

3 May 1943 Meeting with Cs-in-C. Revised plan for Sicily agreed.

7 May 1943 Allies captured Tunis and Bizerta.

12 May 1943 German surrender in N. Africa.

12–25 May 1943 Trident Conference in Washington.

28 May–4 June 1943 Churchill, Marshall and Brooke visited Eisenhower.

11 June 1943 Italian surrender in Pantelleria.

12 June 1943 Dined with H.M. King George VI in Algiers and was invested as G.C.B.

19 June 1943 Final political settlement in French North Africa.

10 July 1943 Allied landings in Sicily.

25 July 1943 Fall of Mussolini.

26 July 1943 Meeting with Cs-in-C in Tunis to discuss invasion of Italian mainland.

1 August 1943 Meeting with Cs-in-C in Malta to discuss plans for Italy.

6 August 1943 Meeting between Italian Foreign Minister and Chief of Staff and Ribbentrop and Keitel.

9 August 1943 Conference with Cs-in-C in Tunis. Plans for Italy approved.

14-24 August 1943 Quadrant Conference at Quebec on 15 August. Churchill's agreement that Supreme Commander for Overlord would be an American.

16 August 1943 Allies captured Messina.

17 August 1943 Last German troops left Sicily.

18 August 1943 Departure of Bedell Smith and Strong to meet Italian envoy in Lisbon.

30 August 1943 German revised plan for occupation of Italy completed.

3 September 1943 Italians signed terms for surrender. Allies crossed Straits of Messina.

8 September 1943 Announcement of Italian surrender.

Night 8/9 September 1943 Allied landing at Salerno.

9 September 1943 Allied landing at Taranto. Germans moved into Italy.

17 September 1943 Visit to Salerno Beachhead.

27 September 1943 Allies captured Foggia.

1 October 1943 Allies captured Naples.

4 October 1943 Hitler's decision to hold south of Rome.

22-27 November 1943 Sextant Conference at Cairo. Eisenhower attended 25th to 27th.

28 November-1 December 1943 Tehran Conference.

3-5 December 1943 Continuation of Cairo Conference.

7 December 1943 Roosevelt informed Eisenhower he was to command Overlord.

24 December 1943 Public announcement that Eisenhower was to command Overlord.

31 December 1943 Departed from N. Africa for discussions and leave in United States.

15 January 1944 Arrived in London.

17 January-11 February Alexander's first bid for Rome, involving crossing of Garigliano, Anzio landing (22 January) and First Battle of Cassino.

19 January 1944 Addressed 120 of the senior officers of Allied Headquarters.

20 January 1944 Visit to H.M. King George VI at Buckingham Palace.

21 January 1944 First Supreme Commander's Conference.

22 February 1944 Preliminary decision on strengthening of Normandy landing and consequent postponement of Anvil.

5 March 1944 Supreme Headquarters moved from Norfolk House to Bushey Park.

21 March 1944 Eisenhower recommended the abandonment of Anvil.

24 March 1944 J.C.S. agreed to postponement of Anvil but not to its abandonment.

25 March 1944 Final agreement on command of strategic air forces during Overlord.

2 May 1944 Establishment of Adv. Command Post at Portsmouth.

11 May 1944 Inception of Alexander's second bid for Rome.

15 May 1944 Final exposition of plan for Overlord to senior commanders involved, at St Paul's School. H.M. King George VI, Churchill, Smuts and Chiefs of Staff present.

4 June 1944 Allies entered Rome.

6 June 1944 Allied landings in Normandy.

7 June 1944 Tour of Normandy beaches by fast minesweeper, visits to Montgomery and Bradley.

9–15 June 1944 Joint Chiefs of Staff in London to be on the scene for Overlord and for Combined Chiefs of Staff meetings.

12 June 1944 Accompanied by J.C.S. visited Bradley in Normandy while Churchill and C.O.S. visited Montgomery.

15 June 1944 In Normandy. First visit to Montgomery and Dempsey's H.Q.

19–22 June 1944 The great storm in the Channel.

22 June 1944 Meeting with Gammel, Chief of Staff to Wilson and demand for earliest possible Anvil.

23 June 1944 Opening of Russian summer offensive.

24 June 1944 In Normandy. Visit to Bradley.

26 June 1944 Opening of offensive to capture Cherbourg and Caen.

27 June 1944 Capture of Cherbourg but Allies held before Caen. Meeting with Churchill to discuss Anvil.

28 June 1944 Churchill's final effort to get Anvil cancelled.

29 June 1944 Roosevelt refused to agree to cancellation of Anvil. Rundstedt and Rommel visited Hitler.

1–5 July 1944 In Normandy with Bradley and for visits to Montgomery.

2 July 1944 Rundstedt replaced by Kluge.

8 July 1944 Allies entered Caen.

17 July 1944 Rommel severely wounded.

18–20 July 1944 Goodwood Offensive.

20 July 1944 Attempt on Hitler's life.

20 July 1944 In Normandy. Visits to Montgomery and Bradley.

25 July 1944 Opening of Cobra Offensive. In Normandy. Visits to Montgomery and Bradley.

27 July 1944 Beginning of break-through on First Army front. Meeting with Churchill and Brooke to discuss Normandy battle.

29 July 1944 In Normandy. Visits to Montgomery and Bradley.

30 July 1944 Opening of Second Army offensive.

1 August 1944 Allies captured Avranches.

3 August 1944 In Normandy. Visits to Montgomery and Bradley.

7 August 1944 Set up Adv. Command Post near Bayeux.

7–10 August 1944 German counter-attack at Mortain.

13–21 August 1944 Battle of the Falaise Gap. (Patton reached Argentan 13 August, Canadians reached Falaise 16 August.)

15 August 1944 Allies landed in south of France.

19 August 1944 Eisenhower informed Montgomery he aimed to take over direct command on 1 September.

23 August 1944 Gave instructions to Montgomery for clearance of Pas de Calais and securing a firm base at Antwerp.

25 August 1944 Liberation of Paris.

29 August 1944 Issued directive to army group commanders for destruction of enemy forces in N. France and Belgium and for the advance into Germany.

31 August 1944 Supreme Headquarters opened at Granville.

1 September 1944 Eisenhower assumed direct command of operations.

2 September 1944 Involved in forced landing and injury to knee.

3 September 1944 Allies entered Brussels.

4 September 1944 Allies captured Antwerp.

12 September 1944 Allies captured Le Havre.

12–16 September 1944 Second Quebec Conference (Octagon).

17–26 September 1944 Battle of Arnhem.

20 September 1944 Supreme Headquarters moved from Granville to Versailles.

22 September 1944 Allies captured Boulogne.

1 October 1944 Port of Boulogne opened.

9 October 1944 Port of Le Havre opened.

15 October 1944 Advanced Comman i ɔ . ᵉsᵗᵃᵇⁱˢhed at Gueux (near Reims).

18 October 1944 Gave instructions to Montgomery and Bradley for operations crossing the Rhine.

4 November 1944 Approaches to Scheldt Estuary and Antwerp cleared.

28 November 1944 Allied advance halted along West Wall. Port of Antwerp working.

16 December–17 January 1944 Battle of the Ardennes (22 December Patton and 3 January Montgomery moved to offensive.

20 December 1944 Promoted General of the Army.

31 December 1944 Issued to army group commanders plan for advance as far as the Rhine.

7 January 1945 Montgomery's Press Conference on the Battle of the Ardennes.

12 January 1945 Russian winter offensive began.

30 January 1945 C.C.S. review of Eisenhower's plans for the invasion of Germany.

31 January 1945 Russians reached the R. Oder.

4–10 February 1945 Yalta Conference.

8 February 1945 Beginning of First Canadian Army attack in Rhineland.

23 February 1945 Ninth (U.S.) Army attacked in Rhineland.

24 February 1945 Supreme headquarters opened at Reims.

3 March 1945 First Canadian and Ninth U.S. Armies linked up on west bank of Rhine.

5 March 1945 Churchill and Brooke visited Eisenhower at Reims.

7 March 1945 First (U.S.) Army seized bridgehead over Rhine at Remagen.

23 March 1945 Third (U.S.) Army secured bridgehead over Rhine.

Night 23/24 March 1945 Main Rhine crossing.

25 March 1945 On banks of Rhine with Churchill, Brooke, Montgomery and Bradley.

28 March 1945 Informed Montgomery that command of Ninth (U.S.) would pass to Bradley after link-up of two army groups east of Ruhr. Personal message to Stalin on future intentions.

1 April 1945 Link-up of 12th and 21st Army Groups near Parderborn.

12 April 1945 Death of Roosevelt.

13 April 1945 Russians captured Vienna.

16 April 1945 Allies reached R. Elbe.

17 April 1945 Meeting in London with Churchill and Chiefs of Staff.

236

21 April 1945 Informed Soviet High Command of his intention not to cross R. Elbe in central sector.

25 April 1945 Russians surrounded Berlin. American and Russian troops met on Elbe east of Leipzig.

30 April 1945 Americans captured Munich.

2 May 1945 British captured Lübeck.

5 May 1945 Czech rising in Prague. At request of Russians Eisenhower halted U.S. troops in Czechoslovakia on line Karlsbad-Pilsen.

7 May 1945 Germans signed act of surrender.

8 May 1945 End of war with Germany.

12 May 1945 Russians entered Prague.

November 1945–May 1948 Chief of Staff of the Army.

May 1948–January 1953 President of Columbia University.

4 August 1949 Signature of North Atlantic Treaty.

19 December 1950 Appointed Supreme Allied Commander Europe.

July 1952 Retired from the army to undertake Presidential campaign.

20 January 1953 Inaugurated as President of the United States.

19 January 1961 Ended second term as President.

28 March 1969 Death.

Index

Index

Other DACAPO titles of interest

**THE COMPLETE WAR
MEMOIRS OF CHARLES DE
GAULLE 1940-1946**
A one-volume edition of the
three books
1,054 pp.
80227-9 $14.95

CRUSADE IN EUROPE
Dwight D. Eisenhower
559 pp., 16 photos, 42 maps
80109-4 $14.95

DOOLITTLE
A Biography
Lowell Thomas and
Edward Jablonski
368 pp., 72 photos
80158-2 $8.95

JAPAN'S WAR
The Great Pacific Conflict
Edwin P. Hoyt
560 pp., 57 photos, 6 pp. of maps
80348-8 $14.95

THE KOREAN WAR
Matthew B. Ridgway
360 pp., 55 photos
80267-8 $12.95

**THE MEMOIRS OF FIELD
MARSHAL MONTGOMERY**
508 pp., 61 photos
80173-6 $10.95

REMINISCENCES
General Douglas MacArthur
440 pp., 30 photos
80254-6 $10.95

THE ROMMEL PAPERS
Edited by B. H. Liddell Hart
544 pp., 17 photos
80157-4 $14.95

THEODORE ROOSEVELT
An Autobiography
New introduction by
Elting Morison
628 pp.
80232-5 $12.95

Available at your bookstore

OR ORDER DIRECTLY FROM

233 Spring Street, New York, New York 10013